CAPTAIN BLIGH
&
MR CHRISTIAN
The Men and the Mutiny

By the same author

THE FLEET THAT HAD TO DIE

ADMIRALS IN COLLISION

THE POTEMKIN MUTINY

DREADNOUGHT:
A History of the Modern Battleship

FIRST SEA LORD:
A Life of Admiral Lord Fisher

THE BLIND HORN'S HATE

CAPTAIN BLIGH
&
MR CHRISTIAN

The Men and the Mutiny

RICHARD HOUGH

NEW YORK
E. P. DUTTON & CO., INC.
1973

For Tom Pocock

Contents

Acknowledgements

I owe a special debt of thanks to His Royal Highness the Duke of Edinburgh, and to Rear-Admiral R. J. Troubridge, Flag Officer Royal Yachts, for inviting me on board H.M. Yacht *Britannia* when, by happy chance, it sailed in the wake of the *Bounty* in the early weeks of 1971. The *Britannia* not only took me to Pitcairn Island and Rarotonga in style, but the officers, petty officers and yachtsmen welcomed me on board with immense and memorable hospitality. I enjoyed equally warm hospitality on board the Royal Fleet Auxiliary *Blue Rover* from her Commander, Captain M. G. Brace, and her officers and men.

Miss Suzanne Mourot, Deputy Librarian at the Mitchell Library, and her staff were both kind and helpful during the period of my research in Sydney.

U.T.A. French Airlines and the manager and staff of the Maeva Beach Hotel in Papeete made my stay in Tahiti comfortable and useful.

The officers and staff at the London Library, the Public Record Office and the Naval Library in London, and of the Library at the National Maritime Museum, Greenwich, provided their usual sterling service which one tends almost to take for granted. And my research into the Cumberland and Manx families who were involved in the mutiny—and notably Fletcher Christian himself— was greatly assisted by Mr Daniel Hay, F.L.A., the Librarian of Whitehaven Public Library, and Mr Kenneth Smith, F.L.A., the City Librarian of Carlisle Public Libraries.

The sectional drawings of the *Bounty* and her launch are reproduced by kind permission of the *Mariner's Mirror*.

I am also grateful to Mr Leo Vernon for his admirable maps reproduced in the end-papers and on page 181.

Professor Christopher Lloyd read this book in manuscript, and I am most grateful to him for his constructive comments.   R.H.

CAPTAIN BLIGH
&
MR CHRISTIAN
The Men and the Mutiny

I

'I am in hell'

A FEW minutes before 4 a.m. on 28 April 1789 Midshipman
George Stewart, acting master's mate, felt his way down the
Bounty's main hatchway to the lower deck. There was a dim light
from the lantern hanging at the bottom of the ladder. Fletcher
Christian's berth was a few steps forward, on the starboard side,
behind a canvas screen. The ship was creaking gently, like the bones
of a tired old man who is in no hurry at all. There had been little
wind on deck and there was not a breath of it down here. The air
was humid and rank with the smell of hot bodies, damp timber, old
clothes and old cooking.

When the screen was lifted, a little light filtered in and Christian
could just make out Stewart's silhouette. The two young men were
friends, Stewart a year younger than Christian, shorter and leaner
too. He had a long neck and a hollow weak-looking chest. But he
was tougher in muscle and mind than he looked. Christian would
miss him, as he would miss so many of the *Bounty*'s crew. They had,
after all, been together for more than nineteen months.

Christian did not need to be awakened for his watch. If he had
slept at all since he had climbed into his hammock half an hour
earlier it was only fitfully. His mind was in a state of agonised

frustration. On the previous evening, and in a rush of nervous energy and mental desperation, he had lashed together the two masts lying in the ship's launch to some planks to make a crude raft with the intention of deserting the *Bounty* in the middle of the Pacific Ocean. He intended to paddle or drift to one of the group of islands through which the *Bounty* was sailing, or perhaps be picked up by a native canoe.

It was, of course, a suicidal plan, and in a more rational state of mind he would have known this. The Friendly Islands had been inappropriately named. Only three days earlier an armed party from the *Bounty* had been molested while collecting wood and water, so a man coming ashore alone and without the awe-inspiring presence of a great ship anchored close by was likely to meet a violent end. There was also a very real danger of being attacked by sharks. Yet Christian had shown himself determined to go through with his plan to desert his ship, and had risked divulging it to the ship's carpenter, William Purcell, in order to obtain the material for the raft, and to several others including Stewart himself. He had even managed to collect together some provisions and articles for trading —a small roasted hog, some nails—which he had stowed in an old clothes bag in preparation for his escape.

Stewart leaned over Christian's hammock and found, as he related later, that his friend was 'much out of order'. This was no surprise. Earlier in the night, after the rain had cleared, he had seen Christian on deck moving about quietly and awaiting an opportunity to launch and paddle away his craft undetected. Although Captain Bligh and several of the officers were below in their cabins many of the ratings were on deck. It was cooler up there. Besides, they were less than thirty miles from an island on which an active volcano was offering a pretty diversion, with a glow of flame intermittently lighting up the sky. Few of the sailors were sleeping. They were restless and talking together most of the time. As well, the *Bounty* was moving only very slowly, which must add to the difficulty of clearing the ship quickly. Christian could not hope to get away without arousing the cry of 'Man overboard!' Feeling more trapped than ever, Christian had decided to postpone his desertion until he took his own watch at four o'clock.

Now Stewart begged Christian to abandon his plan altogether. He told him that it could not possibly succeed. He understood Christian's agony of mind after what he had suffered since they had left Tahiti, and before that too. But he also knew that conditions on board the *Bounty* without Christian as master's mate, second-in-command, and first victim of Bligh's temper, would become intolerable and even more dangerous for all of them.

For Christian had provided both a release for the captain's uncertain temper and a link between the hierarchy and the restless crew of the *Bounty*. With 'the people' (as the ratings were called) Fletcher Christian was popular. From the captain he had suffered savagely, especially over the last few days. But up to now some sort of uneasy balance had been maintained thanks to Christian's involuntary role. If this balance were to be lost Stewart feared that the worst might happen.

'When you go, Christian,' Stewart pleaded quietly, 'the people are ripe for anything.'

Was the midshipman inciting mutiny or offering a warning? Christian's mind was in no condition to discriminate. He had lain down in his breeches and shirt. He had only to swing his feet from the hammock to the deck to be ready to take on his role as officer of the watch—or deserter—or mutineer. While Stewart left him, went to his own berth abreast of the main hatchway on the port side and climbed wearily into his hammock, Christian grasped the rope and pulled himself up the ladder through the main hatchway and came on to deck.

At four o'clock the new moon had long since set and it was still dark. There was a faint breath of wind from the east, hardly enough to fill the sails, and the *Bounty* was only just moving through the water. A light swell lifted the ship and dropped her gently into the next shallow trough. If you looked up you could see the sails swinging across the night sky, slowly masking and unmasking a small area of the star pattern. Most of the off-watch men who had been sleeping on deck had gone below to their berths. Figures were moving about the forecastle and quarterdeck as the second watch was relieved by Christian's morning watch.

Christian himself relieved the gunner, William Peckover, and his men took up their posts without the need for orders, Thomas Ellison at the helm, John Mills as conn directing him. Christian ordered four seamen to coil the ropes ready for washing down the decks and to clear the forecastle.

This was the worst watch, the worst time of the night. It came as no surprise to Christian that his two midshipmen were missing, young John Hallett, at fifteen the youngest of the ship's company—and the shiftiest in Christian's judgement—and Thomas Hayward. Both were slack midshipmen. With John Fryer, the *Bounty*'s master, a difficult, quarrelsome man, they were the officers Christian least cared for. They were always giving trouble.

During the first few minutes of Christian's watch another midshipman appeared on deck. Christian recognised him at once by his walk and burly build. He was Edward Young, tough, ruthless, sardonic, and a close friend of Christian's. He, too, had heard of Christian's plan to desert ship and was as anxious as Stewart had been that he should not carry it out. But Young had different reasons from Stewart's for frustrating Christian's plan.

The two young men—Christian was twenty-four, Young twenty-two—had reacted differently to the crises of the past days. Christian, burdened by guilt and doubt, wounded, confused and angry, wanted to escape. His instinct was to retreat. Young—violent, impetuous, as angry as Christian but less personally involved—wanted to fight. To do so he had to be certain of the support of Christian, the only other officer on board who might be persuaded to join him. Moreover, Christian's good relations with the lower deck were a priceless asset in a rebellion.

Young came up close to Christian and spoke quietly, repeating Stewart's plea and warning. It would be death to desert. The people were ripe for anything. But Young went further. Test out the men, and you will see that I am right. What better time than now, with Bligh, Fryer, Peckover, Cole the bo'sun, William Elphinstone, all asleep below, and before Hayward and Hallett belatedly report on watch? Speak in turn to the men of your watch, Young begged, and those of the people below who will be with you. Speak to them now. Between us we can seize the ship and have done with our sufferings. Do not risk your own life uselessly.

The plan was simple. It could not fail. There was no need for bloodshed, though they would need control of the arms chests. Bligh and his clerk John Samuel, Hayward and Hallet, would be surprised and seized and cast adrift in the ship's small cutter, the jolly boat. They had a better chance (though they did not deserve it) of reaching an island in that than Christian in his lashed-together makeshift raft.

There was no time to elaborate on the plan. Leaving Christian with these fearful thoughts to contemplate, and with no more than a last word of encouragement, and a reminder of the need for swift action, Edward Young went below to await events. He was ready to play his part, though later. The next step was Christian's.

It was about 4.30 a.m. and there was still no glimmer of the new day astern. The *Bounty* was silent and at peace on a calm ocean, thousands of miles from the nearest port and nearest Europeans. Only two men of the forty-four on board knew of the possibility of imminent violence. Christian remained inactive for some time, his mind in a state of turmoil, his conscience struggling against the temptation to desert, and the infinitely more fearful and daunting, yet intoxicating, temptation to incite mutiny.

Two of his friends had now independently told him of the mutinous state of some of the people, and he knew that Stewart and Young spoke the truth. He had seen evidence of it himself, for they were always ready to confide in him. They only awaited a leader. And if Christian was the only man on board who could prevent a mutiny he was also the only man who could successfully lead one.

Bligh, the man to whom Christian owed so much for the advancement and the favours which had been lavished upon him, the man he had so loved and admired, who had promoted him acting lieutenant and second-in-command, who had many times in the past taken him into his house to talk to his wife and play with his children —William Bligh must be deposed, cast adrift, almost certainly to die.

Christian understood the price of mutiny. At best he would experience fear and guilt for the rest of his life. At worst, the ultimate humiliation, death at Spithead at the end of a length of rope, his proud family name soiled for all time.

At what point, as so many of them asked afterwards, did the devil enter Christian's soul? None of them was ever to know, just as no one was ever to know for sure why he yielded to the dangerous temptation to mutiny, although the youngest and most innocent of the *Bounty*'s company recognised how hellish Bligh had made Christian's life in recent weeks, and that a man of Christian's sensitivity could not be expected to endure for much longer the torture of spirit he had been suffering.

When he at length reached the agonising decision for mutiny in favour of desertion, Christian moved quickly to the mizzen mast, drew with a sweaty hand the knife from his belt and cut off one of the sounding leads that were hanging from it together with a length of its line. He tied the line round his neck like a necklace concealing the suspended lead beneath his shirt. This would at least ensure a quicker end, before the sharks got him, if he should fail.

It was five o'clock before Christian approached two members of his watch, Matthew Quintal and Isaac Martin. He had judged them to be riper for rebellion than anyone else. Both had been flogged by Bligh and had not forgotten it. It was not so much the flogging as the fact that Bligh had so often and so unjustly singled them out for blame—or so they judged it—that made them readier to rebel. Quintal was a fair, stocky young man of twenty-one; Martin, the only American in the crew, was nine years older, lean and tough and one of the tallest men on board.

Christian told them of his intention to take the ship—'but there is to be no murder'. Already by that step he was fatally committed, incitement to mutiny being as serious an offence as mutiny itself—a capital offence. He asked for their support and for their opinion on who would join them. Quintal, a violent fellow, showed immediate enthusiasm and willingness. Martin was less certain but at length agreed. That made three, or four counting Young. How many more?

They could certainly count on Charles Churchill—Charley, master-at-arms, one of the toughest men in the *Bounty*. He had once deserted and had been flogged, confined in irons and flogged again. All that made him a near-certain ally. Then there was Quintal's friend Will McKoy, Mat Thompson a hardy veteran of forty, Alex Smith, Jack Williams from Guernsey in the Channel Islands. They had all shown disruptive intentions in the past, and been flogged at Bligh's orders and were probable supporters, or at least unlikely to show allegiance to Bligh when faced with the moment of decision. That would make nine. When it was seen that they had control of the ship's arms there might be others. But surprise was more important than numbers, or even weapons.

There was a figure standing at the stern, beyond where the pigs and goats were stowed in the waist, beyond the wheel and the scattering of hen-coops on the quarterdeck. They could just make out his silhouette against the first grey light now stealing over the horizon. He was Charles Norman, the carpenter's mate, an odd fellow at the best of times, the oddest man in the ship. The volcano's lights did not interest him. He was staring down, unmoving, at the sea, watching a shark. Not quite right in the head, not a reliable ally. Christian decided to ignore Norman. Instead he sent Quintal and

McKoy to raise those below, while he took aside in turn the other men in his watch whom he thought he could trust. Events had already gone so far that he was now at the mercy of the accelerating momentum of insurrection.

By good chance Joseph Coleman—a near-certain mutineer—had the keys to the arms chests, one below the main hatchway, the other on the upper deck on the main grating. Fryer as master would normally have been entrusted with them, but, weary of being disturbed by someone on watch who had taken a fancy to shooting a bird or a shark, he had recently handed them to the armourer for safe keeping instead. He had slept better since then. Sloppy, indolent Fryer, forever grumbling and forever at odds with the world! But for his slackness there could never be a mutiny.

The first act in the conspiracy ran smoothly. Quintal disappeared quietly down the forward main hatchway to the orlop deck. He knew in which tier every man slung his hammock. He roused in turn those they had selected—whispered words: 'Christian is seizing the ship. Are you with us?'

Each man rolled from his hammock and climbed up on deck, at first numbed, then eager and excited at the prospect. Coleman was one of the first to be roused. So they had the keys now.

It was at this point that Quintal made an alarming discovery. One of the missing midshipmen of Christian's watch was asleep on the arms chest. It was young Hallett. By an ironical coincidence, Christian had made a simultaneous discovery up on deck, where his other midshipman, Tom Hayward, was lying stretched out on the top of the second arms chest. So two of the four men they intended to seize were, unconsciusly, barring the way to the first and most vital stage of the mutiny.

The situation was restored, partly by Christian's decisiveness. Informed by Quintal of his dilemma, he went below and brusquely aroused Hallett, ordering him up on deck to attend to his duties. As soon as the boy had gone, Christian opened the chest with Coleman's key and ordered Thompson to stand guard over it and to hand out arms to Burkett and Lamb. Christian himself took no half-measures, arming himself fully, in the style of a pirate, with musket, fixed bayonet, a pistol, a box of cartridges and (the final touch) a cutlass.

Up on deck again, he discovered that Hayward had risen and disappeared. In fact he had been shaken awake, not like Hallett by the officer of the watch but on a whim by Charles Norman who wanted to show him the shark—goodness knows a common enough sight in these waters.

The first crisis had been overcome. It was 5.15 a.m., there was a light spread of dawn in the eastern sky. The sun would rise from the sea in an hour and a half. By then the ship would be in Christian's hands. Only a sudden act of treachery among Christian's followers could save Bligh, asleep in nightcap and nightgown in his cabin. It was astonishing that the mutiny could gather so many followers without the knowledge of a single non-participant. Or perhaps some were awake nursing their fears and suspicions in silence?

At least two men, not yet mutineers, were in fact awake. From the fore scuttle on the starboard side came the reassuringly domestic sound of someone splitting wood. It was the ever-zealous Will Muspratt—perhaps over-zealous considering the time of day, with the second watch only just in their hammocks. Then came a voice raised in protest, identifiable as Michael Byrn's. He was the *Bounty*'s fiddler, blind and therefore especially sensitive to sound. It was important to have a fiddler in a ship's company on a long voyage: blind Byrn was the only man Bligh had been able to recruit.

Christian ignored the incident. He had on deck abaft the mizzen mast, in disciplined near silence, Quintal, Martin, Churchill, McKoy, Burkett and Lamb, all with either a cutlass, a brace of pistols or a musket with a fixed bayonet. Some had all three weapons. Together they made a desperate and fearful impression in the half-light.

A little more than an hour earlier they had been peacefully asleep in their hammocks. Now they faced imminent violence and a hunted future. They could trust no one, least of all one another. But for the moment they were acting in unison and were eager to show their strength. Three more appeared from the hatchway, Able Seaman John Sumner, Alex Smith and Henry Hillbrant, a German from Hanover, all equipped with arms handed out by Thompson, who followed them on to deck. Christian had eleven in all with him; and surely he could count on Young, too, though there was still no sign of him. What had happened to his friend?

Besides Norman there were five more men on deck outside their group—Mills at the conn, Ellison at the helm, Robert Lamb the butcher, Hallett who had discreetly disappeared, and Hayward, still out of sight at the stern watching the white trail of the shark with Norman. The sound of chopping from the fore scuttle had suddenly ceased.

Hayward remained unaware of what was going on until he turned at the sound of footsteps on the quarterdeck. He could just make out a party of men approaching him purposefully. Christian was in the lead, a wild sight with his long dark brown hair falling loose to his shoulders, and his veritable armoury of weapons.

Hayward walked bravely forward to meet him. 'What is the cause of this act?' he demanded of his senior officer.

'Hold your tongue,' Christian told him curtly.

Hayward turned to Mills. 'What do you know of this matter?'

'I know nothing.'

Ellison chose this moment to quit the helm and join Christian's group, begging a bayonet from one of them.

Christian deputed Martin as armed guard over Hayward and also over Hallett, who had reappeared and was standing helpless and terrified by the side of the older midshipman.

With control of the upper deck now established, Christian led Smith, Churchill, Mills, Burkett and Quintal through the hatch and down the ladder to the after cockpit. Bligh's cabin was on the starboard side of the ship. The door was ajar and they could see him asleep on his bunk. Fryer's cabin was opposite, on the port side, the door closed.

Christian, holding his cutlass in one hand and followed by Churchill, Mills, Smith and Burkett with muskets and bayonets, stepped into Bligh's cabin. It measured only six feet by seven feet and there was scarcely room for them all to stand. They would have been hard put to it to raise let alone aim and fire their encumbering muskets.

Bligh was awoken by a rough shaking and was instantly pulled from his bunk to a standing position.

'What is the meaning of this violence?' he demanded. He could see that, besides the threatening men surrounding him, there were others outside the cabin. He struggled and again demanded an explanation.

'Hold your tongue, sir,' Christian told him.

The others were cursing Bligh. As the full danger and horror of his situation struck him he began to call out louder, 'What's the matter? What's the matter?' Then he suddenly cried out at the top of his voice, 'Murder!' over and over again. These cries were heard from one end of the *Bounty* to the other.

The ship's company responded instantly, and in different ways, to the sound of their captain's voice raised, not in anger—they were used to that—but for the first time in the experience of any of them, in anguish. The cry spelt the end of order, the onset of general violence. Some who were awoken by it imagined they were being attacked by native canoes, and these men raced up on deck to repel boarders. Others thought one of their number had gone berserk. For those who did not at once recognise the reality of the situation, the second shock of discovering that some of their shipmates were under arms and intended to seize the ship was as great as their violent awakening.

For some minutes the *Bounty* was in a state of confusion and uproar. Men ran up the ladders colliding with those coming down, shouting curses and the news of the mutiny. One or two hot-heads—Jack Millward, and the slender, bearded wood-chopper Muspratt among them—enthusiastically threw in their lot with the rebels and were given arms. But most assumed a stance of uneasy neutrality, and retained it for the time that was to pass before a decision was forced on them, warily watching the tide of events and the changing attitude of their shipmates. Life in the *Bounty* had suddenly become as precarious as if they had come up with an enemy frigate overnight.

In Bligh's cabin the sounds of cursing and shouting continued for some minutes. One voice became clear above the others, calling up the ladder way. 'Hand down a seizing to tie the captain's hands.' It was recognisably the voice of Charley Churchill, harsh and authoritative. But there was no response, as if even the most deeply committed mutineer flinched from taking the first hostile step. 'You infernal buggers,' he called again, 'hand down a seizing or I'll come up and play hell with you all.'

Mills was the only one to move. He took the knife from his belt and slashed off a length from another of the lead lines hanging from the mizzen mast and handed it down.

Bligh could not understand why no one was coming to his aid. He felt sure that only a handful of the men were concerned in this act of mutiny. What of the ship's master, for instance? Fryer had a pair of loaded pistols always in his cabin at night. He should also have had the keys to the arms chests. How then had these pirates acquired their arms?

Unfortunate John Fryer was asleep on his locker—he found it a cooler place than his bunk on these humid nights—when Sumner and Quintal burst into his cabin. He heard Bligh's cry of 'Murder!' at the same moment, louder because the door had just been opened. He attempted to rise but was held down by the two men and was 'so flurried and surprised' (he said) that he forgot all about his pistols.

'You are a prisoner,' he was told, and when he remonstrated they said, 'Hold your tongue, sir, or you are a dead man.' There was no doubt that they meant it. 'But if you remain quiet there is no one on board who will hurt a hair of your head.'

Fryer lay still, listening to the sounds of tumult on deck, and echoing below in the forecastle messes. From his prone position on the locker he could see the ladder to the upper deck through the glass panel of his door. There were struggling figures climbing up the ladder, amongst them, dressed only in his shirt and nightcap, he recognised his captain, hands bound behind his back. In his haste in tieing Bligh's hands Churchill had caught the tail of Bligh's shirt in the knot, exposing his buttocks.

FRYER: What are you doing with the captain?

SUMNER: Damn his eyes! Put him into the boat and let the bugger see if he can live on three-quarters of a pound of yams a day.

FRYER: Into the boat? For God's sake for what reason?

SUMNER AND QUINTAL TOGETHER: Oh, sir, hold your tongue.

SUMNER: Mr Christian is captain of the ship now. Remember Mr Bligh has brought all this on himself.

FRYER: Consider, my lads, what you are about.

SUMNER: Oh, sir, we know very well what we are about.

FRYER: I am afraid not or you would not persist in your intentions. Lay down your arms now and I will see that you suffer no punishment for what you have done.

SUMNER AND QUINTAL: Oh no, sir. Hold your tongue, it is too late now.

FRYER: What boat are you going to put Captain Bligh into?

SUMNER AND QUINTAL: The small cutter.

FRYER: Good God! The small cutter's bottom is almost out. It is very much eaten with the worms.

SUMNER: Damn his eyes! The boat is too good for him.

FRYER: I hope they are not going to send Captain Bligh by himself.

The two mutineers divulged the rest of the plan. With Bligh were to go John Samuel, his clerk, and the two midshipmen, Hallett and Hayward. Those were all. Fryer now asked to be released and allowed up on deck, and was refused permission. He asked again. There then began a long wrangle involving Fryer, his two guards and Christian and some of his supporters on the upper deck. Christian, rightly judging that the master would be another disruptive influence in an already dangerously confused situation, confirmed that he was to remain in his cabin.

But Fryer—a new Fryer, he was, to all who observed him on that morning—persisted in his appeals and demanded that he should be allowed to talk to his captain before he was cast adrift. Shouted messages continued to be passed between the master's cabin and the upper deck. 'One of you go on deck and ask Mr Christian to let me come up and speak to Captain Bligh,' begged Fryer.

Christian again refused at first, then relented, and Sumner and Quintal escorted him up the ladder.

The scene on the *Bounty*'s upper decks was even more noisily chaotic than anyone below could have imagined who had heard only the cries, the thudding of running bare feet and the creaking of ropes and pulleys. At first sight the situation appeared to be out of control. It was an unreal scene, too. After some seventeen months with these men, for most of the time at close quarters with them, the face and stance of every rating and officer was familiar to Bligh. Each, according to his appearance, his rank and his duties, formed a part of the daily pattern of life in the small vessel. Now all this was broken, and if there was any pattern at all it was only a topsy-turvy nihilistic one.

Some of the seamen were armed and were brandishing their weapons ostentatiously. These were easily enough indentifiable as mutineers. But there were others who were unarmed and were also with Christian; and some who brandished weapons in their excitement—young Midshipman Peter Heywood was one—and yet were not active mutineers. Everybody was, more or less, making a noise, either cursing, jeering or just shouting for the reassurance it gave them to do so. Hilarity was the only missing ingredient. Whatever else was happening, there was nothing to laugh at. Hysteria, yes, but no hilarity.

Bligh was the central figure on this crowded stage, the involuntary star performer, shouting the loudest, threatening and demanding to be released, as full of violent spirit as ever. He was standing abaft the mizzen mast, Christian holding the end of the cord in one hand, in the other hand a bayonet instead of the cutlass he had been brandishing earlier. At the moment when Fryer appeared the stage was suddenly lit, as if the performance was now to begin, by the sun, deep red and larger than life, which heaved itself out of the eastern horizon at eight minutes to seven.

Standing near Bligh and Christian on the quarterdeck were the other lead actors, the hard-core mutineers Churchill, Quintal, McKoy, Martin and Burkett. Forward on the forecastle deck there was a second centre of activity where some ten men were at the booms assisting in clearing and hoisting out the jolly boat—the scene-shifters, preparing for the second act. These remained the busiest people throughout the mutiny, and their shouting was more purposeful.

With Fryer's appearance on the quarterdeck the dialogue here became more coherent, too. Bligh was angrily challenging his guards, who had their muskets cocked and aimed at him. 'I dare you to fire at me,' he shouted at them; and they lowered the barrels and uncocked them. It was a small but notable victory.

'Mr Christian, consider what you are about,' Fryer said, visibly appalled by the scene.

'Hold your tongue, sir. *Mămōō*!' (After their long stay at Tahiti they were in the habit of using expressions they had picked up from the natives, and *Mămōō*—silence—was one of the most popular.)

Fryer persisted, raising his voice above the cries of protest and invective. 'Mr Christian, you and I have been on friendly terms during the voyage, therefore give me leave to speak. Let Mr Bligh go down to his cabin and I have no doubt that we will all be friends again in a very short time.'

Christian said, with truth, that it was too late for that, and repeated, 'Hold your tongue! Not another word or you are a dead man. You know, Mr Fryer, that I have been in hell for weeks past.'

For the first time that anyone could remember, Fryer was showing real courage. Christian was in a half-demented state, 'his eyes flaming with revenge', the bo'sun's mate described him, and he was making constant play with his bayonet, pointing it in turn at Bligh's chest and Fryer's belly. But Fryer did not retreat at once. At least give the captain a chance of getting ashore, he begged Christian, reminding him of the state of the small cutter.

'No, that boat is good enough,' Christian answered.

Fryer edged closer to his captain and, speaking softly, suggested that he, Fryer, should stay on board in the hope of retaking the ship and following him.

Bligh replied with a bellow as loud as before, as if shouting had become his only means of communication. 'By all means stay, Mr Fryer. Isaac Martin is a friend,' he said, indicating with his head the American, who was standing farther aft among the hen-coops, and had earlier given Bligh a glance which he had interpreted as friendly. Then Bligh began to shout repeatedly and hysterically at Fryer and at all and sundry on the quarterdeck, 'Knock Christian down! Knock Christian down! Knock Christian down!'

No one moved except Fryer. He moved towards Christian, not with the intention of knocking him down but of getting nearer to Martin in order to speak to him. Again the shining bayonet swung towards him and was held at his chest. 'Sir, if you advance an inch further I will run you through. Take Mr Fryer back to his cabin,' Christian ordered Quintal and Sumner, who eagerly led the master away.

James Morrison, bo'sun's mate, was at the hatchway, a pale, much-scarred veteran with long black hair. A well-educated man, too, and one of the most interesting and best-informed of the *Bounty*'s company. Fryer spoke to him, eager to learn of any who were not committed mutineers. 'I hope you had no hand in this business?'

Morrison answered that he knew nothing about it. 'If that's the case,' Fryer said quietly, 'be on your guard, there may be an opportunity of recovering the ship.'

Morrison's reply was unencouraging. 'Go down to your cabin, sir, it is too late for that.'

Fryer's attempts to incite a counter-attack were dogged but abortive. Millward joined the others as a third guard. Fryer 'thought he was friendly', unlike Sumner and Quintal, gave him a wink and motioned to him to knock down Sumner who was standing beside him.

Fryer had misjudged the young sailor. 'Mr Fryer, be quiet, no one will hurt you,' he was told, and in seeming contradiction Millward cocked his musket and aimed it at him.

Fryer looked down at the barrel, 'Millward, your piece is cocked,' he said, 'you had better uncock it or you may shoot someone.'

For answer, Millward lifted his musket as if to reassure him. 'There is no one who wishes to shoot you,' he said.

For the next hour Fryer took little further active part in the proceedings. His relations with his guards remained as curiously uneasy and uneven as before. At one point he persuaded them to let him visit the other confined officer, Peckover, who was with David Nelson, the *Bounty*'s botanist, in the gunner's cabin. Peckover was confused and in low spirits, and Fryer—still buoyant, still hopeful—attempted to cheer him up.

'If you are ordered into the boat with the captain, refuse, as I shall,' Fryer told him.

'But then we shall all be judged pirates,' Peckover answered in anguish.

News of this plotting—if plot it could be called—reached Christian on deck, and Fryer's guards were peremptorily ordered to take the master back to his own cabin.

Up on deck the mutiny continued its slow, spasmodic growth, the continuous and querulous wrangling broken from time to time by outbursts from Bligh and Christian and the more vocal and violent mutineers, like Charley Churchill. Christian was still holding with one hand the end of the line that tied Bligh's wrists, the bayonet in the other hand. Sometimes, at moments of exceptional acrimony, he released the cord and held his captain by the shoulder, the two men forming a suddenly intimate statue-like stance together.

Time and again, whenever Bligh started to shout at them, McKoy, Quintal, Churchill, and Christian himself, repeated the word *mămŏŏ* as if it were a barrack-room expletive, following it with threats to run Bligh through or blow his brains out. For a time it seemed as if the mutiny was nothing more than an excuse for exchanging threats and obscenities. At length Bligh appeared to be running out of words and only stood with a furious expression on his face, licking his parched lips. One of his guards, Isaac Martin, stepped forward and fed him a newly peeled shaddock from the *Bounty*'s ample store of fruit. Soon Bligh's voice regained its full volume.

By now everyone was feeling in need of refreshment, the men who were struggling with the jolly boat's tackle and emptying the boat of its store of yams and coconuts, as well as those standing guard over Bligh and the two captive midshipmen. Christian caught sight of John Smith, Bligh's servant and cook, among the crowd on the quarterdeck and ordered him below for bottles of rum from Bligh's cabin to serve out to all the crew under arms. 'And also bring up the captain's clothes,' he added.

Before Smith carried out his new captain's bidding he did something which affected everyone by its dignity. He went up to Bligh at the mizzen mast and untucked his master's shirt-tail from the knot binding his wrists, making him a more decent figure. Then Smith went below and returned with Bligh's trousers and jacket, and a tray of glasses and tin mugs and bottles of rum in the other hand for Christian and his mutineers.

There was a lull in the uproar as he put the tray down on the quarterdeck for a moment while he helped his captain on with his trousers and put the jacket over his shoulders. It made a pleasantly intimate interlude and a touching demonstration of one man's loyalty to his captain.

Then Smith took up the tray again and offered a glass of rum to Christian and made his way forward to where McKoy and Williams were supervising the hoisting out of the boat. Smith returned along the starboard side of the waist, serving several more of the mutineers. Many of them gulped down their dram and took another quickly.

The glasses gave out and the rest got their drink in the tin mugs. Coleman took a dram or more, but Peter Heywood sixteen years old and the first time at sea, refused it without water. Someone went to get some. Back on the quarterdeck the other youngster, Tom Ellison, took a long drink. His task completed, Smith went below to pack Bligh's clothes as if only a routine shore visit lay ahead.

On deck the drinking continued. Every man with a musket also had a mug or glass of potent navy grog in his hand. Bligh watched hopefully, recognising the danger and tensely awaiting his chance. The mood of the men, mutineers and loyalists alike, was as finely balanced as if on a bayonet blade's edge.

Much more of this and it might turn into a drunken orgy, which could have one of two results: a quick end for him, or the chance of making a push. Bligh looked about him, at his sun-tanned, sea-hardened, tattooed crew, from one familiar face to another, seeing some blackly hostile, others uncertain, some hiding their fear more successfully than others.

But there were more than enough who would follow him instantly —the counter-mutiny would be even swifter than the earlier rebellion. Why in God's name didn't one of his men make the first bold move? Were they all cursed cowards?

2

'A fatal turn to the affair'

⚜

WILLIAM BLIGH was thirty-four years old at the time of the a mutiny on his ship. His father, Francis Bligh, had been customs officer in Plymouth and had died nine years earlier. The Blighs were of good West Country yeoman stock, Cornish in origin but more recently living in Devonshire—minor manorial land-owners, some going to sea, others, like Francis, into the civil service. They were typical of many of their kind in the peninsula, respectable and worthy. Francis Bligh did not marry until he was thirty-three and then made up for lost time by marrying in quick succession three widows, the first Jane Pearce when she was forty-one, in 1753. They had a son ten months later. He was their only child. Fifteen years after this, Jane died. Francis married two more widows before he died at the age of fifty-nine.

The son of Francis and Jane Bligh was born on 9 September 1754, and was baptised William a month later at Plymouth. His career was never in doubt. He would go to sea. The comings and goings of ships occupied the life of most of the people of Plymouth. Its maritime flavour was all-consuming. Plymouth had been on the threshold of great nautical events for centuries. Captain the Hon. John Byron (the poet's grandfather) sailed past on his circumnavigation when William Bligh was a boy of nine. Four years later, on 26 July 1768, James Cook in the *Endeavour* cleared Plymouth Sound on the first of his three great voyages to the Pacific.

Francis Bligh took a great deal of trouble over his only son's education. By the time he was fifteen he had a good knowledge of science and mathematics. His clear hand was already well formed. He could express himself well and drew with clarity and imagination.

There were three ways a boy could enter the navy in the 1760s. The first was by the old privileged and traditional route of entering as a 'captain's servant', with all its suggestions of patronage. Captains favoured those in their family or those they knew, and kept them under their wing until they qualified for their midshipman's warrant. This was a comfortably self-perpetuating method that was to prove hard to kill.

Or, since 1729, if you were the 'son of a nobleman and gentleman', you could go to the Naval Academy at Portsmouth and do two years' training. This was viewed with suspicion by those deep-dyed in naval tradition because it smacked of intellectualism and even egalitarianism. Moreover, these entrants lacked sea experience.

Then for a minority there was entry from the lower deck, by way of the rank of master's mate which was not so democratic as it sounds. You had to be nominated. You escaped the roughest work and the roughest treatment. But it was still no soft life. This was the way Bligh came in, and he did not forget it. Nor did some of his fellow officers. Ten years after Bligh's death the Second Secretary to the Admiralty, and the author of the first book on the *Bounty* mutiny, Sir John Barrow, ascribed much—too much—to the disadvantages Bligh supposedly suffered from his third-class entry and training in the Royal Navy. Barrow's is the view of a Victorian looking back to a less class-ridden age. But his comments still retain an uncomfortable measure of truth. They certainly cannot be ignored:

'Seamen,' he wrote, 'will always pay a more ready and cheerful obedience to officers who are *gentlemen*, than to those who have risen to a command from among themselves. It is indeed a common observation in the service, that officers who have risen *before the mast* are generally the greatest tyrants. It was Bligh's misfortune not to have been educated in the cock-pit of a man-of-war, among young gentlemen, which is to the navy what a public school is to those who move in civil society.'

Bligh first went to sea at the age of sixteen as an able seaman in the *Hunter*, a ten-gun sloop. Over the next five years he served in sloops and frigates in home waters and in the Caribbean. He knew that he had to show not just a good record but exceptional skills if he was going to get on in the service. Unlike most of his fellow midshipmen he lacked the patronage of anyone rich and influential who could ensure his promotion. All that he had on his side were a good education and a special aptitude for mathematics and drawing. He decided to specialise, choosing navigation, hydrography and cartography, and worked diligently at them. He had his warrant as a midshipman within six months of going to sea; his passing certificate as a midshipman before he was twenty-one.

The first of the series of events which later brought William Bligh and Fletcher Christian together occurred in 1775. Bligh, then aged twenty-one, was serving his fifth year as a midshipman on board a small and (as he described it) 'very leaky' sloop, H.M.S. *Ranger*. The Colonial Rebellion in the North American colonies had just broken out and there was a good chance of action there, and of war again with France. But the *Ranger* was given the chore of searching suspect ships for contraband in the Irish Sea. She was based on Douglas in the Isle of Man and spent much of her time in port owing to her unseaworthy condition. During one of these long periods of shore leave, some time in 1775, Bligh met the Betham family, and fell in love with their daughter, Elizabeth.

The Bethams were not only influential (as Christian was later to discover), but rich and accomplished in the arts and commerce. Richard Betham had a wide circle of friends from his days at Glasgow University—David Hume the philosopher, Adam Smith the political economist, Joseph Black the chemist, and many others. His wife's family, the Campbells, were equally scholarly and successful in business. Her uncle Duncan Campbell was a prominent West Indian merchant and owner of extensive sugar plantations. He was also a shipowner on a large scale. Her father Dr Neil Campbell was the Principal of Glasgow University and chaplain to the king.

Elizabeth grew up in an unusually cultured and privileged environment. When Bligh first met her and the rest of her impressive family, he found her intelligent, sympathetic, and understanding: all that he had lost when his own mother had died. Elizabeth Betham had charm and liveliness. But she was not especially beautiful. The only extant portrait shows her with wide-set eyes, an oversized nose, a round chubby face with a double chin, and a kind, clever smile.

Elizabeth liked the crisp, clever, self-confident young midshipman, with his definite ideas and determined ambition. Before the *Ranger* left Douglas for the last time early in 1776 the young couple had 'come to an understanding'.

Elizabeth Betham and William Bligh knew that it would be a long time before they met again, for Bligh had just received exciting news. His years of assiduous study were about to be rewarded. News of Bligh's exceptional skill as a navigator and hydrographer had reached the ears of the Sea Lords, of Lord Sandwich, First Lord, and James Cook himself. On 20 March 1776 Bligh received his appointment as sailing master to the world's most famous and successful navigator and explorer, soon to embark on his third and final voyage.

As sailing master in H.M.S. *Resolution* Bligh was Cook's right-hand man as navigator, and in the captain's own words would be 'usefully employed in constructing charts, in taking views of the coasts and headlands near which we would pass, and in drawing plans of the bays and harbours in which we should anchor'. Although non-commissioned and ranking below the lieutenants on board, the master was the most important man in the ship after the commander.

The main purpose of this voyage was to discover (no matter how many had failed before) a north-west passage from Europe to India, the East and the newly opened up Pacific Ocean. Such a short cut would save weeks of sailing time and tens of thousands of pounds a year for British merchants and traders. It would be a revolution in communications. Forty years earlier Anson had proved again, by his suffering and losses, that the southern route round Cape Horn was uneconomic. The British government had offered as long before as 1714 £20,000 reward for the first man to find a northern way through America. James Cook, a national hero since his return a year earlier from his second great voyage and his explorations in the Pacific and Antarctica, was determined to be that man. And he was to make his attempt to find this passage eastwards from the Pacific instead of westwards from the Atlantic.

Cook was, of course, destined not only to fail in his mission but also to die while preparing for a second attempt. William Bligh, unknown to the world, took a leading part in Cook's valiant struggle amid ice-packs north of Alaska; he also became directly involved in the subsequent events that led up to the death of Cook just two and a half years after the *Resolution* cleared Plymouth, Bligh's birthplace and home city, on 14 July 1776.

Like the chance photograph by a background witness to an assassination, we suddenly see William Bligh clearly for the first time on that evil day of Cook's death in 1779. But Bligh is more than a witness. He is, indirectly and accidentally, a participant. It is a scene worth looking at closely because it adds much to what we know about Bligh, and another day of violence in Polynesia just ten years later.

It is November 1778. Cook has reluctantly brought his two vessels *Resolution* and *Discovery*, south from Alaska and the Bering Strait. He has decided to winter in the temperate climate of the Sandwich Islands, discovered and so named by him some months earlier on the outward passage. His men need food and rest, his two sloops are in poor condition and due for a refit.

Bligh's figure and manner are familiar to everyone on board the two vessels. He is twenty-four years old, stands five feet eight inches in height and walks quickly with short steps, his head well back. He has a strong, sharp chin, close-set blue eyes, and a small thin mouth. He is clean-shaven and his complexion is pale and smooth. He smiles rarely and talks only when necessary, and then in practical terms. His work appears to absorb his whole being.

Bligh is known among the lower deck as a man of exceptionally strong will and of uncertain temperament. Cook gets on well with him. But he is regarded as an uneasy man to have on board on a long voyage; especially in the powerful and responsible position as master in the commander's own ship. You never quite know from day to day, or even from hour to hour, what his mood will be. He is a nagger. He has a sharp tongue, hates indolence and inefficiency, admires incisiveness but never gives praise for anything. Whether you admire or despise the man, he cannot be ignored.

The ship's companies of the *Resolution* and *Discovery* acknowledge his real qualities. Above all they cannot deny that the man has courage, and his navigation is sublime. As a cartographer, Bligh regards himself as good as Cook, and so he is. His landscapes in pen-and-ink and his drawings of animals and birds are accurate and have a sensitive line.

Forget for the moment the popular picture of Bligh as a man of uncouth ways, foul language and evil temper. Most language at sea was foul anyway, and there was always some bad temper on all sides when the going was rough. William Bligh was a valuable man to have on board, especially when they had been off Tasmania, or when they were working their way up the dangerous and fog-obscured coast of Alaska towards the Bering Strait six months ago.

On 26 November 1778 they sighted the island of Maui (Mowee). Five days later a broader silhouette rose above the horizon. For the first time in recorded history the island of Hawaii (Owhyee) was noted on a chart: one more landmark on a momentous voyage of discovery.

For some weeks the two vessels, sometimes alone, sometimes together, sailed along the east, south and west coasts of Hawaii, standing off and on at nights, until by mid-January they had almost completed the circumnavigation. Bligh had meticulously charted every mile of the coastline. This is what he enjoyed doing and did so well.

It was an eventful passage. At one time they were becalmed, at another caught in a tropical storm, with thunder and lightning, which carried away some of the *Resolution*'s rigging. For thirteen days the *Disovery* was lost. Whenever conditions allowed, the natives came paddling out from their dwellings set among the trees and plantations, hundreds at a time in canoes ranging in size from two-seaters to twin-hulled thirty-seat ocean-going vessels carrying sails.

Trade and seduction were the natives' first aims. They were swift and efficient at both and there were none of the unpleasant incidents and the pilfering which the Englishmen had experienced in the past. Like the other Polynesians the voyagers had enjoyed before, the women were warm, musk-scented and well-nigh insatiable in their sexual appetites. They liked to stay on board the ships at night, tight-packed with their men in the hammocks, their canoes towing behind the sloops.

The native men, heavily tattooed everywhere except on their faces, came on board wide-eyed with wonder at the size of the vessels, pacing out the decks and staring up at the masts and rigging before they settled down to trade with the deputed officers: nails for breadfruit, knives for green plantains, scarlet cloth for hogs, hatchets for beads, and mirrors for fine cloaks sewn with feathers.

The nature of both the coastline and the people changed after they doubled the southernmost tip of Hawaii. The land, with the snow-tipped volcanic peak of Mauna Loa always towering above it, turned from green to dark brown, which was judged to be the result of the natives' tilling and manuring the soil, until it was discovered to be lava from past eruptions.

The wind dropped on 8 January and their progress was slow, while the natives became more numerous and importunate, swarming over the ships, obstructing the men about their work, thieving relentlessly. In an effort to clear his vessels, Cook at one time ordered a show of power. The crack of muskets and the boom of four-pounders, aimed above the canoes packed about the *Resolution* and *Discovery*, echoed back from the shore. But the natives, though surprised and temporarily silenced, were quite unalarmed and soon renewed their assaults with the determination of termites momentarily startled while working on a pair of logs.

Cook was searching for a good anchorage. But the dark, inhospitable, reef-guarded coastline continued for mile after mile. As William Ellis, assistant surgeon, wrote: 'We now began to be apprehensive that this island afforded no shelter for our ships, as we had nearly made the circuit of it.'

At dawn on 16 January 1779 it was possible to make out a small indentation in the coast, and the hinterland appeared to be more mellow. As usual, Bligh was deputed by Cook to reconnoitre this possible anchorage, and at 8 a.m. the *Resolution*'s pinnace was hoisted out, and with the *Discovery*'s large cutter and under the command of the *Resolution*'s master, the men sailed towards the shore.

Bligh explored the bay with his usual care, taking soundings and drawing a rough chart. It was, he learned, called Karakakooa Bay and was some three miles across at its entrance, with two villages, Kowrowa on the western shore and Kakooa in the centre of the bay. At Kakooa there was a fine sandy beach flanked by a *morai* ceremonial burial place and a fresh-water spring. To the south of it the landscape was softened by groves of coconut trees, cultivated enclosures and native huts in great numbers. There was little else to attract the eye.

Between the two villages there was a high and inaccessible rocky cliff, and Kowrowa itself seemed to offer nothing. The bay, Bligh decided, was by no means ideal, but it would have to do. After

testing the water and making some sketches, Bligh re-embarked in
the pinnace from the stretch of sand and ordered the boat back to
the *Resolution*.

That night Cook wrote in the journal of the voyage:

> In the evening Mr Bligh returned and reported that he had found
> a bay in which was good anchorage and fresh water tolerable easy
> to come at. Into this bay I resolved to go to re-fit the ships and
> supply ourselves with every refreshment the place could afford.

It is the last entry contributed by Cook.

When the Englishmen took their vessels into Karakakooa Bay
they noticed an air of unusual excitement among the natives; nor
was it exuberant, joyous excitement. Nowhere in Polynesia—though
they had experienced everything from warm hospitality to downright
hostility—had there been such a feeling of tension and emotionalism.
There was nothing to account for this, unless it was the density of
the population. Perhaps that was it, a form of Polynesian urban
tension. The huts were certainly tight-packed about the south and
centre parts of the bay, the shore and cliff-tops were lined with
children and women with babies, and everyone who could find room
in a canoe was paddling as fast as they could towards the two sloops,
which were being slowly towed in by their own boats.

Many thousand more natives were swimming out, fearful that
they might miss some happening on this eventful day. They clung
to the gunwales of the ship's boats, obstructing the oarsmen,
climbed up the sides of the *Resolution* and *Discovery*, packing tight
the decks, below decks and high up the masts and yards. The *Discovery* began to take on a list beneath the unevenly spread weight
of the dark bodies.

There did not appear to be any malice or menace in them, though
they purloined everything removable with the same frenetic urgency
with which they did everything. By contrast with those nice people
on the other side of the island, these Karakakooans seemed to be
on the edge of a nervous breakdown.

Cook and his officers never succeeded in sorting out the hierarchy
at Karakakooa. First there was the king, the mild, fat, anxious-to-

please and elderly King Terreeoboo. He was for the present away on a military expedition to the neighbouring island of Mowee. The priests—*arees*—wielded great influence, as Cook was to discover. There were also the women of wealth, power and distinction who appeared to be rated upwards according to their weight; and the chiefs, the *jackanees*.

The first of these chiefs who came on board the *Resolution*, a young man who was to figure prominently in the events of the following days, was called Pareea. Another was named Koah, who, according to Lieutenant James King of the *Resolution*, had once been a distinguished warrior, but was now 'an emaciated figure: his eyes exceedingly sore and red, and his body covered with a white leprous scurf, the effects of an immoderate use of the *ava*', the island's alcoholic brew. A third was Kaneena, a particularly tall and powerful fellow.

When Cook appealed to Kaneena to clear the ships of natives, who were now endangering both his vessels and stripping them clean, the chief at once demonstrated his strength and authority over the masses. At the sound of his voice they leaped overboard in their hundreds until only one defiant man remained. Kaneena simply lifted him up bodily and hurled him into the sea.

These chiefs were also to prove themselves wily and devious. The unsavoury Koah, discovering that the ceremonial presentation of a hog to Captain Cook brought forth abundant gifts in exchange, sent along a succession of commoners under the guise of being chiefs, and at the same time begged back from Cook any surplus hogs. Cook did not realise that he was being duped until he recognised familiar features on a hog that had already been offered to him several times, always with elaborate obsequies and interminable speeches.

After his many years of experience Cook had developed a deep understanding of the Polynesian mind and patience with its vagaries. He had put up with a lot for the sake of peace, and he was genuinely curious about their customs and manners. But he was also a tired man, increasingly given to fits of petulance. This was, after all, his third long voyage to the Pacific. He had seen little of his wife and children over the past ten years. On this expedition alone he had already been absent for two and a half years, and the rigours and disappointments of the recent Arctic search had taxed his reserves. As his ships badly needed a refit, so James Cook required peace and a rest from responsibility. He was to enjoy neither at Karakakooa Bay. First he was to endure again on this new island the pantomine of reception by the chiefs and priests, the speeches and prostrations and processions and meals, including on the menu this time hog meat first masticated by the revolting Koah. The constant pilfering overstrained Cook's patience, too. Each time he made a complaint to the chiefs they answered with extravagant expressions of regret and reassurance, but within a short time the natives were again at their depredations, including swimming under the ships' bottoms to extract the nails securing the copper sheathing on which the preservation of the vessels depended. Attempts to discourage the practice by peppering the swimmers with small shot were futile, and in the end Cook ordered one to be captured and flogged on board the *Discovery*.

Relations between the excitable natives and their exasperated guests were becoming increasingly tense. Yet an outward show of harmony was maintained among the leaders on both sides to the end of the stay. King Terreeoboo returned triumphantly from his campaign. Exchange visits and presentations continued, and when the king heard of the imminent departure of the white men he gathered together vast quantities of hogs and other foodstuffs, which the community could ill afford to spare, as a farewell gift.

Only the young women, who remained freely on board for most of their stay, conceiving Hawaii's first generation of half-breeds, showed grief at the signs of departure: the re-embarkation of a damaged rudder, of newly cut planks for repairing the head rails and the stowage of barrels of salted-down hogs in the hold.

The males no longer bothered to conceal their anxiety about this continuing drain on their food reserves, for not only were the sailors eating prodigiously to make up for the past lean months, but were drawing on the island's precarious surplus for many months to come. A number of the sailors had their newly filled-out bellies stroked with ostentatious admiration by the natives as a hint that they were now full enough.

At last, on 4 February 1779, the two sloops sailed out of Karakakooa Bay, followed by a host of canoes speeding the guests' departure. Cook's intention was for Bligh to complete his survey of Hawaii and the other Sandwich Islands before seeking a more favourable anchorage where they could remain until they sailed north again in search of the elusive passage.

They thought that they had found this ideal anchorage only a few hours' sailing from Karakakooa. Bligh again reconnoitred in the *Resolution*'s cutter, but this time found the water inadequate and the promising-looking bay bound by low rocky shores, with beds of coral adding to the hazards. While Bligh was ashore the skies clouded over and gusts of wind brought with them the smell of a storm. The sea was already getting up when he began his return journey, and the canoes which had followed the ships all through the day were now being vigorously paddled towards the shore. One of them upset in the rough water and Bligh at once made towards it, retrieving two exhausted men and an old woman.

The subsequent storm caused Cook to reverse his plans. Both ships were badly knocked about, splitting several sails, and the *Resolution* sprang her foremast. At the known risk of overstraining the natives' hospitality at Karakakooa Bay again, Cook steered south down the coast, dropping anchor at the same spot as before. Only a week had passed since their departure.

The bay had assumed a new aspect. Almost all signs of life had disappeared. This time no canoes came out to greet them, no swimmers shouted from the water or climbed, brown and dripping, up the sides of the ships. No women waved from the shore or displayed themselves enticingly. It was all very different from those recent days when the women, according to Cook, 'visited us with no other view than to make a surrender of their persons'. Only once or twice did they catch a glimpse of a distant canoe creeping along close inshore.

A new measure of uncertainty and incomprehension overcame the English sailors staring from the decks of the vessels at the familiar but changed scene. 'How very difficult it is,' wrote Lieutenant King philosophically, 'to draw any certain conclusion from the actions of people, with whose customs, as well as language, we are so imperfectly acquainted.'

Had King only realised it, the natives were just as puzzled and dismayed by the situation as the white men. By their reckoning they had committed no crimes. Strange bearded men had come in their giant vessels, without women. Their bellies had been empty and they had filled them. The white men's leaders had been properly honoured. Why, then, had they come again? The first visit was a mystery. This second visit so soon after suggested sinister designs.

During the following twenty-four hours events and tempers

remained unpredictable. When the *Resolution*'s damaged mast was got ashore for repair, priests appeared and *tabooed* the area, as they had done before, by sticking their wands in the ground to ensure its security. This at least was reassuring. But then several of the chiefs drove away from their work a number of natives hired by the *Resolution*'s officers to help roll the water casks down to the shore. Cook therefore ordered out escorts of marines armed with muskets. But old King Terreeoboo visited Cook in the *Resolution* and appeared as harmless and friendly as ever.

Until the evening of 13 February it still seemed possible that a satisfactory relationship might be worked out between unwelcoming hosts and self-invited guests. Cook prided himself on his tact and firmness with the Polynesians, and it is true that however brutally he had sometimes behaved judged by the standards of the twentieth century, no eighteenth-century explorer had avoided more crises or extricated himself so successfully from the few in which he had become involved. But this time, tired and disappointed, irritable that he and his men were having to face again the tedium, and now perhaps the dangers too, of Karakakooa Bay, Cook began to act unwisely and irrationally.

The troubles began when a single canoe, crewed by a party of heavily armed chiefs, came alongside the *Resolution* and remained provocatively and silently for a short while before heading for the *Discovery*. Here a party climbed the ladder and came on board, with protestations of friendship so overdone that the officers' suspicions were aroused and sentries took up station along the sides of the ship.

Later, all but one of the warriors re-embarked in the canoe. This man appeared to be attracted by the activities of the sailors working at the ship's forge. Suddenly he leaped forward, snatched two pairs of tongs and other tools, and before anyone could move had raced across the deck and thrown himself far out into the water where he was picked up by the waiting canoe.

Cook was on shore at this time with Lieutenant King, dealing with an earlier stone-throwing incident. They heard the sound of musket-fire from the *Discovery* and saw that it was directed at a canoe racing for the shore, pursued by one of the ship's boats. Cook and King attempted to intercept it but were too late, and the thieves disappeared inland. It was useless to continue the chase, for the native spectators were, in King's words 'only confusing us with false information'.

The events in Karakakooa Bay now moved swiftly towards their fatal climax. Cook, once the tough unflappable Yorkshireman, was already beginning to lose control of the situation.

The officer and crew of the pursuing boat seized the thieves' canoe drawn up on the shore. At the same moment, Pareea, the handsome young chief who had been first on board the *Resolution* just four weeks earlier, arrived on the scene. His attitude had radically changed since that first joyous meeting. Now he vehemently claimed ownership of the canoe, silently supported at a distance by a growing body of armed natives.

The officer reacted violently by striking Pareea a violent blow on the head. As he fell, the natives advanced in a body, shouting and throwing stones, forcing the boat's crew into the water where they retreated to an offshore rock. In a frenzy of rage the natives began to ransack the boat of all its removable parts and contents, gleeful that at the first serious conflict they had got the upper hand so easily.

Luckily Pareea was as quick to recover as he was to recognise the dangers of the situation. He drove off his own supporters, indicating to the cowering boat's crew that they should return from their rock. It was clear that he was suddenly contrite and thoroughly frightened by this turn of events.

'Will *Orono* [Cook] kill me for this?' he asked anxiously. 'Will I be permitted to come on board again tomorrow?' On being reassured by the officer, Pareea seized him and rubbed noses before leaping into his canoe and paddling rapidly back to his village.

The evening of 13 February was full of other strange happenings, each calculated to increase the sailors' uneasiness. The formidable Kaneena was paddled out to the *Discovery* bearing with him a huge hog. The *Discovery* was commanded by Captain Charles Clerke, normally an admirable and capable officer. But the onset of tuberculosis was already weakening his judgement. He took Kaneena's offering as a gesture of reconciliation. Not a bit of it. The hog was for trade, and in exchange for it Kaneena demanded by gestures 'a dagger as long as my arm'—and he raised his arm to emphasise the required size. To placate him, Clerke informed the chief that he did not have such a great dagger as that, but that he would have one made for him by the morning.

It was a still night in Karakakooa Bay. From the shore came the distant sound of lamentation, a sure sign that the women and children knew that trouble was brewing. 'Their mournful cries,' wrote the surgeon's mate of the *Resolution*, 'struck the sentinels with unusual awe and terror.'

The word had spread north and south along the coast that the white men had returned in their great ships. Last time they had exhausted almost all the islanders' food. Now there was nothing left, and at all costs they must be driven away. At first an exciting curiosity, these invaders had become a threat to their lives. All through the day and far into the night reinforcements of warriors arrived in Karakakooa Bay, bent on a showdown.

On board the *Resolution* that night Cook said to Lieutenant King, 'These people will oblige me to use some violent measures, for they must not be left to imagine that they have gained an advantage over us.'

At dawn on 14 February 1779 Cook was awakened in his cabin with news that Captain Clerke was on his way to the *Resolution*. His message was ominous. His ship's large cutter had disappeared during the night. To preserve the planks against the heat of the tropical sun, Cook often had his boats sunk in shallow water at their moorings, where they were easily retrievable when required. During the night a party of natives had succeeded in cutting through the four-inch cable and towing away the boat. Its permanent loss would be crippling to the *Discovery*.

Cook was furious at this new piece of provocation, and determined to go ashore at once with a party of marines to bring King Terreeoboo back to his ship as hostage—if necessary by force, if possible by gentle persuasion. He had used this method before with unfailing success, as a means of retrieving important stolen items; but never before in the face of such large-scale hostility.

We have now arrived at the most crucial and most controversial moment in the events of this fatal day. The *Resolution* is anchored less than half a mile from the rocky north-west shore of the bay, about three-quarters of a mile from the village of Kowrowa, Cook's destination. The smaller *Discovery* is anchored a quarter-mile south-west of the *Resolution*.

At about 7 a.m. Cook hastens down the gangway, carrying his

musket, one barrel loaded with small-shot, the other with ball. He embarks in the pinnace with Lieutenant Molesworth Phillips, the marines officer, a party of marines armed with swords and muskets, and the boat's crew. Lieutenant John Williamson, with another party of marines, is ordered to follow in the ship's launch to stand offshore as a support group with more marines. All the evidence points to Cook's being confident that a single musket-shot, if even that should be necessary, would subdue any violence. It always had done in the past.

Lieutenant King with more supporting marines is sent in another boat to Kakooa, not to demonstrate force but to reassure the people that Cook means no harm and intends only to recover the cutter and punish the culprits; and that (in his own words) they 'need not be under the smallest apprehension of suffering any evil from us'.

To prevent the escape from the bay of any natives, two ship's boats are to patrol the entrance to the bay. Their marines are to be armed with muskets loaded with ball-shot.

All these arrangements were made and orders issued by Cook between about 6.30 and 6.45 a.m. Although the position was threatening, no one, least of all Cook, appears to have doubted the outcome. And so far the picture remains clear, and all the published and unpublished accounts agree, except in a few small details.

But before violence takes over we must look more carefully at the two patrolling boats, which were to take such an important part in the events of the day. One of these, the *Discovery*'s launch, was under the command of Lieutenant John Rickman. The second was the *Resolution*'s cutter, commanded by Bligh. Rickman, from the smaller of the two sloops, was also junior by several years to Bligh. Bligh, as Cook's right-hand man who had impressed his powerful personality on all ranks over a period of more than two years, would naturally be held in some awe by this young lieutenant.

Cook's orders to Rickman and Bligh, according to Captain Clerke's log, were 'to prevent any canoe going away, and if any attempted it, to drive them on shore'. Nothing was recorded about opening fire if the need arose, let alone about opening fire to kill, the last resort. Cook detested violence and avoided it whenever possible. Did he have words with Bligh on board the *Resolution* before Bligh set off to join Lieutenant Rickman on the armed blockade of the bay? And did Bligh transmit these orders to Rickman couching them in such terms as: 'Captain Cook has emphasised to me that we must use the strongest possible methods to prevent the escape of any canoes, and that includes using our muskets'? Cook had ordered ball-shot. Small-shot was for frightening, ball-shot for killing.

It was in the interests of Lieutenant King (Cook's successor as official narrator) when recounting the events of this day, to preserve the image of Cook as a peaceable man in firm control of events, until they got out of hand because of the savagery of 'the Indians'. Similarly, a direct attack on Lieutenant Rickman or on Bligh would have been inappropriate in the non-controversial pages of an official report.

There was no good landing place for a boat at Kowrowa and the cutter had to use a rocky promontory as a jetty. Cook clambered over the gunwhale on to the slippery rocks and made unhesitatingly for the village above the shore, with Phillips at his side and followed by the marines. The scene at first appeared normal. The women were busying themselves about their morning tasks, and when Cook was recognised, men, women and children prostrated themselves as they always did when he came ashore. They offered gifts of small hogs, partly in honour of *Orono* and partly in the expectation of small gifts in return.

Cook paused to speak to some of them, asking them where the king was. Several natives went off obediently and soon returned from some huts with the king's two sons, who had frequently dined on board the *Resolution* with their father. The boys greeted Cook with respect and at once led him to the entrance to one of the huts.

There now occurred a brief, awkward pause. Was the old man still asleep, or were the boys playing some trick? It would hardly be seemly for Cook to enter and search for the king. Yet the boys showed no sign of bringing out their father.

Cook consulted with Phillips and then ordered the lieutenant to investigate. 'I found our old acquaintance just awake from sleep,' Phillips recorded later, 'when upon my acquainting him that Captain Cook was at the door, he very readily went with me to him.'

The fat old man appeared surprised and bewildered by this early call and squatted down outside his hut, his buttocks on his hands as a sign of respect. Cook was soon convinced that the king—perhaps alone among the natives—knew nothing of the theft of the cutter, and when Cook invited him on board his ship, King Terreeoboo readily agreed to come.

It was at about this time that there was heard the sound of musket-fire from two parts of the bay, followed by the deeper boom of a ship's guns. The firing acted as an instant signal of alarm. The signs of friendliness and respect among the natives dissolved, and Cook and Phillips saw that they were beginning to arm themselves with stones and spears, were donning their close-woven mats which they wore for protection in battle, and were gathering in great numbers, and at great speed, along the rocky shore below the village.

As the two English officers and the king made their way slowly down towards the shore, there was no sign of the earlier obsequies. Instead of prostrating themselves before *Orono*, the natives formed themselves into an increasingly noisy and threatening mob which the marines had difficulty in holding back. It was clear that they suspected Cook's designs on their king. They had never before seen Cook with an armed escort, and the gun-fire from the bay confirmed their suspicions that he was up to no good.

King Terreeoboo still appeared innocently unaware of the crisis that was growing about him and was quite content to continue strolling down towards the pinnace moored alongside the promontory. Then he saw a woman breaking through the crowd towards him. She was one of his favourite wives. She stood before him and 'with many tears, and entreaties, besought him not to go on board'. To add force to her pleas, two chiefs accompanied her and forced the king to sit down, which he did, according to Phillips, 'with the strongest marks of terror and dejection in his countenance'.

Cook still believed with good reason that he and Phillips and their escort could extricate themselves from this increasingly dangerous situation, but that it would be wiser not to attempt to drag the king on board against the wishes of his subjects. 'We can never think of compelling him . . . without killing a number of these people,' he said to Phillips, who ordered his marines to force their way through the closing mob and form up along the shore.

When they saw that their king was safe the crowd opened up and allowed the marines and the officers to continue their walk towards the shore. Although the natives, estimated to number around three thousand, were still noisy and hostile, the temperature had obviously cooled and it appeared to eyewitnesses that there would be no more difficulty in re-embarking the shore party.

At this delicate moment, with Cook some thirty yards from the shore, the mob's fury was suddenly re-energised by news, brought by fast canoe, of slaughter out in the bay. Blood had been spilt as a result of the fire from the ship's guns and the musket-fire. Bligh, it transpired, had chased one large canoe which had attempted to escape, firing at it and supported by the *Resolution*'s guns, but it had escaped by running into the surf. Young Rickman had been in trouble too. He had emulated Bligh, pursuing and firing on a canoe, and killing a man. Unfortunately his victim turned out to be a popular and powerful chief.

This was the news brought by the messenger, and it spread like a shock wave, leaving hysteria in its wake. The men increased their pressure about the beleagured party and the women and children struggled to the rear for safety. The nervous tension among the natives, which had been building up again since the unexpected return of the ships, was about to manifest itself in an orgy of violence.

The horror of the following minutes has been recorded in the reports of several eyewitnesses. The events were too distant to be observed with the naked eye from either of the vessels. But there were officers on the decks of both vessels who followed the sequence of the assassination scene by scene through glasses. They bore out the account by Phillips, a participant and survivor as well as the hero of those terrible minutes at Kowrowa.

A native broke from the threatening circle about Cook and Phillips, raising in one hand his *pahhooa*, a long spike like a spear, and in the other hand a stone, shouting threats and abuse. Cook replied at first by a gesture ordering him to retreat, and when this failed by firing the barrel of his musket loaded with ball-shot.

This had none of the deterrent effect Cook had expected. Quite the reverse. The shot failed to penetrate the native's protective mat, which he flaunted first mockingly at Cook and then triumphantly at his own people.

Stones were already flying, aimed at the marines who stood along the shore with muskets at the ready and at Phillips and Cook. A chief lunged at Phillips with his dagger. Phillips deflected the blow and swung the butt of his musket at the man's head. Another came at him from behind, stabbing him between the shoulders. Phillips turned, discharged a ball and killed him instantly.

The screaming mob closed about Cook, who must now have realised that he was doomed. He fired his remaining barrel at the nearest native. The man fell. But it was ominously clear that these Hawaiians were not as afraid of musket-fire as Cook had anticipated. Instead of falling back, the sound and fury were intensified. The marines on the shore fired one volley, then a second. The marines left behind to guard the cutter also discharged a volley. The front ranks of natives were decimated. The rest came on, running over the bodies, hurling stones, waving their spears.

Before Cook was swallowed in the onrush among the rocks a few yards from the shore he was seen to be waving his hat. Was he calling for help, ordering each man to fend for himself, or signalling a retreat and his own doom? At that tumultuous moment no one knew.

The marines were overwhelmed within seconds. Their shipmates in the boats saw them fall among the rocks, engulfed by such a weight of numbers that they could not even use their swords. As they struggled in the shallow water, their brains were beaten out against the rocks. Four of them, all wounded by stones, somehow extricated themselves from the holocaust and plunged into the surf, trying to make towards the boats.

Cook's end was near. He had already been knocked down by one stone. Beside him Phillips had drawn his sword, had despatched one of his captain's assailants, and was seen holding back the mob for several seconds, though badly wounded, in the hope of covering Cook's retreat. Cook was seen to rise from a rock pool into which he had fallen, but before he regained his feet a chief rushed and stabbed him from behind. When he fell a second time the nearest warriors pounced onto his body, snatching from one another the chief's dagger in a frenzy of eagerness to share the kudos for the assassination.

Phillips could do no more. Still using his sword to great effect, he retreated across the rocks, evading the stones and dagger thrusts, dived into the water and swam out to the nearer boat, the crew pulling him over the gunwale.

But this was not the end of his heroism. The last of the wounded marines was fast sinking in the water. Phillips plunged in again, brought him up, and dragged him to the side of the boat. As soon as they were safely in, the oars were dipped and the cutter was soon out of range of the stone-throwers.

Too late, the *Resolution*'s guns roared, the smoke drifting across the bay as if to salute the death of the great navigator. This cannon-ade was too much for the massed natives, who fled as quickly as they had raced into the kill, disappearing among the coconut plantations and the village huts, leaving behind their fallen and the corpses of the men they had slain.

Already the men in the cutter were asking among themselves why their 'great and excellent Commander' had fallen. The natives' change of temper had been so sudden, their ferocity so fearful. It was easier to account for their own failure to hold off the attack. No one in the cutter doubted that the cause lay in Lieutenant Williamson's reluctance to support them. After the attack began, Williamson had ordered his boat to stand farther off from the shore. This retreat had encouraged the natives. If only Williamson had brought his boat close in, had landed his contingent with fixed bayonets, had led them vigorously into the attack with drawn swords, Cook and the fallen marines would still be alive. Even the support of their musket-fire could have turned the tide. This was what they were saying bitterly in the cutter as the men rowed hard to their ship or comforted the wounded.

(Besides being a cautious fellow, Williamson seems also to have been wily. According to the surgeon's mate, the whole ship's company wanted to have him court-martialled. Williamson in turn claimed that Cook, in his last extremity, had waved the boats away from the shore—and that, in any case, his powder was damp. Later in the voyage, according to this same surgeon's mate, 'He got all the men to become freemasons by bribing them with brandy, and got them to promise, as brothers, that they would say nothing of his cowardice when they came to England.' Williamson apparently had a way with him. He had been promoted first lieutenant before the *Resolution* returned home. His naval career seemed to be set fair.)

Speculation and accusation became more general after the boat's crews had rejoined their ships. Others besides Williamson might be at fault. For example, if orders had been given for the ships' guns to be fired earlier, the beach might have been cleared of natives before the attack. If the marines had stood firm, fixed bayonets and charged, the natives would have been scattered. David Samwell noted that all the marines' wounds were in the back, like the first blows struck against Lieutenant Phillips and Cook himself. The old saying that to face an Indian was enough to make him run away was repeated.

Then, why had not the boats' crews at least returned to retrieve the bodies of Cook and the marines after the shore had been cleared by the cannon-fire? The mutilation of enemy dead was a well-known Polynesian practice. At least their commander could have been spared this final indignity.

It was soon known that Bligh's boat had fired first at a fleeing canoe, and that this had led to the *Resolution*'s opening fire with her guns in support. A minute or two later Lieutenant Rickman had ordered his men to open fire, too. And it was these shots that had killed the chief. But no one believed that the young lieutenant would have fired if Bligh had not fired first.

Feeling against Bligh and Rickman was almost as strong as it was against Williamson. Everyone except Bligh knew that Cook's death was a direct result of the impetuous firing. William Bayley, the astronomer, recorded that 'a man arrived in a small canoe from the opposite side of the bay with the account of a chief of some note being killed by our people in the boats at that side. This intelligence seems to have spread the alarm, as they all began to arm themselves with clubs and spears.' King wrote of the shooting as giving 'a fatal turn to the affair.'

Bligh was the odd one out. He believed that he had been absolutely right to open fire on the canoes. Nor did he believe that the chief's death had had any influence on the events of that tragic day. 'Lieut. Rickman did fire and it was said killed a man; but the attack was over and past before that was known', he wrote some years later. He made no reference to his own part in the affair.

The violence and bloodshed in Karakakooa Bay was not yet at an end. By nine o'clock all but one of the boats had returned to the ships, and all sense of leadership and order had been temporarily lost. Captain Clerke was in a state of near panic, and had forgotten that there was a party still on shore, including Lieutenant King, Bayley, and the men who were repairing the *Resolution*'s mainmast and sails, protected only by half a dozen marines. Their position now was obviously highly dangerous. Moreover, without her mast and sails the *Resolution* was a crippled vessel.

When Captain Clerke at last remembered the plight of this shore party and brought his telescope to bear he saw that King and his men were surrounded by natives. That was enough, and he immediately ordered two four-pounders to be fired into their midst.

This canonade infuriated Bayley and King, who had all along been busily and successfully calming the fears of the natives at Kakooa, according to Cook's instructions . . . No harm will come to you, King had repeatedly told them.

King urgently despatched a boat with a message begging that the firing should cease. Clerke's answer was almost as provocative as a broadside from his ship. He sent Bligh ashore with a party of marines. This was too much for King. Ordering Bligh to take no violent action unless their lives were in danger, King forced his way through the crowds of bewildered natives and took Bligh's boat back to the *Discovery* to remonstrate. He had just reached the top of the gangway when he heard the sound of musket-fire from the shore. Bligh was already in action again.

Any sort of reconciliation with the natives was now out of the question, and when King made for the shore again he had with him a strong escort of marines. By the time they arrived a battle was in full swing, musket-fire against stones and spears again. The natives had been joined by the already blooded warriors from Kowrowa. They were attacking with huge courage, quite regardless of casualties, and in complete contradiction to Bligh's contention that resolute action would always put natives to flight.

The arrival of King's strong reinforcements created a brief lull, in which the men succeeded in getting the mast and sails down to the shore and on board one of the boats. By half past eleven all the officers, marines and ratings were safely back in their ships.

During the four weeks between the assassination of Cook and the departure of the *Resolution* and *Discovery* the crews were able to witness the astonishing post-breakdown condition of the natives, ranging from fear to gloating glee, belated contriteness to aggression again. Captain Clerke, now in command (although almost prostrated by his weak nervous and physical condition), contrived to retrieve piecemeal the remains of his late commander—some flesh one day, and

later his hands, part of his skull and the burned remains of his limbs—
so that they were able to commit most of his body to the deep,
with full honours. But the ships' companies were also treated to
insolent displays along the shore, the natives standing in line, bent
over to reveal their buttocks, which they beat in a triumphant
tattoo.

Yet a few days later a shore party was greeted 'with great earnest-
ness and apparent apprehension'. 'When will the *Orono* come again,
and what will he do to us?' asked the natives. Later, strong measures
had to be used against the Hawaiians when they attempted to interfere with watering parties from the vessels.

King's narratives of these events, carefully bland and designed to
give the least offence, contrasts significantly with Bligh's comments.
These have survived as marginal notes in his own copy of the
published narrative.

Bligh's marginal note to Captain King's account of Cook's assassination reads: 'A most infamous lie for I took down in writing all that
happened here before I slept & particularly the Lieutenant's opinion,
who told me that as soon as the Musquets were discharged they ran
to the Boats, having no time to reload, & was stabed in the back when
unable to make any resistance.'

'A pretty old woman story', writes Bligh against this account of
punitive action:

'It was now found absolutely necessary to burn down some
straggling houses, near the wall, behind which they had taken
shelter. In executing these orders, I am sorry to add, that our
people were hurried into acts of unnecessary cruelty and deva-
station.'

Again on the next page where King regrets the shooting of some natives, and the bringing on board of their severed heads, Bligh comments briskly: 'If this had not been done they would never have been brought to submission.'

Bligh was confident that if he had been in command there would have been a deal more firmness with the natives. As for King, Bligh obviously despised him for his weakness and indecisiveness. For example, when King at a particularly critical moment writes, 'I cannot enough lament the illness that confined me on board this day,' Bligh notes in the margin, 'Whenever any dangerous situation should be taking place he always was ill.'

Nor is there any evidence that he thought very highly of anyone else. He thought that the marines on the fatal day acted like cowards: '. . . for had they fixed their bayonets and not have run, so frightened as they were, they might have drove them all before . . .' And of their lieutenant, Molesworth Phillips, in King's eyes the one heroic figure during the affray, Bligh writes pungently: 'This person, who never was of any real service the whole voyage, or did anything but eat and sleep, was a great croney of C. King's, and he has taken care not to forget, although it is very laughable to those who knew the characters. . . .'

And what did 'the characters' think of William Bligh? There are no known narratives, diaries or records of any kind to guide us. We can judge only by the glaring omissions from the official narrative, which to his fury deprived Bligh of so much credit for the charts and the navigation after Cook's death and their departure from Karakakooa Bay for the last time. For example, King gives no credit to Bligh for his superb feat of navigation as sailing master to Kamchatka and the Bering Strait in one more fruitless effort to discover the north-west passage; and the long voyage home by way of the Cape of Good Hope.

As a concluding tailpiece to this unhappy voyage, we are left with a picture of Bligh four years later, in 1784. He is now twenty-nine, a stouter figure than he had been when he was navigating through the Bering Strait or sketching the coastline of the Sandwich Islands. He has just bought the three large fat quarto volumes of *A Voyage to the Pacific Ocean* and is poring over them at his desk. From time to time he makes pencil notations (later in many cases inked over in red or black). He reaches page 83, volume III, describing the departure from Hawaii and the delicate navigation demanded by the weather over the following days among the islands which, between them, Cook and Bligh had only recently and partly charted. No mention of Bligh's name appears. In his fine clear, hand Bligh writes: 'C. Clerke being very ill in a decline he could not attend the deck, and thus publicly gave me the power solely of conducting the ships and moving as I thought proper. . . .'

'The above is my survey', 'This is a copy of my chart', 'An absolute falsity'—there is no doubt that Bligh was justified in his complaints. But what, one must ask, led to the editing out of anything that might be considered favourable to Bligh in the first two volumes written by Cook, and to Captain King's omissions and distortions in the third volume of the narrative? Was no one prepared to support his claims? It appeared to Bligh that his achievements and real abilities would be for ever overlooked; but at least one copy would tell the truth.

Yet the expedition's sailing master, and in a service in which success and advancement depended so strongly on powerful friends and the patronage they could offer, was to ascend higher and receive greater honours than any of those who sought to denigrate his work. Captain Clerke died at Kamchatka. Captain King was dead within four years of his return. Captain Williamson (as he became) was court-martialled after the Battle of Camperdown—in which Bligh played a notably valiant part—found guilty of cowardice and cashiered. In Nelson's view he ought to have been shot. Lieutenant Rickman was never promoted. None of the others made any notable contribution to naval achievement at a time when opportunities were greater than ever before or since.

William Bligh became a vice-admiral and lived to be sixty-three, his naval and political career a patchwork of mutiny and gallantry, humiliating insurrection and triumphant navigation, hated and feared by some but admired by many more, and earnestly and loyally loved by one woman. He was loved, too, for several years—the most eventful and fateful years of his life—by one man, as emotional, passionate and mercurial as himself, with whom his name will always be linked—Fletcher Christian.

3
'A great man for the women'

F LETCHER CHRISTIAN was twenty-one years old when he first met William Bligh. He was five feet eight inches tall, dark-haired, 'handsome and cheerful', strong and well built, and slightly bow-legged, according to Bligh's own description of him.

He was usually a resourceful and exciting companion, lively and amusing. There was a light-hearted innocence in his manner which his shipmates loved. He was keenly ambitious and had already done well for himself in the service. He was also subject to moods of depression, when his personality suddenly changed, he fell into black silences, and became slack and lackadaisical in his work. Like this, he invited the concerned attention of his friends as if he were a child needing comfort, rather than an unreliable sailor in need of discipline. These moods did not usually last for long. His resilient spirit soon reasserted itself, and he was off again, alert, energetic, ready for anything. 'He had a bright, pleasing counten-ance,' wrote one officer who sailed with him, 'and a tall commanding figure, well adapted to feats of strength and agility.'

Ashore, Christian was the first to attract the women. They loved on the one hand his swashbuckling self-confidence and charm; on the other his seeming vulnerability. 'A great man for the women,' wrote the mate of the ship in which they sailed together for the first time with William Bligh. 'One of the most foolish young men I ever knew in regard to the sex.'

Fletcher Christian was of good Manx-Cumberland stock. In the sixteenth, seventeenth and eighteenth centuries many close links were forged between the landowning, mining and shipping families of Cumberland and the Isle of Man. This was because sea communications were preferable to land communications, especially in this rugged corner of northern England. Centuries earlier, Norsemen who had settled in Ireland and the Isle of Man arrived in great numbers on the north Lancashire and Cumberland coasts. In Christian's time, Whitehaven on the Cumberland coast was one of the three great ports of western England, and at one time was busier than Liverpool or Bristol. It was only thirty-five miles by sea to Ramsey. It took longer by horse to reach the neighbouring county of Westmorland. Farming in west Cumberland was as prosperous as it was in the island. There were rich seams of coal in the Whitehaven area, which became one of several birthplaces of the industrial revolution.

The Christians (from the Norse Kristin?) had been Manx landowners for centuries and had crossed this narrow strip of sea to Cumberland some time in the 1600s. At the time of Fletcher's birth in 1764 they were connected by marriage to other prominent Manx-Cumberland families such as the Senhouses, Curwens and Dixons. Fletcher's branch of the family lived at Ewanrigg Hall near Maryport. When his father, Charles, a lawyer and landowner, married Ann Dixon she brought the house and land of Moorland Close, near Cockermouth, to her husband. Ann had four sons, the last of them Fletcher, named after his godfather, Jacob Fletcher.

Moorland Close is a typical semi-fortified border farmhouse, lonely, heavily walled against raids from the north, its only entrance through a lofty arched gateway closed with heavy doors. To the south the purple and grey fells of the Cumbrian mountains rise up from the pastureland, their tops often obscured by cloud. Nothing is recorded of Ann or of Charles Christian. They were probably a handsome and sturdy couple, though Fletcher's father died when he was only three or four. Local legend tells of a lively, mischievous boy, who played truant to go birds' nesting and fishing in the Ellerbeck, and was soudly beaten by the teacher—'a terrible flogger'.

This was Brigham School in the nearby village to which Fletcher is said to have ridden every morning on a little piebald pony.

At the age of nine, Fletcher was sent to Cockermouth Grammar School where he had a sound, all-round education for seven years. Cockermouth Grammar produced good poets at that time. One of Fletcher's closest friends and contemporaries was Isaac Wilkinson, whose later fame as a poet was admittedly mainly local. Later Wilkinson wrote of Fletcher, 'I can with truth say a more amiable youth I never met with.' In Fletcher's last year at Cockermouth another and more renowned poet, William Wordsworth, entered the school. It would be nice to think that Fletcher took a kindly interest in him; and he may well have done, as the Christian and Wordsworth families knew one another well.

Two of Fletcher's older brothers followed their father into the law, and one of them, Edward, was reading law at Cambridge at this time. The Wordsworth-Christian bond was strengthened when Edward came down from Cambridge to become for a short time a schoolmaster. By then the Wordsworths had moved from Cockermouth and William was at Hawkshead Grammar School some twenty miles away over the mountains in Westmorland, and there, for one year, William's master was Edward Christian.

The close relationship between the families continued for many years. Edward became a fellow at St John's College, Cambridge, and the first occupant of the Denning Chair of Law and a leading counsel in London. In this capacity he acted for the Wordsworth family in their epic case against the Earl of Lonsdale, from which they eventually derived, after the Earl's death, £8,500 in unpaid debts. William Wordsworth described Edward as a 'very, very clever man', and his sister Dorothy wrote to Jean Pollard (26 June 1791), 'I am very well acquainted with him and a charming man he is.'

The Wordsworths, ever loyal to their Cumberland roots and their old friendship with the Christians, were among the first to rush to the defence of the Christian name after the mutiny and when Fletcher himself was being publicly vilified, and they actively supported Edward in his campaign of defence.

Edward Christian once wrote of his younger brother that 'he possesses extraordinary abilities, is an excellent scholar, and everyone acquainted with him from a boy . . . can testify that no young man was ever more ambitious of what is esteemed right and honourable among men, or more anxious to acquire distinction and advancement by his good conduct in his profession.'

This, of course, must be taken as a highly subjective view. But it is true that everyone seems to have liked Fletcher. And how happy that they did! For he was a young man who needed to be liked by all about him all the time.

There was no strong maritime tradition in the Christian family, and he was eighteen before he made the surprising decision to join the Navy for adventure and travel. Exploration had seized popular interest in England as strongly as it had in Spain and Portugal in the sixteenth century. It had about it an aura of romance and the reality of profit. Many older people could remember Commodore Anson's return, loaded with riches, from his famous circumnavigation. The voyages of Wallis, Carteret, Byron and Cook himself in the Pacific in the 1760s and 1770s had instilled a new spirit of adventurous curiosity among the country's young.

Fletcher Christian was among those who succumbed to the attractions of the sea. He had no interest in an academic career or in the law. Quite simply, he yearned for travel and adventure. The Royal Navy offered both. In 1782 the country was at war with France, Spain and the Netherlands, and was still attempting to stamp out the revolt among the North American colonists. Whatever military follies the Army might be committing, Admirals Rodney, Howe and Hood were in action from the Caribbean and Chesapeake Bay to the Texel.

Christian took readily and happily to life at sea, the squalor and privations as well as the physical demands, the boisterous company and the delights of new places and peoples and climates. He got on well and fast. His good education, his lively mind and manner, ensured that. In 1784, as a twenty-year-old midshipman on the homeward passage from his first voyage to the Far East, he was given a watch in H.M.S. *Eurydice*, a new sixth-rate. This was unusual for a young man with only two years' service.

England was at peace again, and the strength of the Navy was being run down. When the *Eurydice* was paid off, Christian found himself without work. This was the sort of situation in which a large family with wide connections showed its strength. The word was spread among friends and relatives that young Fletcher Christian wanted to continue his career at sea. Who could help?

At length a hopeful word was received. Christian's cousin John, eight years his senior, had first married a Margaret Taubman of Castletown in the Isle of Man. She had died shortly after giving birth to a son, and John had subsequently married into the Curwen family. Close ties remained with the Manx Taubmans, and it was from Captain Taubman himself that Christian heard about a Lieutenant William Bligh, lately sailing master to the great James Cook.

Bligh had led a busy and sometimes dangerous life since he had navigated the *Resolution* back to England at the end of 1780. As soon as his ship had paid off he made his way to the Isle of Man. Elizabeth Betham had remained loyal to his memory and Bligh renewed his courtship. There was a brief engagement, and they were married on 4 February 1781. Elizabeth, like her husband, was twenty-six years old.

This marriage secured Bligh a clever and talented wife whose support over all the troubled years that lay ahead was unswerving. The marriage also secured him a wide range of connections, all powerful and potentially valuable, like the Campbells, and others who were to prove to be more trouble than they were worth, like the Heywoods and Christians.

Meanwhile, his country needed Bligh. Within ten days of his marriage he was appointed master of the captured French frigate *Belle Poule,* in which he saw action for the first time at the bloody but indecisive engagement at the Dogger Bank. Later in the war, and now as a junior lieutenant, Bligh took part in the relief of Gibraltar. He reached England again on 14 November 1782, just in time for the birth of his first daughter, Harriet Maria. It was his last naval appointment for nearly five years, and half pay was a mere two shillings a day, hardly enough for a growing family. Bligh settled down briefly with Elizabeth and their baby in their modest home in Douglas, Isle of Man, and began enquiring among his wife's relatives for work.

The Campbells rapidly proved their worth. This was not surprising, for Bligh, with his wide experience in every ocean and his fine record with Cook, was an attractive proposition to any shipowner. In July 1783 he wrote to Duncan Campbell at his offices in London: 'I am glad to hear you think it likely I may soon be wanted in Town as I am anxious to show you that whatever my services may be, my endeavours in every respect will not be wanting either in exercise or care. I shall be ready at an hour's notice.'

The call soon came. Campbell showed his confidence by in turn appointing Bligh to command one of his merchantmen, putting under Bligh's care his own son John, and appointing him his agent at Port of Lucea for several months. Now well paid, giving satisfaction to his employer and seemingly in a settled career, Bligh rented a house in London and brought his family over from the Isle of Man. While he was bringing shiploads of sugar and rum across the Atlantic, Elizabeth gave birth in turn to two more daughters, one of them, unhappily, a mentally retarded epileptic.

In the late summer of 1785 Bligh was due to take command of Campbell's fine new ship the *Britannia*. His crew was complete and they were soon to sail. It was at this point that he received a letter from one of the Taubmans, who were old family friends of Elizabeth. Bligh had often met them and knew Captain Taubman, the writer of this letter. Its purpose was to recommend Midshipman Fletcher Christian and to ask if Bligh might have a berth for him on board the *Britannia*.

Bligh had never met the young man but knew the Christians as one of the more important families in Cumberland. He would like to oblige, he wrote back, but regretted that he already had a full complement of officers.

Fletcher Christian now took the step that was to link his name with Bligh's for all time. He was desperate to get back to sea, and of course to sail under William Bligh would provide priceless experience. Christian wrote to him direct, asking if he could not change his mind. 'Wages are no object; I only wish to learn my profession, and if you would permit me to mess with the gentlemen, I will readily enter your ship as a foremaster, until there is a vacancy among the officers. We midshipmen,' he continued, 'are gentlemen, we never pull at a rope; I should even be glad to go one voyage in that situation, for there may be occasions when officers may be called upon to do the duties of a common man.'

That seemed to Bligh to be the right spirit, and Christian's persistence paid off. Bligh wrote back that he would be welcome on these terms: working as a rating, messing as an officer. Bligh owed his own situation to family influence. He welcomed the chance to repay his own opportunity in some small measure by oiling the family-connexion machine.

Christian sailed on two voyages to the West Indies in the *Britannia*, first as a gunner. On the second voyage he was promoted to second mate. The special favours he was offered aroused resentment and jealousy, certainly in the heart of the first mate, one Edward Lamb. Seven years later when Bligh, in his turn, was under fierce attack, Lamb wrote that it was a lie that Christian was made an officer in the *Britannia*. 'I recollect you putting him in the articles as a gunner,' he told Bligh in a blistering, bitter letter, 'telling me at the same time you wished him to be thought an officer and desired I would endeavour to make the people look upon him as such.'

Next we read in this same letter the first evidence of the closeness of the relations existing between the twenty-one-year-old midshipman and the 'passionate' ship's captain who was ten years older. 'When we got to sea I saw your partiality for the young man, I gave him every advice and information in my power, though he went about every point of duty with a degree of indifference that to me was truly unpleasant; but you were blind to his faults and had him to dine and sup every other day in the cabin, and treated him like a brother in giving him every information.'

If Christian was a slack and indifferent seaman, it seems more odd than ever that Bligh gave him such favoured treatment, 'blind to his faults'. It was, after all, accepted that there was always a point when you ceased to favour and support your friends and relatives if they failed to match up to expectation; moreover Bligh of all men did not suffer gladly laziness or incompetence on board his ships.

Bligh's success in the service of Duncan Campbell had attracted the attention of a lot of people. The most important of these was Sir Joseph Banks (1744–1820), scientist, entrepreneur, explorer, naturalist and visionary, a man of great wealth, energy and influence who had sailed at his own expense with Cook on his first Pacific voyage and was now President of the Royal Society, already a venerable and deeply respected institution in the worlds of science and philosophy. By 1787 Bligh's reputation, especially as a navigator, was well known to Banks.

Like Campbell, Banks had substantial financial interests in the West Indies, where the profits from colonial exploitation were as satisfactory as anywhere in the world. But for more than a decade the cost of feeding the slaves working on the sugar plantations had been a constant worry. The main problem was that most of the food had to be imported from North America. The War of Independence had underlined the need for some sort of action to make the West Indies more self-sufficient. This was the kind of problem that Banks relished because it exercised his scientific bent and in its solution lay ever-greater profits.

As long before as 1775 the Society for West India Merchants had offered to underwrite the expense of importing a cheap food-yielding plant to the 'West India Colonies'; and in its turn the Royal Society added as a further inducement the offer of its prestigious Gold Medal to the first person who succeeded in conveying 'six plants . . . in a growing state'. The plant that the merchants and the Royal Society were chiefly interested in was the breadfruit.

'The breadfruit grows on a large tree', wrote William Dampier, pirate-explorer, when he observed it during his circumnavigation in 1688, 'as big as our largest apple trees: It hath a spreading head, full of branches and dark leaves. The fruit grows on the boughs like apples; it is as big as a penny loaf . . . of a round shape, and hath a thick tough rind. When the fruit is ripe it is yellow and soft, and the taste is sweet and pleasant. The natives gather it when full grown, while it is green and hard; they then bake it in an oven, which scorcheth the rind and makes it black; but they scrape off the outside black crust, and there remains a tender thin crust; and the inside is soft, tender, and white like the crumb of a penny-loaf. There is neither seed nor stone in the inside, but all is of a pure substance, like bread . . .'

Hawkesworth, describing the voyage on which Banks accompanied Cook, wrote that to procure the breadfruit cost the Tahitians 'no trouble or labour but climbing a tree. . . . If a man plants ten of them in his lifetime, which he may do in about an hour, he will completely fulfil his duty to his own and future generations as the native of our less temperate climate can do by ploughing in the cold winter, and reaping in the summer's heat, as often as these return.'

For the few months when it was not in season it could be made into a durable paste; and from the fibre beneath its bark a useful cloth could be made.

Many other navigators reported on this succulent fruit in glowing

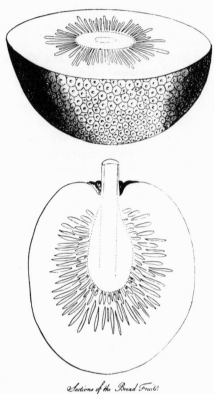

Sections of the Bread Fruit.

Sketch of bread fruit

terms, and most seamen (usually notorious for their conservatism and dislike of tropical fruits) were glad enough to break the monotony of ship's biscuits with some warm, doughy breadfruit. It was prolific, tough and grew readily all over Polynesia.

Early in 1787 Banks and Lord Sydney, one of King George's Principal Secretaries of State, began informal discussions on the problems involved in transporting some breadfruit plants from Polynesia to the British West Indies colonies. It would be a delicate, complicated and expensive operation, but its benefits would be immense. Think of it! No more plantains and maize, which were so temperamental and expensive to grow. No more risks of famine in the West Indies. Free nourishing food for twelve months in the year.

Until now no attempts had been made to exploit the discoveries made by the numerous English-sponsored voyages to the Pacific. Their aims had not been entirely altruistic; but neither had they brought back with them the riches of the tropics. By contrast with the earlier voyages of Dampier, Anson and Drake—to say nothing of the Portuguese, Spanish and Dutch trading and colonising expeditions to the East—these had scarcely been profitable exercises.

The voyage now being planned by Banks and Lord Sydney was considered in profit-making terms from the start. George III, 'our farmer king', was, of course, an enthusiastic supporter. Everybody seemed to be in favour of it. It was a marvellous idea. Formal authority for the voyage was given in a letter from Lord Sydney to the Lords Commissioners of the Admiralty on 5 May 1787, while Bligh and Christian were arranging to embark one more rich cargo of sugar from Campbell's Briscoes Estate into the *Britannia*.

The vessel to be selected by the Admiralty 'for the transportation of the Bread-fruit and other valuable productions of the East' was to proceed to Tahiti for the collection of upwards of one thousand breadfruits by way of Cape Horn, thence through the Torres Strait to Cape Town, to St Helena 'where she will receive orders from England pointing out the places in the West Indies at which she is to touch and deliver cargo'. Time was short if the worst Cape Horn season was to be avoided, and urgent consideration was given by Banks and Lord Sydney to the choice of vessel, of master to command her, and of a botanist to supervise the vital horticultural aspects of the voyage. All this was accomplished in the months of May and June.

The selection of botanist, or gardener, was no problem. David Nelson was the man. Banks knew him well. He had been first recommended to Banks by old James Lee of the Vineyard Nurseries at Hammersmith. Another notable botanist, one Robert Bran, had named a genus of *Acanthacea* after him. Nelson was a quiet, unassuming, diligent man. He was also the most travelled gardener in the world. He had sailed with Cook on his last voyage, had successfully collected plants and seeds and knew how to look after them at sea. He had already been to Tahiti, and even had a fair smattering of the islanders' language. On one of the Friendly Islands he had stoically survived being stoned and stripped when caught botanising alone by some natives. In him the spirit of adventure burnt as brightly as the spirit of science. So, when the call came from Banks, he gladly gathered together his books on botany, his Polynesian notes, his plant presses and drying papers, his wooden boxes and casks. For his assistant he chose William Brown, a tall, slim gardener of twenty-five years.

Banks had no doubts about the choice of commander either, although it would be up to the Lords Commissioners to make the final decision. Duncan Campbell warmly confirmed Banks's choice, although it meant the loss of his most valuable master. As early as 2 May it appeared likely that Bligh would be selected, for on that day Duncan Campbell was writing that 'I wish Bligh home soon, as thereby he may stand a chance of employment in his own line, but of this more by and by'.

The *Britannia* raised the Downs on 31 July, and tied up in the Thames on 5 August, when Bligh heard the first official news of his appointment. It was the greatest honour that could have been paid to the thirty-three-year-old lieutenant. He knew who had been responsible for it, and he wrote off to Banks that 'I have heard the flattering news of your great goodness to me, intending to honour me with the command of the vessel which you propose to go to the South Seas, for which, after offering you my most grateful thanks, I can only assure you I shall endeavour, and I hope succeed, in deserving such a trust. . . .'

Bligh's vessel had been chosen in his absence. The Navy Board had advertised for a suitable ship on 10 May, and by the 16th were already considering five vessels offered, all of them under the maximum specified burthen of 250 tons. These were narrowed down to two, both in the Thames, the *Bethia* of 230 tons and the *William Pitt* of 240 tons. The *Bethia* was selected on the recommendation of the assistant to the Surveyor of the Navy, and approved by Sir Joseph Banks. She was a three-masted merchantman built at Hull two and a half years earlier, ninety-one feet long overall on the upper deck, with an extreme breadth of twenty-four feet ten inches; handsomely ornamented with a figurehead of a woman dressed in a riding habit.

Under the direction of Banks, Nelson and the assistant surveyor, modifications to the *Bethia* for her unusual new function were put in hand without delay: copper sheathing for protection against the notorious *teredo navalis*, especially damaging in tropical waters; guns for protection against hostile natives and piratical attacks *en route*; special accommodation for the plants. She was, in short, to be a floating and armed conservatory.

'The difficulty of carrying plants by sea is very great,' Banks emphasised. 'A small sprinkling of salt water or of the salt dew which fills the air even in a moderate gale will inevitably destroy them if not immediately washed off with fresh water. It is necessary therefore that the cabin be appropriated to the sole purpose of making a kind of greenhouse, and the key of it given to the custody of the gardener; and that in case of cold weather in going round the Cape a stove be provided by which it may be kept in a temperature equal to that of the inter-tropical countries.'

The whole of the lower deck from a point midway between the main and mizzen masts and the stern, normally the most comfortable and commodious area in a ship, was sacrificed to the greenhouse—its rows of pots to accommodate over one thousand plants, its lead-lined deck and elaborate drainage system for recovering the fresh water used for watering the plants, and its large gratings in the deck and scuttles in the side for ventilating them. 'The master and crew,' Banks crisply observed, 'must not think it a grievance to give up the best of her accommodation.'

So Navy Board parsimony in limiting the size of the vessel was bound to lead to overcrowding on a voyage that was certain to last nearly two years. And, because of the length and nature of the voyage the ship's complement would number no fewer than forty-seven, to work the watches, carry out running repairs, feed the men, man the guns in action and tend the plants. There could certainly be no accommodation for any Royal Marines either for punitive measures ashore or to give edge to the captain's authority on board. The ship's commander would have to fend for himself.

Honoured and flattered as he was at this appointment, Bligh was from the beginning alarmed that he was to have no marines on such a long and hazardous voyage, nor any commissioned officer to share his responsibilities and support him. He had every confidence that he would avoid any trouble with his men. But you never knew on a voyage as long as this would be. He also hoped to avoid any situation as dangerous as Cook had met in Hawaii. But Polynesians were not always friendly, it was not always possible to avoid conflicts with them, and he would be trading with them and living among them for a long time.

He was to be ship's commander and purser, responsible for the

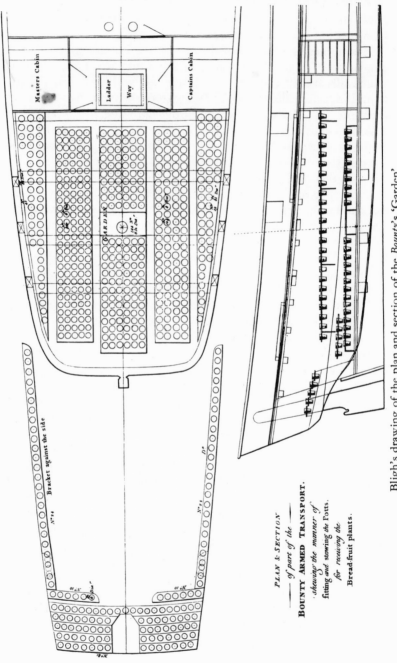

Masters Cabin

Ladder

Way

Captains Cabin

GARDEN

Bracket against the side

PLAN & SECTION
of part of the
BOUNTY ARMED TRANSPORT.
shewing the manner of
fitting and stowing the Potts.
for receiving the
Bread-fruit plants.

Bligh's drawing of the plan and section of the *Bounty*'s 'Garden' safe passage, the issuing of rations, the health, welfare and discipline of the crew: a total and solitary dictator—all for £70 a year instead of the £500 Campbell had been paying him.

Bligh's authority would have been strengthened if he had been promoted captain. But this was not to be. All that Lord Howe, First Sea Lord, would promise him was promotion on his successful accomplishment of the mission. Bligh was not pleased at this further evidence of navy meanness and complained widely to his friends and relatives. To Duncan Campbell he wrote angrily, 'The hardship I make known I lay under is that they took me from a state of affluence in your employ . . . to perform a voyage which few were acquainted with sufficiently to ensure it any degree of success . . .' His father-in-law wrote sympathetically, 'Government I think have gone too frugally to work; both the ship and the complement of men are too small in my opinion for such a voyage.' Lord Selkirk complained strongly to Banks that Bligh was sailing on such an important mission only with the rank of lieutenant and that the 'establishment of Bligh's vessel is that of a cutter . . . highly improper for so long a voyage, without a lieutenant or any marines'.

Bligh was not pleased with the ship either. He travelled to Deptford Yard to examine the *Bethia*—now more appropriately named *Bounty*—on 16 August. For a start, he found her too small for the task, and the accommodation appallingly cramped for such a long voyage. Under Nelson's supervision, the great cabin had been entirely taken over as Banks had directed by five rows of double-tiered planks, pierced to receive the pots, with narrow aisles between for tending the plants. There was nothing to be done about this and he would have to make the best of the situation. The garden was the *raison d'être* of the voyage, and of the *Bounty* herself. But as Bligh walked the decks of the ship in the yard, studying the rigging and specification, he determined on a number of modifications which would improve her sailing qualities and safety, and the comfort of the men.

The *Bounty*'s masts had already been cut down but he considered that she would still be carrying too much top weight for Pacific weather and ordered them to be further shortened. Nor did he like the weight of ballast being carried and arranged for this to be reduced from forty-five to nineteen tons. Bligh learned that, besides the two cutters—the large eighteen-foot cutter and the sixteen-foot small cutter or jolly boat—a twenty-foot launch had been ordered

Dimensions of masts and yards of the *Bounty* after Bligh's final modifications.

	Masts			Yards		
	Length		Diam.	Length		Diam.
	Ft.	In.	In.	Ft.	In.	In.
Main Mast	55		16	41		$11\frac{1}{4}$
Topmast (the whole length)	35	10	$10\frac{3}{4}$	35	2	$8\frac{1}{8}$
Do. Head	4	9				
Gallt. Mast (to the Hounds)	18	2	6	24	$8\frac{5}{8}$	5
Polehead	9	1				
Fore Mast	51		$16\frac{1}{2}$	38		10
Topmast (the whole length)	34	3	$10\frac{3}{4}$	30	6	7
Do. Head	4	0				
Gallt. Mast (to the Hounds)	17	3	$4\frac{3}{4}$	24	8	5
Polehead	8	7				
Mizzen Mast	48	2	$11\frac{1}{4}$	21	2	$6\frac{1}{8}$
Topmast (the whole length)	24	$3\frac{1}{2}$	$6\frac{7}{8}$	24	0	5
Do. Head	3	1				
Bowsprit	35	4	$18\frac{1}{4}$	30	6	$6\frac{3}{8}$
Do. Housing	10	2				
Jib Boom	27	1	$8\frac{3}{4}$			
Cross Jack Yard				30	6	$6\frac{1}{2}$

from John Burr, the naval contractor. He approved of the jolly boat but persuaded the Navy Board that the large cutter should be a twenty-foot six-oared one, and that the launch, too, was not large enough.

This was an odd decision—one might say a prescient one. Bligh insisted on a twenty-three-foot launch, the standard naval size it is true but far oversize for a modest brig like the *Bounty*, and awkward to stow. This new launch would accommodate four additional men.

On 3 September the *Bounty* was removed from her dock and towed out alongside a hulk in the river. For the next five weeks Bligh was continuously engaged on completing and fitting out his ship. The Navy Board emphasised 'the utmost despatch' and Bligh was able to spend little time with Elizabeth and the children at their house in Lambeth. He was familiar with all the tasks and the dockyard officers were put on their mettle. At the victualling office arrangements were completed for the stowing below of supplies for eighteen months.

The *Bounty*'s provisions consisted largely of the basic—and notorious—ship's biscuit, laughingly called bread, tough, weevil-ridden and virtually indestructible; salt pork and beef in casks, dried peas,

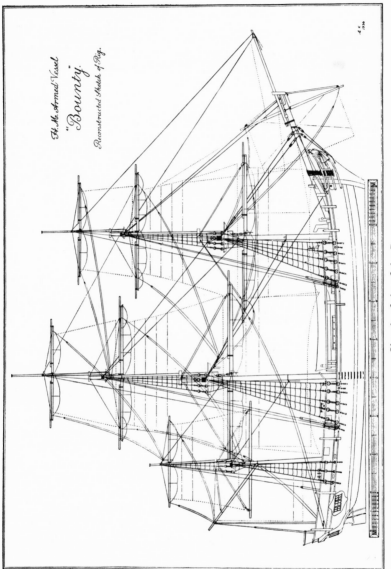

Sketch of rig of the *Bounty*

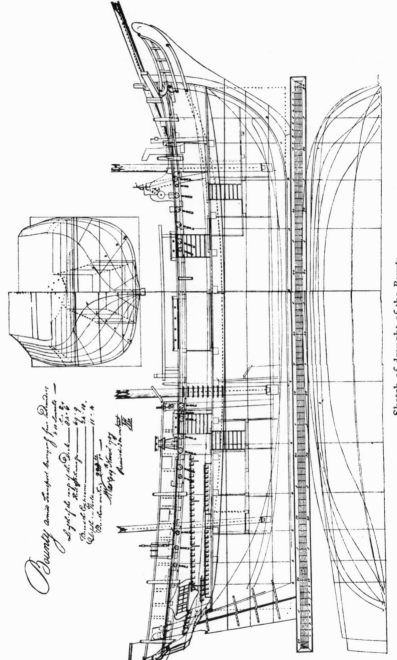

Sketch of draught of the *Bounty*

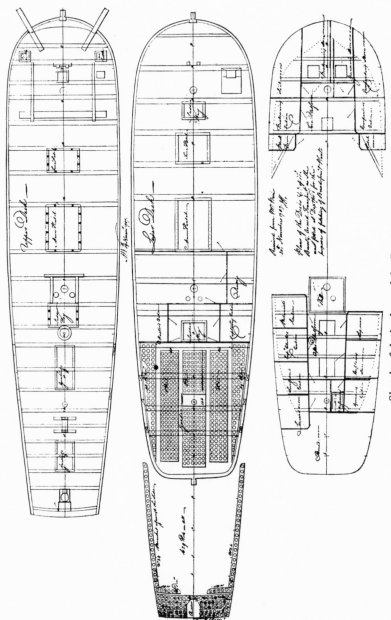

Sketch of deck plans of the *Bounty*

grog (rum), beer, and wine. In addition there was stowed below supplies of the new lifesavers, essence of malt, barley, wheat and oatmeal, *sauerkraut* and—marvellous new invention—portable soup. This concoction was regarded as an acceptable substitute for fresh vegetables, and therefore anti-scorbutic. It was made by boiling vegetables until finally the remaining juice solidified, when it lasted for ever. (There is a piece in the National Maritime Museum, Greenwich, today.)

Finally, it should be added that in traditional service manner, all these fancy new foodstuffs were treated with the gravest suspicion by the lower deck who believed that the only things that kept them alive, and were worth consuming, were grog, beer, wine, biscuit and salt meat.

The *Bounty*'s mission was regarded primarily as a trading one. The only successful method of acquiring one thousand breadfruit plants was to buy them. Any other method must lead to trouble. It was Bligh's job to buy 'on the best and cheapest terms' with what the Board called 'the toys and chisels for the Indians of the Islands in the South Seas from whom breadfruit trees are to be procured'. This meant no fewer than 2,800 steel blades in five different patterns, one thousand knives with wooden handles and sheaths, several thousand nails, forty-eight saws and numerous hatchets and gimlets, rasps and files—all beloved by the Polynesians and worth a king's ransom in local currency—though a mere £125 in England. Those old favourites, threepenny and sixpenny looking-glasses, coloured beads and stained glass drops for ear-rings, were included along with six dozen coarse shirts for special presents and trading.

The one hundred gold ducats were for more sophisticated trading places, like Batavia or Java, for the replacement of lost plants *en route*—if any could be found—and for purchasing provisions.

By 9 October the victualling, storing and refitting had been completed, all on time and with no special problems. The carpenter's crew had built four cages on the forecastle deck for their live cargo of a dozen hens, some pigs and half a dozen sheep which they would take on board at the last minute. Somebody appeared with a dog, the inevitable pet, mascot and butt of many a joke. There had to be a dog.

The *Bounty* was ready to proceed down river to Longreach where the four carriage light four-pounder guns and her ten half-pounder swivel guns were awaiting collection, along with the muskets and pistols, the ammunition and the cutlasses for the ship's two arms chests.

Meanwhile, on top of all this work and supervision, Bligh's most important task was the selection of his officers and ratings. This is worth looking at very closely. Living conditions, food, the style of discipline, the route and the timing of events—all these must play an important part in bringing about any threat of trouble at sea far from home. Finally, it is the quality of the officers and men, and of the commander himself, which will avert this threat, or turn it to violence.

It is easy enough to cite examples of the breakdown of control and the discipline in a ship, when the men suddenly and spontaneously explode into violence. Take that tyrant Hugh Pigot, commander of the *Hermione* and a great flogging man. He even began flogging the last man down from the yards as a matter of course. One day off Puerto Rico two men fell in their haste and were killed. The men seized the captain, murdered him, mutilated his body and threw it overboard—along with the corpses of eight other officers they murdered for good measure.

It is more difficult to cite cases when a commander, by firmness and diplomacy, has snuffed out the threat of imminent mutiny. They are not usually considered worthy of record.

The first thing to remember about the *Bounty*'s company is that, except for the gardener and his assistant, they were all chosen by Bligh personally. He had no clearly defined powers to select his officers and men, and the Lords Commissioners of the Admiralty could certainly bring pressure to bear on a commander, or simply deprive him of his command if he did not yield. The system was deliberately left open, and on the whole it worked well enough. A good commander would certainly listen to the appeals of his senior officers and his more powerful friends and relations in his selection; but a good commander would not put these considerations above those of the true worth of candidates; for his success and promotion, and even his life, might depend on the quality of his crew. He favoured those he had sailed with and had proved themselves—and friends of those who had proved themselves. If he was a good commander he was a good judge of men; and a commander learned at close quarters the qualities and failings of his men on a two-year voyage to the Pacific and back, through long and uneventful periods of tedium and sudden alarms, in a vessel of less than 300 tons.

First the midshipmen. The *Bounty*'s rating officially permitted Bligh to appoint only two. But there was nothing to stop him from including supernumerary midshipmen, who were ranked as able seamen but did duty as midshipmen and messed with the officers. This encouraged friends and relations to press the claims of their eager sons if the voyage sounded an attractive and profitable one. So, when news of Bligh's appointment reached the Isle of Man, the Bethams began busily putting forward names to their son-in-law, William.

One of the first was Peter Heywood, son of a close friend of the family—father a Manx deemster and steward to the Duke of Atholl. Young Peter (he was only fourteen) was a lively lad and everyone liked him. His elder sister Nessy doted on him, and he was 'the idol of the family'. Peter had been mad about the sea since he could remember and had entered the navy a year earlier. Bligh had often met him at the Heywood's house, and when Elizabeth's father wrote recommending this 'ingenious lad', this 'favourite of mine', Bligh willingly complied, and even had him to stay with his own family at Lambeth while the *Bounty* was fitting out.

Elizabeth had already staked a claim for John Hallett, brother of her old friend Anne. And the Bethams asked Bligh to include, too, Tom Hayward, one of another old Manx family.

Then there was Edward Young, a saturnine young man, reputed to have West Indian blood in his veins, nephew of Sir George Young. His mother could trace her lineage back to Queen Mary Stewart and to earls created by James IV of Scotland.

When the *Resolution* had put into Stromness in the Orkneys on the last leg of her passage back from the Pacific, Bligh had been entertained by the Stewart family. He had taken a fancy to their boy George, and when this young man wrote to Bligh now, reminding him of his suggestion that he should apply for a berth in his ship when the opportunity arose, Bligh was ready to accept him. He had 'the look of an able stout seaman', though later Bligh was to comment that 'he fell short of what his appearance promised'.

These, then, were the midshipmen, all young, all enthusiastic for the adventure that lay ahead, all seemingly able.

Bligh also knew, either personally or by reputation, most of the warrant and petty officers—William Peckover, for instance, the gunner, a veteran if there ever was one, who had sailed on all three of Cook's Pacific voyages, and the proven if overweight quartermaster, John Norton. John Fryer, the *Bounty*'s master was unknown to him but he came with a good reference and Bligh told Banks that he was confident he was a good man.

The *Bounty*'s surgeon met with Bligh's approval, too. Dr Thomas Huggan was another overweight officer, and he also appeared to be a very steady drinker indeed. However, 'the doctor has a good character', Bligh wrote cheerfully to Banks, and he believed he 'may be a very capable man'. He needed to be congenial company, too, for Bligh, Fryer and the surgeon were to mess together—every meal for many, many months.

There was no shortage of ratings to choose from, and Bligh believed that when he had sorted through all the candidates he had chosen well. Several came with a recommendation, tough little Tom Ellison among them, only fifteen years old but highly regarded by Duncan Campbell himself. Fryer asked that his young brother-in-law, Robert Tinkler, should be included as an able seaman. He was making the Navy his career and hoped to become a midshipman. For the responsible job of sailmaker Bligh himself chose a tough old veteran who had been in the *Britannia* on her last trip, Lawrence Lebogue.

Bligh was insistent on having a musician in the ship's company, both to cheer the men and to provide the music for dancing on board. He knew how slack the men could become on a long voyage, especially across the Pacific from the southern tip of South America to the Society Islands where the south-east trades blew steadily for day after day and there was little for the men to do. There was some difficulty in finding a fiddler prepared to face the rigours of a two-year-long circumnavigation, and in the end he had to make do with a nearly blind fellow. This is how it came about that Michael Byrn, twenty-six years old, a fair-haired, slender and amiable young Irishman from Kilkenny came to be on board the *Bounty*.

As for Fletcher Christian, now twenty-two years old, experienced in all branches of seamanship, and, thanks to Bligh's tutoring, a first-class navigator, he was one of the first to know that he would be sailing to the South Seas, now promoted again to master's mate. The master-pupil relationship with Bligh had developed into something deeper, and more intimate, as all on board the *Britannia* on her second voyage to the West Indies had recognised. The young man and the young middle-aged man seemed to be constantly together. Christian was often in Bligh's cabin in the evenings, and besides dining there every other day while at sea, Christian had a key to Bligh's liquor chest so that he could help himself when he felt inclined.

According to Edward Christian, his brother told him that he had not regretted for one minute his decision to sail as a foremastman on the *Britannia*'s first voyage. Bligh had taken great pains to instruct him. Christian could not, he said, have had a finer master. His judgement of Bligh as a man was brief and ambivalent. While grateful for all the instruction and special treatment, he found Bligh 'a very passionate man, though I believe I have learned how to humour him'. Christian does not appear to have explained this relationship more fully to his brother.

This, then, was the full complement list of the *Bounty* when she sailed, including all the final changes and additions:

Lieutenant William Bligh	Commander
John Fryer	Master
William Cole	Boatswain
William Peckover	Gunner
William Purcell	Carpenter
John Huggan	Surgeon
Thomas Denman Ledward	Surgeon's Mate
Fletcher Christian	Master's Mate
William Elphinstone	Master's Mate
Thomas Hayward	Midshipman
John Hallett	Midshipman
George Stewart	Acting Midshipman
Peter Heywood	Acting Midshipman
Edward Young	Acting Midshipman
Peter Linkletter	Quartermaster
John Norton	Quartermaster
George Simpson	Quartermaster's Mate
James Morrison	Boatswain's Mate
John Mills	Gunner's Mate
Charles Norman	Carpenter's Mate
Thomas McIntosh	Carpenter's Crew
Lawrence Lebogue	Sailmaker

Joseph Coleman   Armourer
Charles Churchill   Master-at-Arms
John Samuel   Clerk and Steward

ABLE SEAMEN

Thomas Burkett, Michael Byrn, Thomas Ellison, Thomas Hall, Henry Hillbrant, Robert Lamb, Isaac Martin, William McKoy, John Millward, William Muspratt, Matthew Quintal, Richard Skinner, Alexander Smith, John Smith, John Sumner, Robert Tinkler, Matthew Thompson, James Valentine, John Williams.

David Nelson   Botanist
William Brown   Botanist's Assistant

The only officer holding the king's commission was Bligh. The king's warrant was held by Huggan the surgeon, Fryer the master, Cole the bo'sun, Peckover the gunner, and Purcell the carpenter. The other officers were petty officers, with limited privileges. Christian and the other midshipmen—really apprentice officers—were classed as ratings (and could therefore be flogged) but messed separately and had other privileges.

The nature of the *Bounty*'s voyage, and her imminent departure, aroused wide interest in London. The details of her route and timing were kept confidential, even from her crew, and this naturally increased the curiosity. The West Indies' merchants were, of course, delighted that, between them, Banks and Campbell had succeeded in organising the voyage. Merchants with interests in other parts of the world, with eyes on profits and the main chance, wondered if there could be anything in it for them. Among these was Sir George Yonge, the Secretary of State for War, who had extensive estates in India. He and others sought out Bligh at Deptford, supposedly to 'make his acquaintance' while the *Bounty* completed her fitting out. Yonge, Bligh reported later to Banks, 'was particularly inquisitive and anxious about my proceedings and orders'. Bligh remained courteously evasive throughout the inspection and interview. Yonge understood that Bligh was to collect plants from the South Seas—could he arrange to deliver some to Madras, or to Java for on-shipment to Madras? Bligh thought this unlikely and was maddeningly vague.

Yonge wrote crossly to Banks on 7 September. Bligh appeared

to be in the hands of his gardener, he complained, who was nowhere
to be found for interrogation. 'I am sorry to say I found Captain
Bligh likely to sail without his errand, he expected several instructions from the Admiralty—he knew he was to go to the South Seas
and some other places but he new little or nothing of the object
of his voyage, had no idea of going to the East Indies or to the West
Indies. A captain of the King's service can not and ought not to
be contented with doing as a gardener bids.'

Later Banks congratulated Bligh on his discretion—and Bligh
wrote back shortly after this incident with the news that Lord Howe
himself, First Lord of the Admiralty, had also visited him at Deptford. Why not, suggested Howe, take in on your outward voyage
a cask of wine at Tenerife for your patron Banks? It should be nicely
matured for him by the time you get back. A circumnavigated wine:
that would add spice to the talk at any dinner table.

Though many frustrating delays still lay ahead before the *Bounty*
cleared the English coast for the last time, Bligh received his orders
to proceed to Spithead on 15 October, and sent his family ahead of
him so that he could spend his last days with them at Portsmouth
in the lodgings he had found there for them.

It was a terrible passage down the Channel, extending the men to
the fullest and revealing at the outset their strengths and weaknesses
—or so Bligh thought. He found little to complain about except the
weather itself, which threatened to throw them on to the French
coast. Fryer gave every satisfaction, the men worked well together.
Bligh thought that he would soon 'have them all in very good
order'.

Only the surgeon was a bit of an anxiety. Fat John Huggan
lurched about the ship, within an ace of breaking a rib or a leg at
every uncertain step, cursing and forever swigging a bottle. Like
the *Bounty* herself he was provisioned for eighteen months, and
there was no chance that he would run short and sober up in the
foreseeable future. 'His indolence and corpulency,' wrote Bligh
mildly to Banks, 'render him rather unfit for the voyage.' But Bligh
was unable to get rid of him and had to resort to taking an additional
crew member, one Thomas Denman Ledward, as surgeon's mate
and as insurance against the day when Huggan broke his neck or
died of grog.

'I think I cannot have much worse weather in going round Cape Horn', Bligh wrote to Banks when the *Bounty* anchored safe at last at Spithead on 4 November. He was better pleased with his ship now. The *Bounty*, inadequate in size though she might be, was a good steady sea boat and had stood up well to her hammering.

But now, briefly, the tone of Bligh's letters changes. He is suddenly no longer blandly optimistic. He is angry and frustrated. The reason for this is what he reasonably describes as Admiralty inefficiency. At Spithead he is under the direct command of Lord Hood, C.-in-C. Portsmouth, and Hood has not yet received Bligh's final sailing orders. Six days later, with a fine east wind blowing, he is still stuck at Spithead. 'To see so fine a wind expending itself and so late in the season as I am, has given me much uneasiness.'

As the days pass he becomes more and more angry. The prickliness reasserts itself and old resentments to which we think he has now become reconciled again erupt. This is how he addresses Duncan Campbell: 'If there is any punishment that ought to be inflicted on a set of men for neglect, I am sure it ought to be on the Admiralty for my three weeks' detention at this place during a fine fair wind which carried all outward bound ships clear of the Channel but me, who wanted it most. This has made my task a very arduous one indeed for to get round Cape Horn at the time I shall be there. I know not how to promise myself any success and yet I must do it if the ship will stand it at all or I suppose my character will be at stake. Had Lord Howe sweetened this difficult task by giving me promotion I should have been satisfied.'

Banks made a last attempt to persuade the members of the Board to change their minds and promote Bligh but they remained obdurate.

At last, on 24 November, Hood received what Bligh had been fretting for. By then the weather had changed for the worse and when at last he did make sail and got clear of the Needles and into the Channel he was beaten back again. Bligh's only consolation was that he was able to spend a little time longer with 'my dear little family'. Almost two months had been needlessly lost before a fair east wind again blew. It was two days before Christmas, and he was now more than ever anxious about conditions round Cape Horn. However, the Admiralty at the last minute gave him discretionary powers. Do not risk your ship unnecessarily. If the weather in the sub-Antarctic is bad, go by way of the Cape of Good Hope.

'If you do not hear from me in '89 you will know that I had to go by Cape Good Hope', wrote Bligh in a last message to Banks.

Sunday 23 . . . at 4 A.M. hove Short & got up Yards and Top-masts and at ½ past 6 Weighed and lay too until day light. Then I made Sail and took on board off Cowes John Low Pilot to carry me through the Needles and discharged the Pilot. At Noon St Albans head NNW 4 leagues . . .

Thus read the entry in Bligh's log for the first day at sea on a voyage to Tahiti that was to take far longer than he could ever have calculated. The very next day, with the English coast still in sight, the *Bounty* was struck by a fierce gale which 'increased with such fury on us that I could not with any safety attempt to bring the ship to. . . .' Some of the ship's biscuit was spoiled, seven barrels of beer swept overboard, the ship's boats damaged, yards were carried away, the stern stove in and the great cabin breached. At one moment, in driving sleet and high seas, one of the men fell while furling the main topgallant sail. By an extraordinary chance, he caught a stay just before he would have struck the deck, and so saved himself.

However, on Christmas Day the gale abated, the men were able to dry out their clothes, and Bligh ordered rum and beef and plum pudding for Christmas dinner. . . .

4

'Songs were made on him extolling his kindness'

William Bligh, on himself

✣

BLIGH's orders were to sail from England to Tahiti, a distance of over twelve thousand miles, with only one stop. The *Bounty* was to anchor at the Canary Islands, then sail clear across the South Atlantic to Tierra del Fuego and half across the Pacific Ocean to the Society Islands, arriving in late March or April 1788, when the breadfruit—according to Nelson and Banks—would have finished flowering and be ripe for transplanting. To accomplish this long voyage successfully required the most careful and disciplined husbanding of their victuals, and a great deal of luck as well as good seamanship at the Horn.

It was 270 years earlier that Ferdinand Magellan had first discovered that there was a way through the American continent to the *Mar del Pacifico*, providing a theoretical saving of many weeks to the riches of the East and the Spanish possessions on the west coast of South America. Fifty-eight years later, Francis Drake observed that there was an end to the American continent, that Atlantic and Pacific oceans 'meet in a large and free scope'.

Round the Horn or through Magellan's Strait, it did not matter. Both were fearfully hazardous, and few mariners attempted the passage against the williwaws of the strait or the adverse winds and currents of the Horn.

For the sake of saving three months, the Admiralty Board, and Banks himself, considered that it was worth taking the risks of the westward passage with the *Bounty*: she was a new, well-found vessel, commanded by an experienced navigator—and it would mean getting that cheap food for the plantation slaves a year earlier.

For the twenty days of their passage to the Canaries, only Bligh and Nelson in the *Bounty* knew the details of their route and their eventual destination. Everyone, of course, understood that they were going to the South Seas, that they would be away for a long time and that—by the nature of the modifications to the ship and the presence on board of two gardeners—their main business would be something to do with plants rather than trade or exploration.

Except for their brief, merciful break on Christmas Day, the gales and high seas continued unabated until the third watch on 28 December. The following days, with moderate winds and clear skies, were spent in shaking down, drying out clothes and bedding, and repairing the damage caused by the gales. Fires were lighted between decks to dry out the ship, the hatches and scuttles were kept open, the carpenter's crew repaired the launch—the most damaged of the boats—and the ratings on watch spent many hours laboriously picking through and drying out the damaged store of ship's biscuit. 'To our mortification', wrote Bligh in his log, 'found a great quantity more, wet with salt water.' A few days later still more damaged bread was discovered, and when Bligh ordered a cask of cheese to be broached it was found to be rotten. Nor was that all. On 31 December a cask each of salt pork and salt beef were broached. Both were short in weight. Four four-pound pieces of pork and three eight-pound pieces of beef were missing—pilfered at Deptford or deliberately sold short by the notoriously dishonest contractors. It was not much, but this sort of thing aroused suspicion and anxiety among any ship's company, especially at the outset of a long voyage. Perhaps in a few months when they were in dire need, they would find more serious, perhaps life-or-death, shortages.

The weather turned hazy and heavy, there were no signs of fish or birds, only an occasional sail was seen—an English ship *Fanny* out twelve days bound for Guinea, a French ship bound for Mauritius. During this first leg the men learned one another's ways and eccentricities, the habits and weaknesses of their officers, and above all watched warily their commander, on whose dictatorial will and power of discretion their well-being and their lives were going to depend, perhaps for several years. Was Bligh going to be just and steady? Unpredictable? A tyrant and a flogger? It would take a week or two to get the measure of the man. Meanwhile, those who had sailed with him before—Lebogue, Norton, Peckover, Christian —were closely questioned about him.

Ledward was not the only one who quickly formed the conclusion that Bligh was 'a passionate man'. There were other things about him that were already causing a measure of uneasiness—the uncertain nature of his temper and his moodiness, the way he would nag, nag, nag away on some failure, real or supposed, large or small, one day, then ignore some serious piece of mismanagement the next day. There wasn't any consistency about the man. They were all used to bad language. There was nothing shocking about that. But Bligh never seemed to stop, even when he was talking conversationally. When he was reprimanding someone on deck, especially in a high wind, the volume of his voice was only equalled by the foulness and range of his vocabulary. They had never heard anything like it before.

They sighted Tenerife in cloudy, heavy weather on the morning of 5 January, with Grand Canary visible to the south, and twenty-four hours later the *Bounty* came to with the small bower anchor and moored off Santa Cruz. This was a neat, trim little Spanish town, all church spires and straight roads flanked by low houses, a fort, a jetty, the land rising to vineyards and the mountain peaks lost in clouds. There were several ships anchored here, including an American brig, probably trading corn for the local wine.

Bligh ordered Christian, who combined respectability with experience, to go ashore and pay his respects to the Marquis of Brancheforté, the island's governor, and request permission to repair the damage sustained in the storm and buy food and water. Bligh, always a stickler for etiquette, would salute on the understanding that he would be saluted with the same number of guns. Christian was told by the marquis to compliment his captain on his safe arrival and to ask for all that he needed from the port contractor. But the marquis declared he never returned an equal salute to officers of inferior rank ('an extraordinary answer!' Bligh commented). However, the marquis would be honoured to welcome the *Bounty*'s captain at his dinner table if he could spare the time.

It took four days of hard work to take on board the fresh provisions and water. Bligh complained at the high price of everything except the wine. The beef was scarce and of the lowest quality, the corn, pumpkins and potatoes twice the summer price. But with no other port on his route, Bligh had to pay out, and stowed 230 pounds of fresh beef as well as the corn and pumpkins and some poor figs and oranges—'all the fresh supplies I could get'. A goat and its kid were added as livestock to the chickens, sheep and pigs which had somehow survived the storms in their small cages. The wine, however, was excellent, and he bought $863\frac{1}{2}$ gallons of it—over nineteen gallons a head—in view of their loss of beer. Wine was considered a better drink in the tropics anyway.

Nor did Bligh forget his patron. For Sir Joseph Banks two hogsheads of two-year-old wine ('it may challenge the best Maderia') were brought on board and lowered into the deepest recesses of the *Bounty*'s hold.

It was unlikely that there would be another chance of writing home, so Bligh left behind at Santa Cruz reports for Banks and Campbell to be taken by the next ship bound for England. All was well, according to Bligh—a cheerful and happy ship's company all in good health and spirits. He was even able to reassure Campbell about his protégé, Tom Ellison—'He improves and will make a very good seaman'. Only the drunken doctor and his own clerk, who was seemingly ignorant and worthless, gave cause for complaint. As to the *Bounty* herself, she had survived her battering bravely and Bligh had quite altered his mind since he had first set eyes on her at Deptford. She was 'the completest ship I believe that ever swam, and she really looks like one fit to encounter any difficulties'.

(There is one minor and unsolved mystery about the *Bounty*'s stay at Santa Cruz. Strict health and quarantine control was exercised by the Spanish administration, smallpox being regarded as the worst danger to the islanders. Bills of health were demanded from ships before they could have contact with the shore, and while the *Bounty* was there Bligh was asked if he could vouch for the crew of an English vessel newly arrived without a bill of health, 'that no epidemic disease raged in England at the time they sailed'. Besides these early quarantine regulations, smallpox was also, it seems, kept at bay by regular inoculation. This was 1788. Jenner's revolutionary findings on vaccination were not made known until 1796.)

Once clear of Tenerife on 11 January, Bligh called together the ship's company and read an announcement. Its terms are important and have a direct bearing on much of what happened later. There is no recorded comment on it by Christian. Bligh refers to it in his log and in his narrative. Morrison wrote of the occasion in some detail in his journal and noted that it was 'cheerfully received'.

'We are proceeding to Otaheite (Tahiti) without stopping and by way of Cape Horn. But because of the delays in England,' Bligh continued, 'the season is now far spent and we may be defeated in our efforts to reach the South Sea by this short route. But I am determined to try. If I fail in the attempt I shall put about to the Cape of Good Hope and proceed by the easterly route to the Society Islands. In either event, it is necessary to be careful of our provisions, especially our biscuit. I shall therefore now reduce the allowance to two-thirds, all other provisions remaining at full rations.'

Then as some sort of cheering compensation: 'In view of the length of the passage I can assure you that all those that merit it will be promoted on your return.'

Second, the ship's company was to be put on three watches. This meant that the men would work four hours on watch and eight off, instead of four hours on and four off. 'I have ever considered this among seamen as conducive to health, and not being jaded. . . . It adds much to their content and cheerfulness,' wrote Bligh. The men were also told that after four o'clock on each day the evening would be laid aside for their amusement and dancing. This was the time when Byrn would play his part—music and dancing on the forecastle.

As to the watch-keepers, the master and gunner would be in charge of watches as before. For the third watch, Mr Christian would be in command.

Bligh now ordered grog to be served to the ship's company; and for the midday meal there was fresh meat and a pint of wine for everyone.

What an oddly uneven announcement this is! On the one hand it shows caution, and care and consideration for the men. Cook had been a pioneer of this new enlightened school of commanders. For centuries, and out of habit as much as anything else, the well-being and morale of a ship's company was given small consideration

—by the Spanish, Portuguese, Dutch, French, Venetian and Genoese as well as English commanders. The tradition of slave-manning died hard. Of course there were notable exceptions—the Spanish Nodal brothers and a number of the Dutch captains, and Francis Drake among the English—but generally the common crew—'the people'—were still treated like slaves, or the pressed scrapings off the tavern floors of seaports, which many of them were. Disease was regarded, by minds steeped in fear and superstition, as an act of fate or God. Paternosters and promises to patron saints were the only answers. The sea was regarded as an alien, hostile, unnatural and unhealthy element for man, and those who took to it for gain must perforce risk paying the price. This price included scurvy, which was associated with salt water and sea breezes rather than to an unhealthy diet and stinking bilge water.

It was not until the long voyages of the mid-eighteenth century that commanders gave deeper thought to morale and health. These reforms were born as much out of practical sense as compassion. Bougainville and La Pérouse, Cook and Cartier, recognised that on the health of each man depended the survival of the ship's company and the successful, and profitable, conclusion of the long voyage. Every man who was taken sick or died added to the burden on the others. If half the ratings were down with the scurvy—and that was not unknown—the ship could not be worked and a sudden squall could mean disaster.

Cleanliness and hygiene, a balanced diet, healthy and happy off-watch occupations—these were some of the ingredients of success when men were crammed together, through storm and calm, hot and cold climates, for months at a time. Cook had learnt this, and Bligh had witnessed his success at first hand. It was one reason why he had such large stocks of *sauerkraut* and portable soup among his provisions.

A rigid economy of victuals, a careful regard to a balanced diet, dancing and games in the evenings—all these made good sense and improved the likelihood of a satisfactory conclusion to the voyage. The three-watch system obviously meant a more relaxed and easy life. But Christian was no better qualified to be the officer of the third watch than the other master's mate, Will Elphinstone, or the established midshipman, Tom Hayward. Bligh's choice showed the same favouritism towards his family friend as he had shown in the *Britannia*, where it had led to some resentment. Already Christian was being invited frequently to Bligh's cabin in the evenings and to dine, and soon after this he was shot up to the rank of acting lieutenant, over the head of Fryer, to whom he had been mate, and to the position of second-in-command.

In the copy of Bligh's *Narrative* in the Naval Library in London, against the entry on page 25 noting Christian's promotion, someone long ago has added in the margin: 'an injury to the Master— unwarranted'. Fryer certainly felt the injury, and his relations with Bligh became increasingly tetchy, until the two men were scarcely on speaking terms. (Bligh could not stand his whining.)

But what is more surprising and significant, Fryer did not show any resentment against Christian, which he might reasonably have done if Christian had flaunted his new rank. This was the last thing he would do. On the contrary, he always tended to identify himself with 'the people' rather than with authority in times of difficulty and disruption. To be admired and liked by the youngest boy was as important to him as it was to be loved by his captain.

This double role of Christian's did not seem to bother him. His high spirits continued to endear him to one and all.Only midshipmen Hayward and Hallett, and Bligh's dour, disapproving clerk, John Samuel, showed their resentment. Even Christian's black moods became everyone's concern, as if, like the *Bounty*'s dog, he were a cherished pet or talisman of good fortune.

It took the *Bounty* more than four weeks to reach the Equator— some seventy-five miles a day—through fair but humid weather. 'Very sultry and damp air' appears in Bligh's log, and the ship was aired whenever possible and washed down below with vinegar. Everything was quickly covered with a fine white mould, and even the sails—often hanging limp in the still air—were spread with mildew. Like all those who had sailed south through the tropics, from the time of Henry the Navigator's explorers and Magellan, every day that passed increased the longing for the cooler weather of the south. Sometimes the sultriness reached an unbearable weight and then burst into a thunderstorm, with lightning illuminating the oily swell for many miles around them. Bligh ordered awnings to be spread to catch the rain and filled many hogsheads with fresh water.

On some days the hot grey misty sky and the hot gently undulating grey sea seemed empty of life. On other days, unpredictably, the sea and sky became suddenly alive. Bligh noted 'prodigious numbers of porpoises', sharks, dolphins and shoals of flying fish; while white boobies and brown petrels, sheerwaters and man-of-war birds were identified and entered in the log.

It appears from this log and from the journal Bligh published later to defend himself against personal attacks, that it was a happy voyage during those first weeks to the Equator. On the crossing of the line there was much hilarity and tipsiness. Three bottles of rum were shared out, and everyone had half a pint of wine. Bligh would not allow the ducking part of the ceremony—'of all the customs it is the most brutal'—which suggests a humanitarian consideration for his men. The twenty-seven officers and ratings who had never crossed the line before were just tarred and shaved with a piece of iron hoop. Byrn was kept busy with his fiddle and there was much dancing.

The same appearance of contentment is reflected in a letter to Duncan Campbell which, by a happy chance, he was able to send on 16 February when they came up with a whaler, *British Queen*. 'We are all in good spirits,' wrote Bligh hastily before ordering the jolly boat hoisted out to take his letter to the whaler, 'and my little ship fit to go round half a score of worlds. My men all active good fellows . . . my officers and young gentlemen are all tractable and well disposed.'

Only the doctor was excluded from this panegyric. 'I have trouble to prevent him being in bed fifteen hours out of the twenty-four.' Earlier in the voyage Bligh had located the surgeon's grog store and had described Dr Huggan as 'a drunken sot. He is constantly in liquor, having a private stock by him which I assured him shall be taken away if he does not desist from making himself such a beast.'

Was the *Bounty* really such a happy ship two months after leaving Spithead? If there had been troubles, it would hardly have been in Bligh's interests to recount them to Campbell, causing anxiety to his own family and relatives and gratuitously casting doubts about his leadership. There is only one significant entry in the log, and that does not appear until 10 March: 'I found it necessary to punish Matthew Quintal with two dozen lashes for insolence and mutinous behaviour'.

Morrison tells another story. In his journal (see below, page 312) the bo'sun's mate writes of restlessness and discontent within a few days of leaving Tenerife. First there was the matter of the missing cheese. Bligh ordered a cask to be brought up and opened in front of the ship's company, as was the custom at sea to prevent any suspicion of malpractice. Two cheeses were missing. 'They have been stolen,' Bligh declared angrily.

'This cask has been opened before, sir,' said the cooper, Henry Hillbrant, daringly. 'It was opened by the order of Mr Samuel [Bligh's clerk and steward] while we were at Spithead and the cheeses were sent to your lodgings in Portsmouth.'

Bligh turned on Hillbrant. 'I'll give you a damned good flogging if you say any more of this,' he told him. Then to the ship's company: 'The allowance of cheese for the officers as well as the people will be stopped until this deficiency is made good.'

The men dispersed. Later seaman John Williams confirmed the cooper's allegations and revealed that he had been ordered to take ashore in one of the ship's boats not only the cheeses but also a cask of vinegar 'and some other things'.

This sort of pilfering was commonplace and everyone knew that it went on, especially when a commander was also ship's purser as Bligh was. It was not a cardinal sin, whether or not Bligh had committed it on this occasion, or Hillbrant was justified in his accusation. Wherever the truth lay, this was only the first of many food incidents, the last only hours before the mutiny.

'On the next banyan day' (the one meatless day a week), wrote Morrison, 'butter only was issued, this the seamen refused, alleging that their acceptance of the butter without cheese would be tacitly acknowledging the supposed threat.'

The matter of missing cheeses was allowed to drop. It was followed some three weeks later by the pumpkin affair. With the temperature in the eighties, in this high humidity the pumpkins Bligh had bought so expensively at Santa Cruz began to go bad. In order to avoid waste and consume them quickly, Bligh ordered Samuel to issue them instead of biscuit.

'What is the rate of exchange?' the men demanded suspiciously of the clerk.

'One pound of pumpkin for two pounds of biscuit,' they were told—and they refused with one voice.

When Bligh heard of this near-mutinous protest 'he came up in a violent passion,' declared Morrison, 'and called all hands telling

Mr Samuel to call the first man of every mess and let him see who would dare to refuse it.'

'You damned infernal scoundrels,' Bligh shouted at them. 'I'll make you eat grass or anything you can catch before I have done with you.'

According to Morrison, discontent and suspicion increased further after this second crisis. The men noted that whenever a beef or pork cask was broached the contents were never weighed and that the prime pieces were taken out for the captain's table. The men at last took their complaint to Fryer, to 'examine the business and procure us redress'. Considering what had gone before, this was bravely optimistic of them.

Bligh again called together all hands. 'Everything relative to the provisions is transacted by my orders,' he told them. 'It is therefore useless to make any complaint for you will get no redress as I am the first judge of what is right and what is wrong. I will therefore flog severely the first man who dares attempt to make any complaint in the future.' There were more threats of violence, underlined with obscenities, before he dismissed the company and returned to his cabin.

The voyage continued tranquilly with fair winds from the Equator until the *Bounty* had the first taste of Horn weather 4,000 miles and nearly six weeks later, when the temperature had fallen from the upper eighties to the mid-forties. There were no more outbreaks during this leg. The officers, who received the same rations as the men, 'made frequent murmurings among themselves' about the small rations; the ratings, more accustomed to ill-usage, reconciled themselves to their food and spent much of their time off watch fishing, sometimes with success. Shark flesh made a fine supplement to the dreary round of dried peas and oatmeal, biscuit, portable soup and *sauerkraut*.

As for Bligh, slackness and dirt remained his first enemies. The surgeon personified these vices, and Bligh continued to regard him with outrage and contempt. Day after day Bligh preached his gospel of exercise and hygiene, and kept all but Huggan up to the mark. The men scrubbed themselves down every day. Never before had they been obliged to keep themselves and their clothes so clean. Bligh examined them with eyes as keen for dirt as any housekeeper.

In hot weather awnings were got up, and beneath their protection the men worked at making chafing mats from spun yard and old rope, plaiting cord to make reef points, and gaskets—the cords used to secure the furled sails to the yards—and cable plaits. Every day, except during heavy rain, the *Bounty* was thoroughly aired between decks, scrubbed down with vinegar and washed and dried. In humid weather Bligh ordered fires to be lit to counter the unhealthy dampness, and every afternoon the men combined exercise with hygiene by pouring water down one pump to the bilge and pumping it up again with the second pump. Bligh was satisfied only when the water coming up was pure as the water poured down.

Bligh equated a sick man with personal failure, and he could record with complete satisfaction—and did so—that the *Bounty* survived the tropics with no serious sickness: and Huggan could drink himself to death if he wished.

The first southern gale struck the *Bounty*—as it had struck so many ships bound for the Horn in the past—between Cape Virgin Mary at the eastern entrance to the Magellan Strait and the Falkland Islands. The violent squalls that accompanied it took them by surprise and hardly gave them time to bring the ship to under the mizzen staysail. Bligh altered course to close the coast of Tierra del Fuego. The gale died as quickly as it had come up, and two nights later, in bright moonlight, the ship's English dog and the Spanish goat both gave signs that they smelt land. At two o'clock in the morning the coastline and mountains of Tierra del Fuego, the first land they had seen since the Canaries, emerged in the moonlight to the south-east.

Bligh ordered a sheep to be killed to celebrate. 'It gave them a pleasant meal,' he recorded. Morrison tells the story differently. The sheep, he says, had died of starvation, was all skin and bone, and though Bligh claimed that it weighed fifty pounds, they had to throw most of it overboard. Moreover, it was a substitute for the day's ration of meat, not a supplement. But Morrison also tells us that they were all in high spirits because the weather in this most dreaded area was fine and clear—almost balmy—and it looked as though they would soon be round the Horn and into the South Sea—the *Mar del Pacifico*, the Pacific Ocean—of which they had heard so many tales: the mellow, sunny climate, the rich fruits and spices, and, above all, the eager, dark-skinned women.

This is how Anson fifty years earlier had found the Cape Horn seas, and many others before him: by contrast with the brutal shoreline, sunny skies and calm seas and a gentle wind. It looked set fair for ever. No wonder that the men were happy, scrawny mutton for supper notwithstanding.

Bligh navigated the *Bounty* round Staten Island, with its insanely white-tipped silhouette, and far south with the intention of avoiding the strong adverse currents near to Cape Horn. He was as optimistic as the ship's company, but more cautious, determined to push on while the weather held. On the afternoon of 24 March the weather remained fine and clear, and Bligh noticed how the sky appeared 'very much streaked and appearance of wind', and he judged that they were not to escape the baleful spell of the Horn after all; that they were in for a hammering. The next morning he ordered the ship to be cleaned and dried, perhaps for the last time for many days, and brought down the top hamper.

Bligh's experienced eye recognised every element in the pattern of the change. First there came the thick cloud, then at night the fog. At dawn it was suddenly calm with a wet fog clinging about the ship. Later in the day came fresh breezes alternating with banks of fog, then the wind got up in earnest and the fog cleared, and as the sea increased he ordered double reefs and then close reefing. By midday the wind was screaming through the rigging, and albatrosses, like morbidly eager spectators, began wheeling close about the *Bounty*.

The ship's long ordeal began in earnest on the night of 28–29 March. The westerly gale brought strong slanting rain and the seas often broke right over the deck—'it exceeds any I have seen', Bligh noted.

No early attempt to double Cape Horn has been as fully and movingly recorded as that of the *Bounty* in March and April 1788. Bligh knew what he was up against and his profound respect for the power of the elements was as massive as his determination to defeat them. His weapons were his ship and his men, and he nursed them both devotedly and unremittingly from 29 March until 22 April—nobody on board ever denied that. For day after day, as he tacked and wore, gaining a few miles in a few days, and losing them all and more in a few hours: as he took his observations lashed to the mast, watched every change of the weather from hail and snow storms to squalls and brief periods of moderating gales; ordered the sails furled, or reefed, or set according to the constant and unpredictable changes in direction and strength of the wind—all this time, sodden, half frozen and weary himself, his first thoughts were for the state of his ship and the welfare of his men.

This was William Bligh at his best, gladly agreeing to the men's request for straight grog instead of watered to keep out the cold, deputing two men from each watch to supervise the only fire below to dry out the clothes and the hammocks of the others, ordering hot soup for all and hot breakfasts of boiled wheat and sugar, and a pint of decoction of ground malt once a day. With the gale at its worst on 19 April, and everyone showing signs of the immense strain, he ordered one of the last hogs to be killed to cheer them on. For a commander who had previously husbanded his resources to a point of obsession, and had already seen most of their livestock die in the cold and the wet, this was a decision demanding high resolution.

The *Bounty* and her company both reacted stoutly. There were moments, described in Bligh's cool narrative as 'highly dangerous' —the wind swinging suddenly to another quarter, a sea like the cliffs of Dover racing at their stern—when it seemed as if they must be swamped and capsize, like Drake's *Marigold* and many another suffering vessel in these waters. Bligh would certainly have read the account by Drake's narrator Fletcher of that earlier navigator's ordeal in these waters, how 'God seemed to set himself against us . . . as if he had pronounced a sentence, not to stay his hands, nor to withdraw his judgement, till he had buried our bodies, and ships also, in the bottomless depth of the raging sea'.

For two weeks of this battering the *Bounty* showed few signs of the strain she was undergoing. Then 'she begins to be a little leaky', Bligh notes flatly, and orders the men to the pumps every hour.

On this same day, 12 April, he gives similar concerned attention to his men by sacrificing his cabin at nights, which allowed more room between decks and 'rendered those happy who had not dry beds to sleep in'. In spite of all Bligh's efforts and concern for his men, the injury and sick list began to increase after two weeks of the contest. Huggan, whose services were for once in need, was one of the first to tumble. A sudden lurch, and down the after ladder he went, landing heavily on his shoulder and dislocating it. Quartermaster Peter Linkletter fell into the fore cockpit and one of the seamen, Richard Skinner, was badly hurt. No one could move about the upper decks without clutching the ropes that were rigged during the whole of this Cape Horn ordeal.

By 18 April four more men were immobilised by rheumatism and heavy colds, and there were other more significant casualties. Tempers were running short and the galley was sometimes a shambles as the cooks went about their duties and the men struggled for their food and tried to remain on their feet. Tempers became frayed. One of the cooks was attacked in a sudden brawl in the galley and fell to the deck with two broken ribs. A few days later Charley Churchill, always liable to fits of vicious temper, badly scalded his hand in a scuffle.

There were one or two brief lulls in the weather, brief moments of cheer when the sun broke through the scudding clouds and Bligh could get a reading with his sextant and the men could fish again. The sky seemed more promising than the sea and everyone tried jigging—floating a line with hooks beyond the bait, a sudden jerk catching the feet or the body of a bird. By keeping it alive and cramming it with corn for a day or two, it fattened well for the pot. Albatross was a special delicacy.

By the middle of April Bligh was beginning to lose hope. Because of the sails' weight and stiffness from snow and ice, the weakened men found it well-nigh impossible to haul them up and furl them, and when they came down from the yards they were unable to speak and scarcely able to stand. When they at last struggled down the ladder to the forecastle, they were met by a thick cloud of smoke from the stove and the sound of coughing and retching and the stench of vomit from the sick who had succumbed to the smoke and the tossing of the ship.

On 13 April Bligh wrote: 'It is now three weeks since we came round Staten Land, a time we have spent with much fatigue and almost constant bad weather. Few ships could have gone through it as we have done, but I cannot expect my men and officers to bear it much longer.'

Eight days later, with nine men out of action, the *Bounty* badly leaking and no sign of the weather easing, Bligh knew that he had been defeated, and in his heaving cabin was writing: 'It was with much concern I saw it improper and even unjustifiable in me to persist any longer in a passage this way. Towards the evening the wind and heavy falls of snow became so violent that I must have laid to, and the wind backing to the westward became so fixed with a high sea running led me to determine to bear away for the Cape of Good Hope. . . .'

Just before five in the afternoon Bligh called all hands aft and told them that he was going to put over the helm and bear away east for Africa. 'You have endured much and I congratulate and thank you all.'

The whole ship's company—sodden, frozen, hungry and until that moment close to despair—were suddenly beside themselves with relief and spontaneously burst into three cheers for their commander.

In an ordeal on this scale, no ship's company could have been more loyal, determined and tenacious: and Bligh had proved himself, too, an unsurpassed captain in a time of adversity. To have survived those weeks of Horn weather without the loss of a man, of a spar or even a yard of canvas was a stunning achievement.

The *Bounty* made good speed across the South Atlantic sometimes running at up to nine knots with a strong westerly wind from astern. But the weather remained consistently foul and their discomforts unrelieved. The wetness of everything on deck and below decks, the everlasting pitching and tossing, the dreary rations and the overpowering smoke and smell of bodies and wet clothes, tested them to the limit. At one point in the passage there were eleven 'rheumatic invalids', and this put very heavy pressure on the rest of the men.

Bligh characteristically claimed that no voyage of this duration, touching at only one place, had ever been accomplished with 'such health among seamen in a like continuance of bad weather'. And of course he was right. His obsession with cleanliness ('and in cleaning ship all dark holes and corners the common receptacles of all filth were the first places attended to') and a change into dry clothes, contributed greatly to this record. Bligh fussed over his men like a nursemaid, seeing that they got proper and regular exercise—compulsory dancing to Byrn's fiddle regardless of the weather —and ensured that they had a good balanced diet, with hot oatmeal when it was especially cold. 'They must be watched like children', he noted in his log.

It was not until they were almost in sight of Table Mountain that the weather at last eased; and just before noon on 24 May the *Bounty* came to anchor in False Bay, Cape of Good Hope, where seven other ships, mostly Dutch East Indiamen, were already at anchor. It was their first sight of other human beings for eighty-six days. Bligh ordered a thirteen-gun salute, and this time received the appropriate thirteen-gun reply from the Dutch fort.

The *Bounty* remained at Cape Town for thirty-eight days, which seems a long time, but there was a great deal to do, and in fact Bligh congratulated himself that he was away as soon as he was. The ship was in poor shape after her five months at sea and her Cape Horn battering. All the rigging and sails had to be completely overhauled, and the carpenter and his crew had a lot of repairing work to do. The seams had to be caulked, and every day the boats plied between the shore and the ship, bringing casks of water (forty-one tons) and wine (deemed excellent), fresh meat and vegetables, tons of stones to replace the coal ballast which had been almost exhausted during their long period of cold weather, some livestock—five sheep, some goats and pigeons—and a mass of miscellaneous stores. These included apple-tree saplings and all sorts of seeds from corn to lemon and oranges for Nelson to plant on their travels in the Pacific.

Although it was mid-winter in Cape Town, and rainy and cool for much of the time, the crew thrived on their healthy diet of fruit and vegetables, fresh meat and real bread instead of ship's biscuit. There was good fishing in the bay and this helped to augment their diet so that they were all fit and filled out after five weeks here.

David Nelson, as always busy and incorrigibly curious, was ashore most days, head well down like any good naturalist, studying the flora and fauna, collecting specimens and writing reports. Bligh, too, spent much time ashore, noting with approval the neatness and cleanliness of the town which had grown so fast in the eight years since he had last been here, applauding Dutch hospitality and courtesy, but deploring the condition and treatment of the slaves, brought in by the French from Madagascar, Mozambique and Sumatra. 'It is distressing,' he wrote, 'to see some of them carrying weighty burdens naked, or what is worse in such rags that one would imagine could not fail to reproach the owners of a want of decency and compassion in not relieving such a degree of wretchedness.'

At four o'clock in the afternoon on 1 July the *Bounty* weighed anchor and made sail from False Bay. Ahead lay the longest leg of the voyage, clear across the Indian Ocean for well over 6,000 miles to Tasmania (Van Diemen's Land), which was still thought to be the southern tip of Australia.

It seems almost miraculous today that a navigator equipped only with suspect charts, a compass, a chronometer, nautical tables and a sextant, could make accurate and unhesitating landfall not just on a coast but on a particular rock—in this case the Mewstone off Tasmania—twenty-three days after leaving the Cape of Good Hope. But then Bligh was a peerless navigator. He had no patience with those who were inferior to him, and also those who perpetuated errors by printing them incorrectly on charts. 'A madness seems to have got among these publishers of errors about fixing places in their true longitude,' Bligh observes in his log. 'And in the meantime they have neglected the grand point, the latitude, which they err as much in, when it might be known to within five miles.'

During this winter passage across the southern Indian Ocean Bligh had cause time and again to regret his failure to double the Horn, and to curse the Admiralty Board which had delayed his departure. Although the winds were at first favourable, and the *Bounty* sometimes logged little short of 200 sea miles in twenty-four hours, it was a rough, chilly and damp voyage. The miseries they endured can be read between the lines of every entry in the log. Yet in Bligh's 'Remarks' in his log, in his journal, and in James Morrison's journal, the moments of wonder and splendour they experienced in these little known waters are also evident.

A month out of Cape Town, in squally weather—though it was better than it had been—they come upon the isolated little island of St Paul, right in the centre of the southern Indian Ocean, no more than a five-mile-long lump of rock, stark and hostile.

This first landfall is first sighted at a distance of ten leagues at dawn on 28 July after Bligh had made a small correction in the *Bounty*'s course. The skies are grey and cloudy and worse weather is coming up. Later in the morning the *Bounty* is within one and a half leagues of the southern tip, and they sight whales, like guardians of the 'iron-bound shore'.

Everyone is on deck, some with a glass, watching for signs of life on the cliff-tops, for this is one of the loneliest and least-known corners of the world. 'Saw no place where a landing might be made with safety,' notes Morrison. 'The island is high and barren affording but a very few trees and shrubs.' Bligh has read that there is fresh water on the island and a hot spring in which some enterprising mariners once boiled fish. Bligh and Nelson, both once protégés of Cook, are keen to anchor and go ashore, to explore, to record, to plant and botanise and collect rocks. But this place is hardly better than Tierra del Fuego in mid-winter. A gale breaks over the *Bounty* at 11.30 a.m. and Bligh has reluctantly to bear away and take in sail, catching a last glimpse through driving rain of the black cliffs at midday, twelve miles distant. None of them will ever see again that island with its spectral gauntness and mystery.

The weather continued stormy and cloudy and the thermometer fell to the low forties as the *Bounty* continued on a east-south-easterly course, suffering conditions and temperatures little better than at Cape Horn. 'The weather of this day,' wrote Bligh on the afternoon of 5 August, 'has been very bad, being almost constant rain and thick, with a very strong gale and the sea breaking constantly over us. . . . The ship being wet below I had two good fires between decks and kept the men as comfortable as possible. All wet clothes were kept by the galley fire and got dried by the time they were wanted. . . . Got no observation of the sun, it never once being out in twenty-four hours.' Only Cook and one or two other navigators had ever sailed these waters, and Bligh kept a scrupulous record of the birds that flew with them for day after day in these stormy waters—blue petrels and sheerwaters, pintadas and albatrosses.

In spite of the difficulty in taking observations, 'perfectly to my most sanguine expectations', the Mewstone Rock on the south-west corner of Tasmania hove into sight at 2 p.m. on 19 August, and Bligh worked the *Bounty* carefully—noting every detail for future navigators—into Adventure Bay.

The duties and activities in which the men were engaged here were typical of the time and the nature of the voyage. Christian took a wooding party ashore, others took casks in the launch to fill with water, the men fished with the seine and with hook and line—with little success on this occasion, although Christian succeeded in shooting some birds for the pot.

At Adventure Bay they found evidence of past English visits to this land. Bligh and Nelson recognised the stumps of trees which they had cut when they had called here with Cook in the *Resolution,* and Tom Hayward, straying from Christian's wooding party, found an old tree-trunk marked with a knife 'A.D. 1773', 'as if it had been cut a month' instead of fifteen and a half years earlier by the men of Furneaux's voyage of exploration. Nelson discovered living evidence of his own earlier visit when a party of natives suddenly appeared on the shore, among them a deformed cripple whom he remembered, proving at least that these people were not nomadic and tolerated the disabled.

They were all curious about the natives. Bligh sent parties ashore to try to lure them from the forests, but they always retreated silently inland before they could be approached with gifts. At night the glow of their fires a short distance away up in the hills exasperated Bligh and made him more determined than ever to establish contact with them. Nelson's assistant, Brown, was the only one to succeed in doing so. One day he strayed far from the shore in search of plants and when he emerged again on to the beach it was impossible to get a boat to him through the surf at that spot. Brown signalled to the ship that he had been with the natives. Bligh at once manned the cutter, taking with him Nelson and bags of nails and trinkets, and came in as close to the shore as the surf allowed.

Suddenly the natives broke from the forest on to the beach a mere twenty yards away. They were a smallish people, black as coal, stark naked and with woolly black hair. Their teeth were beautifully white and some had painted themselves in red ochre or added another coat of black on their faces and shoulders. They were all making a tremendous noise, chattering away and waving their hands above their heads. Although some carried knobkerries, they appeared peaceable enough and even invited the Englishmen ashore by sign language.

Bligh stood up and began hurling the bags of trinkets towards them, which they caught with the accuracy of zoo monkeys, but at once put aside as if of no further interest.

Back on board the *Bounty*, Brown described to Bligh and Nelson how he had met in the forest an old man, a young woman and some children. The man sent the woman and children away, crying and frightened, but Brown succeeded in reassuring the man by giving him a knife and calming him down 'so that we became good friends'. They lived in a crude bark wigwam with some kangaroo skins on the ground and their only visible possession a reed woven basket, presumably for carrying the shellfish up from the shore, as this appeared to be their staple foodstuff: there were piles of empty shells everywhere. The Tasmanian aborigines Bligh judged, from this rather slight evidence, to be 'the most wretched and stupid people existing'.

At Adventure Bay, David Nelson, busy and diligent as ever, planted some fruit trees, vegetables and seeds in a clearing, notching the nearby trees to mark the spot. Bligh did not think that they were likely to survive as the natives were always lighting fires which often got out of control and spread rapidly through the forests in dry weather.

By 4 September Bligh was ready to embark for the last leg of their journey to Tahiti. They had taken on board all the water and wood they needed, Nelson had completed his planting and his collections of soil and specimens, Bligh himself had written up in detail his observations and a summary of the passage from Cape Town.

From the evidence available it is not easy to date and define with any precision the first signs of trouble that led to the disaster in the *Bounty* seven months later. But certain conclusions can now be drawn. We have already seen how superbly commander, officers and men worked together during those hellish weeks off Cape Horn. There were few troubles on the turbulent and stormy passage from Cape Town to Adventure Bay. In the dark, gloomy, misty, chill and squally weather which followed them on the earlier part of their passage from Tasmania to Tahiti, there is no record of any restlessness. Bligh concerns himself with his men's health and diet, ensures that they are kept warm and dry when the temperature falls to the lower forties again, inspects them daily for cleanliness, keeps them fit with compulsory dancing between five and eight every night, performs divine service on Sundays. He demonstrates again that there is no better foul weather commander in the service.

Four hundred miles south-east of New Zealand on 19 September Bligh sights and names after his ship some rocks, which in misty weather might be a hazard to ships taking this southern route to the central Pacific. Soon the weather becomes warmer, the sea calmer: the *Bounty* has almost completed her eastward passage and Bligh will take her north-east, north and then north-west in a circle to pick up the prevailing easterlies that will bring him swiftly to the Society Islands.

The first major trouble with one of his officers while at sea occurs, significantly, on the day with 'the wind as steady as a trade', the temperature at a mellow 60 degrees fahrenheit and the weather fair. Again it is Fryer who makes the trouble—Fryer, the master, passed over for promotion, a petulant, uneasy man with chips on his shoulders. It is the morning of 9 October and there are clerical formalities to be carried out—expense and monthly books to be signed both by the commander and the master. Bligh examines them, signs and calls for his clerk, Samuel, to take them to Fryer's cabin for his signature. Instead Samuel brings back a note saying that the master will not add his signature unless Bligh himself signs a certificate confirming Fryer's own good behaviour during the passage so far: something for the record in case there is trouble later, and for when they get back home.

Bligh is livid and sends Samuel to summon Fryer to his cabin. Confronted by his commander, Fryer again refuses and leaves Bligh without another word. Bligh turns up all hands. When they have assembled on deck, with Fryer at his side Bligh reads aloud the Articles of War, with particular reference to the Printed Instructions with all their hints of dire retribution. Samuel produces again the books and a pen and Bligh holds them out to Fryer while the whole ship's company watches with fascination. 'Now sign them books,' Bligh orders.

Fryer takes the pen, and in a voice so loud that none will miss his words, he says, 'I sign in obedience to your orders, but this may be cancelled hereafter.' And he does so.

According to Morrison, this was only one of several rows between commander and master before they reached Tahiti.

Bligh's relations with Surgeon Huggan were also going from bad to worse. During the long periods of bad weather which they had suffered Bligh was so preoccupied with running his ship and looking after his men that he did not notice the deteriorating condition of his surgeon. The illness of one of his able seamen, James Valentine, again drew Bligh's attention to what had been going on for a long time. In short, Huggan was drinking himself to death, and in the meantime was incompetent to carry out his duties.

Valentine had been taken ill in Adventure Bay, and in accordance with usual practice had been bled in the arm by Huggan. This arm was obviously looked after carelessly by Huggan and probably by Valentine, too. It became inflamed and he retired to his hammock where he developed what seems to have been an asthmatic complaint as well. (He was probably suffering from a pulmonary embolism.) Huggan applied blisters to his chest, but only towards the end when Valentine's shortness of breath was causing him great pain, and failed to apply them to his back as he should have done.

Bligh visited Valentine in the forecastle and found him in a very poor condition. A few days after this, Huggan informed Bligh that he was much better. It came as a bad shock, therefore, when news was brought to his cabin that Valentine had died. His few possessions —some shirts and trousers, that is all—were given to the seamen who had nursed him during his last days, and Valentine was buried 'with all the decency in our power' at four o'clock on the afternoon of 10 December.

Bligh was very put out by this event. He had hoped to complete his voyage without a casualty. That would be the most impressive confirmation of his quality as a commander. Now the clean record which he had tried so hard to maintain had been broken, and Bligh suspected that Huggan was responsible. He began to watch the man more carefully.

As the *Bounty* sailed into the tropics, and the temperature and humidity rose daily, more men were taken ill, complaining of rheumatic pains. Huggan said it was scurvy. Bligh was outraged. It was a personal affront to suggest that he could allow his men to succumb to this dread disease. Only inferior commanders, with dirty ships and dirty men eating a poor diet, experienced scurvy among their crew. Bligh examined the men with care, especially their gums, because he knew that a general loosening of the teeth was one of the first effects of scurvy. He did not believe that Huggan's diagnosis was correct. Nevertheless, he ordered the sick men off all salt provisions and gave them flour instead and a daily dose of essence of malt. He also took greater care than ever in his inspections for cleanliness of both men and ship. Nothing escaped his eye. Even the cables were got up and scrubbed, and he put his men on the pumps again every evening, although there was no leak in the ship, just to keep the water and air in the bilge circulating. Two men discovered to be shirking their evening dancing had their grog stopped, with threats of worse punishment if they persisted in continuing to risk their health.

Bligh inspected the sick men again on 18 October. 'It appeared to be nothing more than the prickly heat,' he wrote in his log, with some relief and a good deal of anger directed towards his surgeon.

Nevertheless, more fell foul of the 'rheumatick complaint' and Bligh became very worried. He asked for the full sick list from Huggan and was astonished to discover that only one name appeared on it. Huggan was obviously quite unable to carry out even the simplest duties.

By this time captain and surgeon were no longer on speaking terms. As Bligh's relations with Fryer were no better and Huggan was incoherent for most of the time, it seemed sensible to give up their messing arrangements together, which had continued since they had left England. With the advantage of hindsight it seems surprising to us that these three men with such different characters and tastes had continued to eat together for as long as they had. The conversation could not have been very sparkling. They now took all their meals separately, in their own cabins. 'After which,' Morrison notes, 'they had several disputes and seldom spoke but on duty; and even *then* with much apparent reserve.'

Under Bligh's care the health of the men improved as Huggan's condition grew worse and worse. On 24 October Bligh discovered that his surgeon had been lying on his bunk in an alcoholic stupor for four days. Disgusted and exasperated, he ordered his cabin to be cleared out and his stock of liquor removed and hidden, an operation which Bligh found 'offensive in the highest degree'. Huggan was later seen lurching about the ship—seemingly half paralysed down one side—searching for his bottles. He failed in his quest and eventually returned, thwarted, to his cabin.

Two days later Huggan's condition had so improved that Bligh felt that he was capable of carrying out one last important duty before they landed. They had almost reached their destination. Already they had sailed close to the island of Maitea, only twenty-five leagues from Tahiti. Cook and Wallis before him had been accused of allowing their men to spread venereal disease among the innocent natives. 'To free us from any ill-founded suppositions,' Bligh determined that none of the men suffering from the disease would be allowed to have any relations with the women whom he knew from past experience would be swift and eager in their seductions. Every officer and man was therefore ordered to report to Huggan for venereal inspection. That night Bligh wrote with satisfaction: 'Every person is totally free from the venereal complaint.'

Early on the evening of 25 October 1788, dead on course as

always, Bligh sighted the towering green volcanic peaks of Tahiti. The sky was clear, a favourable and gentle trade wind fanned them, the temperature was 78 degrees.

It was ten months since they had left England, many months since they had seen a woman. They had sailed over 27,000 sea miles, 108 miles for each twenty-four hours.

The *Bounty* closed the island during the night and by the following morning, a Sunday, they could make out the deep valleys between the shoulders of the mountains, the thick, rich forests, the proud and elegant coconut palms along the sandy shoreline and the natural groves of breadfruit trees. Here and there, in small groups, they could pick out natives' huts. Even at this distance it truly appeared

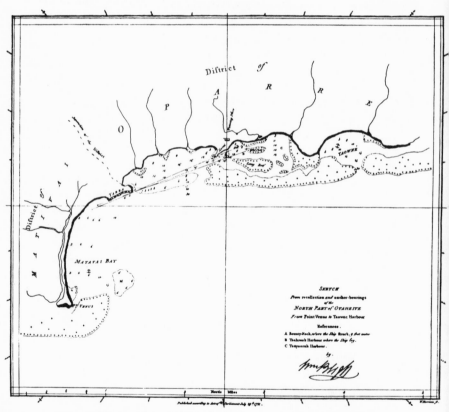

Matavai Bay, northern Tahiti. A sketch map drawn from memory by Bligh. Note the *Bounty*'s track to Oparre after the December storm

the paradise on earth of which they had all heard such extravagant accounts.

Off the *Bounty*'s starboard quarter was another island, Tahiti's satellite Moorea, with the same jagged configuration in miniature, green precipitous slopes rising to razor peaks which seemed to create their own clouds like the smoke from the volcanoes they had once fringed.

Ahead was Tahiti's reef, a narrow ring of coral against which the Pacific rollers tore themselves to pieces in a white frenzy and sprayed the air above with a line of mist. When they got nearer they had to shout to make themselves heard above the thunder of this reef. Bligh worked the *Bounty* through a break in it that he knew well, and into the clear calm of Matavai Bay.

Nature had been kind as well as clever at Tahiti. Everything seemed to be arranged for the pleasure and comfort of man, and it was all beautiful beyond description. Long before the *Bounty* had made her achoring point the long canoes came out from the shore in their hundreds, and they could see that the Tahitians were among the most attractive people they had seen on all their voyages.

The young women and girls standing up in the canoes, some holding armfuls of fruit or young wriggling hogs, were tall with hair, woven with hibiscus flowers, falling to their shoulders and half across their breasts, their skin a rich olive in colour, their eyes as black as their hair. Cook had been here in 1769, and with Banks observed the transit of the planet Venus. Now it seemed magnificently appropriate—with the first of these eager, lissom girls coming aboard the *Bounty*—that the nearest point of land should have been named Point Venus, and that this was to be their headquarters for the paradisical months ahead.

5

'The Paradise of the World'

William Bligh

✤

ON this, his second visit, Bligh fell in love with Tahiti. It was, indeed, the paradise of the world, as all the *Bounty*'s company agreed—a benign climate, scenic perfection, unlimited and delicious food, a kindly, attractive, happy people (with, it is true, some rather odd practices) who enjoyed life to the full. 'If happiness could result from situation and convenience, here it is to be found in the highest perfection,' Bligh comments. 'I have seen many parts of the world, but Otaheite is capable of being preferable to them all.'

The *Bounty*'s welcome off Point Venus was characteristically Polynesian. The Tahitian men and girls swarmed by the hundred from their canoes up the sides of the *Bounty*, cluttering the upper deck, climbing the rigging, scuttling down the ladders, chattering, laughing, shrieking. For a while it was total anarchy. Bligh wanted to work his ship closer inshore. 'I was so crowded with the natives I could not attempt it for I could scarce find my own people.'

At first it was excited curiosity that brought them out. Were they from Pretanee or Rima? From Britain like the great chief Cook (*Toot* they pronounced it) or were they Spaniards from Lima, Peru, who had once visited the island?

'Where is the great Cook?' they asked. It was a natural enough question. Captain Cook had already become a legend. How was Cook? When will he come again? They had his framed portrait, by Webber. It hung like a crucifix in the regent's hut. But Bligh had warned his men that they must not refer to the assassination.

'Here is the son of Cook,' David Nelson told them in their own tongue, pointing proudly to Bligh.

Soon they were busily trading, and the minor chieftains exchanged gifts of live hogs and fruit for hatchets and mirrors. The coconut harvest was at its peak and the crew all drank deeply of the restorative milk as they bartered and made their choice of the girls who showed off their bodies with uninhibited enthusiasm.

At first there was little thieving, to Bligh's surprise and relief. When one native was seen stealing a tin pot, and Bligh caught him

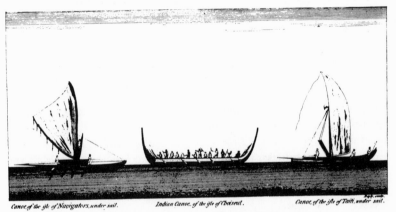

Canoe of the isle of Navigators, under sail.   Indian Canoe, of the isle of Choiseul.   Canoe, of the isle of Taiti, under sail.

Contemporary drawing of Polynesian canoes

red-handed, a chief flew into a rage and beat the culprit about the deck and drove him overboard into the sea. Then the chief turned to Bligh and begged him to apprehend any other robber, tie him up and flog him without mercy. 'This was a mode of conduct I never saw in any Otaheite chief before,' commented Bligh approvingly.

As the sun went down over Point Venus the native men were ordered ashore. Only the lucky chosen girls, sometimes two to a man, were allowed to remain, sharing hammocks or lying linked with their lovers on deck through the hot night.

With this sudden change in their lives, from the brutish diet, the discomforts, the harsh discipline, the enforced celibacy of the past ten months, there now began a long and lazy period of self-indulgence. These new circumstances wrought great changes in the officers and men and revealed new strains in their characters. Until this time the men of the *Bounty* had known one another only as mariners, bound by their masculine tasks and shared arduous experiences. Now, though they were still confined to their vessel for much of the time and had to carry out their daily routine duties, their lives had become domesticated, and the *Bounty* began to look like a small village, with the womenfolk settling in comfortably, stowing the hammocks at dawn, folding the bedding, fetching and preparing the food, gossiping among themselves and making love to their men.

There was a constant flow of canoe traffic to and from the shore. Children came to visit their sisters, parents their daughters, bringing with them fruit and meat and fish, pausing to gaze wonderingly about this great strange vessel.

The person most changed by this new life was Bligh himself. From 26 October 1788 to 4 April 1789 Bligh became the benevolent autocrat of northern Tahiti instead of the stern commander of a ship at sea; the respected and honoured viceroy of King George III of the distant and legendary kingdom of Britain. Bligh had watched at close quarters how Cook had succeeded time and again, with firmness and kindness, in acquiring the affection and respect of the Polynesians, and Bligh had learned his lessons well—above all the lesson of his own angry impetuosity at Karakakooa Bay when he had been a young man.

From the moment when the *Bounty* dropped anchor a quarter mile from Point Venus in Matavai Bay, Bligh set about the task of 'cultivating a friendship with the natives' with patience and restraint. At first he showed only scant respect for the minor chieftains until he had sought out and established relations with the one man—the ruler of this part of Tahititi—on whom he would depend for the success of his whole breadfruit enterprise. It was Sir Joseph Banks's trust in Bligh's diplomacy which had helped to lead to the Board's selection of him as the expedition's commander.

But there was a second and equally important quality in Bligh which Banks had long ago recognised. Bligh was an enquirer. He was as deeply infected by the eighteenth-century enthusiasm for knowledge, and for recording it, as his old commander. His role as unproclaimed viceroy of King George III was only one of several he was expected to play at Tahiti. He was also diarist and observer, botanist, astronomer, geographer, artist and anthropologist. From his arrival in Tahiti, the log of the *Bounty*, at sea a sailor's hour-by-hour record, becomes a fascinating account of all that he sees and hears. Nothing escapes his observation, and the result would be a credit to any present-day research team.

The ruler of this area of northern Tahiti was Tynah, a fine, dark, sturdy figure of a man, six feet four inches tall, fearless in his canoe in any weather, a stern authoritarian among his people, yet timorous in war. With Bligh he was cunning, wily and devious, his eye ever on the main chance. But it is clear that he also became deeply attached to Bligh, and not only for what he could cadge from him. He was saddened as well as chastened when Bligh was angry with him and transparently delighted when he was reinstated in his esteem.

Tynah's wife, Queen Iddeah, was an equally formidable figure, a veritable giantess. Bligh describes her as 'a very resolute woman, of a large make, and has great bodily strength'. She had once been the champion wrestler and remained overall supervisor and umpire at the frequent wrestling competitions. Sometimes she could not resist showing off her old prowess, when she always proved that there was still no match for her in all Tahiti.

Tynah and Iddeah had four children under six years, the eldest boy, in accordance with local custom, being made nominal king at birth. Tynah reigned as regent until his son became a man.

Bligh had his first meeting with Tynah on the second day after the *Bounty*'s arrival. He had picked up a smattering of Tahitian on his earlier visit. David Nelson had given him lessons on the passage out. This was to prove highly advantageous for Bligh. In order that neither side should lose face a mutually acceptable compromise was reached about the arrangements for the meeting. If Bligh went ashore with his gifts it would be regarded as paying obeisance, and the same interpretation would be made of Tynah's journeying to the ship in his canoe. So Tynah indicated that Bligh should send his own boat to take him off. This satisfied everybody and Christian was deputed to the task. With half a dozen men at the oars, the launch made its way to the beach, collected the royal passengers—Tynah, Queen Ideeah, Tynah's aged father and their considerable retinue—and out again to the *Bounty*.

'Are you a friend of Cook?' were Tynah's opening words at the head of the gangway. Bligh assured him that he was. 'Then please take care of my wife,' Tynah requested.

It was no easy business hoisting Queen Ideeah up the gangway, but at length the entire party was safely on board and Tynah and Bligh, in Polynesian custom, rubbed noses enthusiastically and exchanged names.

There followed an orgy of gift-swapping which worked out advantageously to the Tahitians: it usually did. They gave a bread-fruit and a quantity of cloth. For these Tynah received hatchets and files, gimlets and a saw, knives, looking glasses, two shirts · and some spectacular red flamingo wings which Bligh had acquired at Cape Town for this very occasion. There were beads and ear-rings and necklaces for Queen Ideeah, who quickly showed that she expected as well the more masculine gifts her husband had received; and then said she wanted to see Bligh's cabin.

Bligh knew only too well what this would lead to, but deter-mined that nothing must go awry on the first morning and led the way reluctantly down the ladder. As he had feared, Tynah and Ideeah took a liking for everything that they saw, and Bligh presen-ted them with as good grace as he could summon. Back on deck the scrounging continued relentlessly, officers were asked for their handkerchiefs and shirts and the last two of the live English pigs were taken from their pen and handed over for safe-keeping to one of the royal retinue. It was a relief when Tynah asked that one of the cannon should be fired: this at least was a distraction. Two of the four-pounders were loaded with ball-shot and fired. Tynah in turn expressed terror at the sound and wonder at the distant fall of shot in the sea; and then, thank goodness, it was time to eat.

The men ate apart from the women, Tynah voraciously, fed by a servant who sat beside him and took nibbles himself from the same chunk of meat. When this was over Tynah asked that the queen and her servants should now be fed. Hospitable as ever, Bligh at once arranged this in privacy below decks, and was amazed to see Tynah settle down again with the women and 'eat as hearty as before'.

Thus began a curious five-month-long close relationship between the Royal Navy lieutenant and the regent of northern Tahiti. Bligh, a sentimental man with those who showed him affection, returned the friendship of the muscular ruler and his massive wife with ardour. Tynah had a questioning mind, too, and the men would talk for hours on end—Bligh's command of the language improving daily—about Polynesian and English manners and customs, history and daily life in the royal palaces in England, especially the last: Tynah could not hear enough about King George III. Tynah, often with his entire family and entourage, took dinner, and sometimes supper too, on board the *Bounty* with Bligh almost every day; and when Bligh went ashore Tynah accompanied him and often arranged some entertainment, perhaps wrestling or dancing.

Bligh was not much impressed with the wrestling. Although he recorded with interest the elaborate ritual preliminaries—the beating of cupped hands on naked flesh like the sound of an axe against a tree-trunk, the bending of arms, the pointing of fingers—and admired the strength of the contestants, he found the Tahitians neither very skilful nor very courageous.

The dancing interested him, but also failed to impress him. This is what he saw at one of his first *heivas*. He is sitting on the ground, the guest of honour, Tynah at his side. It is damp and hot, for the rainy season has just begun, but the air is tolerable in this clearing under the shade of the breadfruit trees. Propped up beside them is the framed portrait of James Cook. Both Bligh and the portrait of his old commander are draped in lengths of white cloth—in Tahitian eyes the effigy of a demi-god and his living son, his Christ. A priest appears, harangues the crowd, and then turns to Bligh, to the portrait, and to Tynah. That evening Bligh writes in his log:

'The priest now spoke again, when an old man with one eye came running up to me in a superstitious kind of manner, and placed a piece of plaited coconut leaf at my feet. The same was done to Tynah and one piece was thrown under the picture. The priest left off speaking and the *heiva* began by the men jumping and throwing their legs and arms into violent and odd motions, which the women kept time with, and as they were conveniently clothed for the purpose, their persons were generally exposed to full view, frequently standing on one leg and keeping the other up, giving themselves the most lascivious and wanton motions. As this was for some time performed, at the farthest part of the ring from us, out of compliment the women were directed to come nearer, and they accordingly advanced with their clothes up, and went through the same wanton gestures which on their return ended the *heiva*.'

Some of this dancing was too much for Bligh. Later, when a band of itinerant male entertainers put on an elaborate display to show what could be done to their private parts with strength and lengths of twine, he ordered them to stop although everyone else was roaring with laughter.

Bligh was horrified by some of the Polynesian sexual practices— the public ritual of deflowering a little girl (seven years was not considered exceptionally young) by an experienced and hearty youth, the uninhibited acceptance of sodomy, and what he called 'numerous sensual and beastly acts of gratification' including oral intercourse. Some four weeks after he had first met Tynah and Iddeah he heard from Tynah's brother that the queen shared her bed equally with her husband and his servant, the same one who fed him at meals. Bligh could not at first believe it, but eager witnesses were found who confirmed this arrangement and treated it as normal 'that both men cohabited with the wife in the same hour, and in the presence of the other'. Clearly promiscuity was also accepted as normal between families, and brothers freely slept with each other's wives. Outside the family it was something different, and while Bligh was at Matavai there were cases of knifing and other violent retribution for infidelity outside the family.

Day after day Bligh reported on everything from sexual deviations and burial practices, childbirth and infanticide, to religion and alcoholism. Sometimes there is evidence of his shock and outrage at what he sees, but mostly he is content to record with affectionate interest. He is never patronising. Although there had in the past been occasional outbreaks of inter-tribal fighting, overpopulation was a greater anxiety than war and conditioned many of their practices. The *erreeroys* horrified yet fascinated him. They belonged to a highly privileged society formed under a vow of celibacy. *Erreeroys* could demand food at any time, could take from anyone clothes that took their fancy, were not expected to work, and spent their lives wandering about in a state of dissipation and idleness. If they conceived a child—which they frequently did—it was summarily strangled at birth. Only in time of war did they have to pay for their privileges, for the *erreeroys* were the professional fighting men, and when fighting was imminent they were expected to be celibate 'that they might not weaken or enervate themselves'.

Bligh was deeply concerned with the Tahitian problem of over-population, and characteristically produced a possible solution. Why not use the rich emptiness of Australia?—mass migration from

Polynesia. 'How greatly the two countries might be made to benefit each other,' he wrote. 'A great continent would be converted from a desert to a populous country; a number of our fellow creatures would be saved; the inhabitants of the islands would become more civilised.'

But not for one day does Bligh forget the main purpose of his visit to Tahiti. Above the moral comments and philosophising, the recording of the minutiae of native practices, and his close relationship with the royal household, his first concern remains the progress of David Nelson's nursery gardens and the potting and cultivation of the breadfruit plants. On many days at Tahiti he notes in his log the number of plants successfully potted, and their condition. Ten years earlier at Hawaii he had seen what difficulties Cook had encountered in repairing on shore his masts and rigging in the face of a suspicious and later hostile population. The breadfruit cultivation was going to take months, not days. And however generously nature had provided the islanders, the taking away of one of their basic sources of food required delicate handling. Look what had happened to Cook when the islanders of Hawaii thought he was threatening them with starvation. The creation of a nursery garden was a delicate business, and, of course, the slightest disturbance could mean the destruction of weeks of Nelson's painstaking work.

The first thing Bligh had to do on his arrival, therefore, after establishing cordial relations with Tynah, was to raise the object of his visit, without seeming to do so. Ashore with Tynah on 1 November, a warm day with lightning and much rain from which they sheltered in a hut, Bligh talked to the regent.

BLIGH: You have many good friends in England, including King George. When ships come again to Tahiti they will bring more presents and other good things for you.

TYNAH [*'much pleased and satisfied'*]: How long will you stay at Matavai?

BLIGH: Five months among the islands.

TYNAH [*uneasily*]: Stay at Matavai. Do not go to the other islands. We have everything here, breadfruit, coconuts, plantains and hogs.

BLIGH: King George has sent you many presents. You should let me carry back in return presents to King George.

TYNAH: I will gladly send anything your king might prefer—hogs plantains, bananas, coconuts, breadfruit—

BLIGH: The breadfruit is a very good idea. King George will like that.

TYNAH: I shall see that you carry away a great deal of breadfruit.

And so the matter was concluded and Bligh congratulated himself on his shrewdness. The minor chiefs were informed by Tynah that King George was to be presented with as many breadfruit saplings as the great ship could carry, and Bligh as a result was treated with additional respect and gratitude as the chief who would do the islanders the kindness of transporting them to 'Pretanee'. The following day he went ashore with Nelson and Brown and sought out the most suitable place on Point Venus to create their nursery garden.

Point Venus marks the northern extremity of the Tahitian coastline, a low rich promontory. Today at the tip there is a monument where Cook and Banks set up the telescope for the observation of the transit of Venus in 1769, some pretty grassy gardens with shrubs and bougainvillaea, a museum of relics (usually closed) and a rather splendid piece of *avant garde* sculpture placed just above the shore bearing the names, in order, of the first three European navigators to land at Tahiti, Wallis, Bougainville and Cook himself, with the dates also inscribed. It is still an idyllic spot. From the black lava sand beach you can see the bay of Matavai sweeping in a shallow curve to the distant town of Papeete, administrative capital of the French island; and above the long low cloud of spray which is poised for ever over the coral reef off Papeete five miles away, the riotous silhouette of Moorea sits on the horizon, usually with clouds brushing its higher peaks. A crescent of more coral reef, like the white tip of a nail to the finger of land, protects Point Venus from the Pacific rollers.

Inland the sharp-edged green-clad hills rise steeply, to seven thousand feet in a few miles. A valley like a knife cut, the Valée de Toouoo, slices deep into the mountains. Tumbling down its base flows one of Tahiti's biggest rivers, which meets the sea on the eastern side of the promontory. This river was one of the features that attracted voyagers to this part of the island, and from it they drew their casks of water before sailing away. It was also, as we shall see, nearly Bligh's undoing.

David Nelson chose a spot close to the estuary of this river for his garden. Today full-grown breadfruit trees rise about this area, living 200-year-old memorials to this determined and much-travelled gardener. From that time, and until the *Bounty*'s departure, the area became forbidden territory to the natives—Tynah and his chiefs saw to that. But to help reinforce security Bligh ordered Christian to collect his belongings and come ashore as commander of the *Bounty*'s shore-based establishment. He was to bring with him his fellow midshipman, young Peter Heywood, and Peckover the gunner. Four armed ratings, working in rotation, provided the defence force.

A tented encampment was set up beside Nelson's garden on Point Venus. The *Bounty*'s mainsail and mizzen, firmly lashed, provided large tents for the main living quarters and protection for the young plants; the small sails made good individual tents. This arrangement worked well. But as time passed the encampment was elaborated with water tanks and footpaths and other small conveniences, and the natives erected permanent huts. Point Venus thus became a comfortable little English colonial outpost and the first point of call for all those from the *Bounty* when they came ashore. When the rainy season broke, as it did soon after the encampment was set up, there was adequate shelter. And because of its exposed situation, the fly and mosquito nuisance which could make life ashore a misery was greatly diminished.

Only five people made permanent homes at Point Venus: Nelson and Brown, who rarely returned on board the *Bounty* until she sailed; Will Peckover, the trade supervisor; Peter Heywood; and Fletcher Christian, permanent commandant. So, once again, Christian had been given a situation of comfort and privilege. Again no one seems to have resented this or showed signs of jealousy. Christian himself settled down happily to a life of almost total indolence. Like all the *Bounty*'s men he had many girls to choose from and for a time lived a promiscuous life. Then he found a real *tyo*, a young girl called Mauatua, daughter of a chief, whom he renamed Isabella. She is described as tall and beautiful. He also acquired, as many of them did, a male *tyo*—a servant-cum-friend.

In the eyes of the men of the *Bounty* all the Tahitian girls were beautiful: but it does appear as if there was something especially radiant about Christian's Isabella. Certainly side by side they must have made a splendid-looking pair. Except for a brief period after the *Bounty*'s departure, they remained together as man and wife right until the end. Their tall son grew into a magnificent figure of a man, as many people testified.

The *Bounty*'s ratings were allowed ashore on leave two at a time and were free to do as they liked so long as they adhered to the rules of conduct laid down by Bligh shortly before they had arrived at the island which forbade them to trade privately and adjured them 'to study to gain the good will and esteem of the natives'. There was not, in fact, very much for an uneducated naval rating to do ashore except chat to the natives—'we found it very easy to converse by signs at which these people are adept', remarks Morrison—play with the children and see how the breadfruit plants were getting on. We can see them, tanned and fit, without shoes or jackets, strolling about for a few hours, flirting with the girls and plucking and eating the fruit which grew so freely. Then they would be quite glad to get back to the ship, to their *tyos* and their possessions, perhaps showing off to one another their new tattoo marks. Officers and ratings alike admired the elaborate tattooing with which all the natives adorned themselves, on their chests, arms and buttocks, even their faces and their private parts. Tattooing was almost unknown in England. Only a handful of seamen who had sailed the Pacific with Wallis or Carteret, Byron or Cook, enjoyed the distinction of tattoo marks, flaunting them like campaign medals in taverns. Now almost without exception, the *Bounty*'s company suffered the pain of native tattooing, vying with one another for the most elaborate design.

On shore or on shipboard, on watch or off, the demands made on most of the men were very light. One or two were kept busy. Peckover, for example, was kept fully occupied with his trading and bartering. The carpenter and his crew were also busy for the first few weeks. Purcell grumbled a good deal, as he always did, but without good reason. A carpenter usually had plenty to do after his ship had been at sea for a long time. Of his crew, Charles Norman was seriously ill for a while, so that added to the burden on McIntosh, who worked hard without grumbling.

Another busy man was Joseph Coleman the armourer. He set up his forge within a few days of their arrival and was never without work. The natives brought their precious iron tools and toys which they had acquired from Cook or Bougainville and were in need of repair. They also discovered that, given an old bit of metal, Coleman could form it into any shape, useful or just diverting. Bligh encouraged the armourer and the carpenters to meet the natives' needs. It all helped to cement relations.

During November and the early part of December the men on watch were engaged in the usual tasks when a ship was at anchor off a friendly shore. Peckover traded for hogs in large numbers for salting down and casking for the voyage to the West Indies; the remaining biscuit, which one day would again be their staple food-stuff, was sorted, the bad bits thrown to the fishes, the good restored. The yards were tarred, the boats inspected, and the ship cleaned down daily.

As Christmas approached the routine tasks of maintenance had been completed and there was very little left for the men to do. From Morrison's and Bligh's journals and other observations we can visualise the scene on a December evening with the *Bounty* now anchored a mere hundred yards from the beach. Bligh is ashore with Nelson, and most of the *Bounty*'s company are on deck, lying about with their *tyos*, chatting, fishing with lines over the side. Earlier the women have cooked the evening meal in the galley below—fish, pork, breadfruit beaten into a paste or eaten whole, plantains, bananas and other fruit. It is dark, the air is still, the bay calm, the temperature in the lower eighties. It has been cloudy during the day with threatening thunder but now the skies are clear.

On one side the mountains rise dark against the starlit sky, towards the open sea a mile distant the breaking rollers on the reef cast a white scar line separating the lagoon from the Pacific. The natives, as usual, are out fishing in their hundreds, their favourite evening occupation, each canoe and the sea about it illuminated by a splash of yellow light from a burning reed bundle. Some, like the *Bounty*'s men, are using a line—everyone is very up-to-date with a steel hook from Europe now—and others are trawling with nets. Close to the reef the lights are brightest, the fishing best and most risky, the outrigger canoes the largest, a dozen men in them, some holding the rushes close to the water, others with spears poised for the strike.

As always, the beating of the surf on the reef is the predominating sound—a deep boom with a barely audible cadence as one roller smashes from end to end of the reef and the next begins before the first extinguishes itself. The other sound that is with them day and night, however calm the lagoon, is the creaking of the *Bounty*'s timbers, the eternal living sound of a ship afloat anywhere at any time. Sometimes the fishermen can be heard calling to one another, and there are murmurs of conversation on the *Bounty*. Byrn strikes up a tune on his fiddle; the women chat among themselves and later drift off with their men below or to a corner of the forecastle deck. There is little quarrelling among the men or the women, and the atmosphere is bucolic rather than maritime. For the Englishmen it is all rather like any village green on a summer's evening outside the tavern.

Bligh's time became increasingly filled with his study of the Tahitian people and their practices, by entertaining Tynah and his wife and their large family, and by his anxious observation of the progress of the breadfruit plants. Although fond of the Tahitians, his judgement of them is often oddly ambivalent. Taken ill suddenly with sunstroke and nursed by them tenderly, he conceived 'every favourable idea of these people, surely they may be supposed to possess every degree of sensibility and affection'. Yet he continued to express disgust at their more obscene dances, surprise at their burial practices and contempt for their lack of courage and their scrounging habits. Sometimes he was frankly puzzled. While walking amongst the breadfruit groves he heard the sound of lamentation and found a group of women, apparently in the last stages of grief, standing about the corpse of a baby. As soon as he was observed their expressions changed and they all burst into uncontrollable giggles. 'This strange behaviour,' Bligh observes, 'would incline us to think them hard-hearted and unfeeling, did we not know that they are fond parents, and in general, very affectionate: it is therefore to be ascribed to their extreme levity of disposition; and it is probable that death does not appear to them with so many terrors as it does to people of a more serious cast.'

Bligh was amused by their teasing ways. At one dance the natives put on a special act imitating the Englishmen rowing their boats and the officer in charge 'finding fault if anything is wrong'. He was amused, too, at the way they often lied for the fun of it. That was all right. Thieving was another matter. He had of course prepared himself for it. Ten years earlier he had seen at first hand how counter-action against the thieving tendencies of the Polynesians could lead to tragedy. He was obviously determined to take every possible step to prevent it, and before their arrival lectured the officers seriously. It was part of their nature to steal, he told them, but if anything was stolen it was the fault of the officer of the watch. On 4 November, when something was stolen from the large cutter under the nose of Alex Smith, he was punished with twelve lashes.

The women on board at the time were very upset by this, 'which marked them', in Bligh's judgement, 'to be the most humane and affectionate creatures in the world'. Tynah and his chiefs, however, always advocated the most savage punishment for any of their subjects found guilty of theft. On at least one occasion they received it.

On a dark night a native stole into the shore encampment and took an empty water cask, part of a compass, and the bedding out of Peckover's hammock. Bligh was so outraged that Tynah and his chiefs fled to the mountains. Bligh sent him a message saying that unless the thief was discovered and brought to him, they would no longer be friends.

Within a few hours, Tynah was seen approaching the encampment, personally leading the thief by the arm. 'This is the thief. Kill him,' he begged Bligh, who replied by telling Tynah that they could be friends again now. There was much embracing. Then the thief was taken out to the *Bounty*, spreadeagled against a grating and given one hundred lashes.

Even by eighteenth-century standards in the Royal Navy, one hundred lashes must be regarded as a savage and exceptional punishment. None of Bligh's own men received at one time more than two dozen, even for the most heinous offence. 'He bore it surprisingly,' noted Bligh, 'and only asked me twice to forgive him although he expected he was to die.' Not content with that, Bligh confined him in irons. Five nights later the prisoner broke the bolt of his irons, which required remarkable strength, found his way up on deck and dived overboard. Stewart, mate of the watch, went off in a boat in search of him without success. Bligh spent all the next day with Tynah and Queen Ideeah 'as usual'. All had apparently been forgiven.

The breadfruit cultivation went ahead satisfactorily for the first two months. By 5 November the natives had caught the spirit of the operation and were eager to assist. Nelson and Brown trained several of the more attentive as assistants and even learned several tips from them. The plant, after all, had been cultivated on Tahiti for centuries and although their methods were crude they were effective. The onset of the rainy season encouraged their growth, and soon Bligh was able to record: 'I have now 168 plants potted at the tents, and if we continue to go on as we have done, a fortnight or three weeks more will complete our business. No time, however, is lost, and I must do Mr Nelson the justice to say he is very diligent and attentive. The plants in general, although suckers, have very fine roots, and I hope he will soon be able to remove them to the ship out of the way of the natives.'

This did not mean that the cultivation would be complete in such a short time. The plants had to develop size and strength for another three months at least before Nelson would judge them fit for the long sea passage. In any case, the whole transplantation, and even the *Bounty* herself, was placed in jeopardy a few weeks later when a tropical storm struck Tahiti.

It was the afternoon of 5 December. The seas broke over the reefs, converting Matavai Bay from a tranquil lagoon into a boiling cauldron, 'threatening us with instant destruction', and breaking right over the ship. The rain came down in torrents, and that night all hands worked to save the *Bounty*. Bligh ordered yards and top-masts struck early in the morning, and had to draw on all his skill to ride out the storm.

In the midst of this turmoil Bligh was astonished to see the royal canoe putting out from the shore. This was a new Tahiti, a new Tynah. With everyone in the canoe, including the queen, wielding the paddles to bring it through the tumultuous seas safely, they succeeded in coming alongside the pitching *Bounty*, and then, overweight Ideeah included, grasped ropes and hauled themselves on to deck. In turn Tynah and his wife embraced Bligh in a flood of tears and told how they had been praying all night for his safety. They had even brought food with them to give the crew strength to survive the ordeal.

Ashore, the tents were flooded, the river burst its banks, and the plantation was soon threatened with destruction. Nelson and Brown struggled to save their breadfruit by digging a trench through the beach to divert a part of the floodwater. Mercifully the rain eased off later in the day, the river subsided, and in the end few of the plants were damaged.

Matavai Bay, as Bligh had now learned, was by no means an ideal anchorage, and he determined to find a better bay. This was discovered at Oparre, some six miles west of Point Venus, a little bay with sufficient depth, better protected by a reef from the sea, and by a headland from the trades. Bligh had hinted that he meant to try the island of Moorea. This outraged and frightened Tynah, who had gained vast kudos and wealth from his patron and was deter-

mined to keep him as his own to the end. Oparre had been Tynah's
idea.

Over Christmas the encampment on Point Venus was dismantled,
the tents struck, and over 700 potted breadfruit plants ferried out
and stowed in the ship.

As the young breadfruit plants matured and then flourished in their
new garden ashore at Oparre, so the seeds of the mutiny four months
later germinated on board the *Bounty*. It is not possible to put a
date to the beginnings of the trouble. Duties had been neglected at
Matavai, too. There had been plenty of slackness at the old anchorage.
It is to the gradual breakdown in leadership that we have to look
for the undermining of discipline and the lowering of morale that
culminated in the violence of 28 April.

Significantly, it was on the brief voyage out of Matavai and along
the coast that the extent of the decline in spirit and efficiency among
the *Bounty*'s company becomes evident. It was Christmas Day, fine
and warm. All 774 pots of plants were safely stowed in the *Bounty*'s
garden, and Bligh had sent the launch ahead to meet the ship at the
entrance to the anchorage to show the way in. Bligh weighed, and
with Tynah, the queen and the entire royal retinue on board, ran
out of Matavai. Three-quarters of an hour later the *Bounty* began to
make her way through the reef, the launch ahead, Fryer on the
fore yard keeping a lookout, a leadsman in the chains calling out
the depth and Bligh himself, one of the most experienced navigators
in the world, beside the helmsman.

Yet in a sudden sequence of miscalculations, everything began to
go wrong. The launch drifted into the lee of the ship, was becalmed
and fell astern. Fryer failed to see the danger ahead. Suddenly they
were no longer moving. Bligh did not even realise what had happened until Fryer came down from the yard and said, 'We are aground
for'ard, sir.' The *Bounty*'s bows had struck a reef and the fore part
of the ship was no longer afloat.

The weather was deteriorating. Black clouds were rolling in from
the north-east. A sudden squall now must mean the end of the
Bounty. The Tahitians realised this as clearly as the crew and became
alarmed. Bligh ordered all the women ashore and asked Tynah for
some of his menservants to help the crew. He himself went in the
launch to the bows, took in the bower anchor and carried it astern,

while Fryer was ordered to send out the kedge anchor astern on the port quarter in an attempt to drag the ship off manually.

Slowly the *Bounty* was drawn from the reef and refloated. Unfortunately, further neglect led to the two anchors and their cables becoming foul on the reef, and it took more than twenty-four hours to free them. By a merciful chance the weather remained fair.

Bligh was becoming increasingly exasperated with his officers. These men whom he had chosen with such care, for their temperament and experience, on whom he had earlier reported so favourably to Banks and Campbell, now became the victims of Bligh's foul tongue and fitful temper. The first recorded trouble occurred on 5 December when the carpenter refused Bligh's order to cut with his chisels a grinding stone for the natives' new hatchets. It will spoil my tools, Purcell protested. For this 'mutinous and insolent behaviour' he was confined to his cabin.

'Such neglectful and worthless petty officers I believe never were in a ship as are in this,' Bligh wrote on 5 January. A few days later, Will Cole the bo'sun and Fryer are again vilified. 'If I had any officers to supersede them, or was able to do without them, considering them as common seamen, they should no longer occupy their respective stations.'

After further evidence of neglect—this time by the mate of the watch on the night the thieving native escaped—Bligh delivered himself of another attack in his log, embracing them all and not just the guilty Stewart. 'I have such a neglectful set about me that I believe nothing but condign punishment can alter their conduct.'

The worst sufferer was Fletcher Christian. By contrast with the voyage out, Bligh saw him less frequently now that Christian lived ashore, and meetings only occurred as a result of Bligh's displeasure at some actual of imagined failure in his duties. Nor were his attacks made in private. Bligh liked an audience because it added to the culprit's humiliation. Against an officer it was always a bad practice on shipboard for the obvious reason that it reduced the man's authority over his subordinates. It was even more undesirable in front of native chiefs whose hierarchical society was acutely status conscious. On several occasions Christian's slackness led to fearsome rebukes from Bligh in the presence of Tynah and his family and Christian's male *tyo* who so admired and was so proud of his master. Bligh also made it clear to this same young man that he was quite wrong if he thought Christian was second-in-command of the *Bounty*. 'He is no more than one of the people,' Bligh explained with much satisfaction.

Things were no better among the ratings. As the grounding of the *Bounty* on Christmas Day highlighted the decay of leadership and seamanship, so the death of the surgeon betokened the declining spirit of the men. Huggan had continued to drink himself senseless every day since their arrival, rarely emerging from his cabin and never going ashore. His assistant and successor, Ledward, one of the few who still visited him, found him in a dreadful condition on 10 December, hardly able to breathe. Fryer and a party of seamen later went below with the intention of dragging him up on to deck to get some air. But the cabin was empty. Some last instinct for survival had caused the pathetic, bloated and stinking surgeon to drag himself up the ladder, and he was stretched out unconscious on deck when they found him. Someone tried to give him a sip of coconut milk. But he was really past all aid, and he died at nine o'clock that evening.

One of the last duties Huggan had been able to perform was checking 'the venereal list'. With the promiscuity that began within minutes of the *Bounty* dropping anchor at Matavai, it was hardly surprising that venereal disease spread rapidly. Even though Bligh, for the record, had seen that his men were inspected before they arrived, these medical examinations were always perfunctory affairs and it is possible that several of them were still carrying latent germs or were acting as carriers. The same applied to the women of Tahiti. Cook and other early navigators suffered under the guilty impression that their men were staining the pure Polynesian islands with a corrupt Western disease. Before Bligh left Tahiti he had come to the conclusion—now, of course, long since confirmed—that gonorrhea was rife long before the arrival of the Europeans. Bligh also believed, this time quite incorrectly, that the Tahitians had a simple cure. 'Many women have absented themselves from us on the men telling them they were diseased,' he wrote. 'However, they have returned again in a short time, and kept with other men without infecting them.'

Venereal disease began to spread among the men at the beginning of December, and the number of 'venereals' continued to increase during this month and after the move to Oparre. Sometimes as many as seven were down at one time. In all eighteen officers and men, or nearly half the ship's company, had to apply to the surgeon for a venereal cure; and, incidentally, be fined.

The spread of venereal disease in a ship's company, even at this exceptionally high level, does not alone prove demoralisation. Cook had had the same trouble on all his voyages and Bligh had prepared for it. 'It could not be expected,' he noted, 'that the intercourse of my people with the natives should be of a very reserved nature.' We have to look for more evidence than this for proof of the disintegration of discipline. It is not difficult to find. The frequency of floggings began to rise steeply soon after the *Bounty* had anchored—Smith on 4 November, Thompson 'twelve lashes for insolence and disobedience of orders' on 5 December, Muspratt a dozen for neglecting his duty on 27 December, Robert Lamb another dozen two days later.

This was followed by worse trouble. At some time between midnight and 2 a.m. on 5 January, Muspratt, Millward and Churchill, the *Bounty*'s corporal, stole a complete arms chest, climbed into the small cutter and deserted ship. This was not difficult as Hayward, mate of the watch, was asleep as usual. The theft was discovered when the watch was relieved at 4 a.m. Bligh was not informed until half an hour later. He ordered Hayward confined below in irons and at once went ashore. The hunt began at dawn.

The cutter had, it seemed, gone to Matavai where the men had left it and taken a large canoe and then made out to sea, heading for the small islands of Tetiaroa twenty miles to the north. It was obvious that the three deserters intended to hide there until the *Bounty* sailed and then return to the good life on Tahiti. Bligh returned to the *Bounty* with Tynah, one of his brothers and a chief, and sent them off in pursuit with Fryer. On their way to Matavai they met the missing cutter being rowed back to the ship by some natives who had found it. Bligh was delighted and rewarded them. The loss of the boat had been more serious than the loss of the men. But Bligh made clear to Tynah that he would not leave Tahiti without them, and asked him if he would take a party to Tetiaroa to recapture them. Tynah enquired, reasonably enough, how was he supposed to seize three desperate men armed with muskets when he was without firearms. Use guile, was Bligh's answer to this problem. Pretend to be friends, then leap on them and bind them with cords. 'Show them no mercy if they resist.'

Later Bligh discovered a piece of paper in Churchill's sea chest on which was written the names of three of the shore party. Was this the beginning of a full-scale mutiny and not just a desertion? Bligh hastened ashore again, sought out Christian and accused his men of being implicated. According to Morrison 'they persisted in their innocence, and denied it so firmly, that he was inclined from circumstances to believe them'.

Because of a sudden change in the weather, the affair dragged on for nine more days during which no canoe or ship's boat could safely put to sea. It was not until 14 January that a strong party of natives set out for Tetiaroa to search for the deserters. Four more days passed and Bligh became increasingly anxious about what had happened to his men. 'Do not fear,' Tynah reassured him, 'they will be brought back.'

As it turned out, the three men came back on their own to Tahiti after being captured by the party of natives and escaping again. The locals had been equally hostile, and in wet, squally weather, Muspratt, Millward and Churchill had sailed their canoe south, missing Moorea where they hoped to land, and being cast ashore six miles from Oparre, sodden, miserable, their ammunition ruined and some of their arms lost. Bligh himself set off in the launch to bring them back, and returned to the *Bounty*, his mission completed, on the evening of 23 January.

The next morning, still in pouring rain, the ship's company was mustered. Bligh read out the Articles of War, publicly rebuked Hayward, and then ordered twelve lashes for Churchill and two dozen each for the others. This was not the end of what was the most serious threat to his authority that Bligh had so far suffered. The three men were confined in irons until 4 February, when they were brought up and given the same punishment as before.

There was one more ironical—and potentially disastrous—consequence of this affair. Hayward's male *tyo*, a man by the name of Wyetooa, had been on board the *Bounty*, standing close behind Bligh and with a club in his hand, on the morning when the three deserters had been flogged and Hayward had been publicly rebuked and ordered below in irons again. Bligh never knew how close to death he had been. If Hayward had been flogged, Wyetooa had planned to fell Bligh on the first lash, then leap overboard and gain the shore before anyone could reach him.

Instead, Wyetooa had bided his time, bitter at Hayward's humiliation and the loss of the company of his friend. Then on the black wet night of 5–6 February, he swam out and with a knife severed all but one strand of the *Bounty*'s bower cable. There was a gale blowing, and the Tahitian reckoned that the remaining strand would soon snap and the *Bounty* be cast on to the shore. This way, according to Morrison, 'he hoped to get his friend out of Mr Bligh's power, as he supposed that all hands would be forced to live ashore. . . .'

However, Bligh knew nothing of all this and was—besides being furious—'at a loss to account for this malicious act' which was providentially discovered before the last strand snapped.

All through the Tahiti rainy season the men were given little to do except the daily routine tasks of washing down the decks, picking biscuit, caulking, repairing the rigging. Bligh was on shore with the royal family almost every day, bringing them back on board for supper, and taking only spasmodic interest in the men and the ship. The *Bounty* was becoming a slack ship—no doubt of that. On 17 January he ordered the sail room to be cleared and the sails taken on shore to air. Among them were the unused spare sails which were found to be rotten and mildewed. They had previously been reported in good order. So his officers were liars and slackers. 'Scarce any neglect of duty can equal the criminality of this.'

The failure to inspect regularly every part of the ship for signs of decay—the duty of any commander and especially of one who mistrusted his officers—led to other discoveries of damage, some of it irreparable. The small cutter was a case in point. By the time of the mutiny in April both the smaller boats were in poor shape and the small cutter was no longer seaworthy. Everybody knew this, no one did anything about it. The stock of the bower anchor—the most important anchor—was allowed to rot through, eaten by *teredo navalis*. No one had checked it for months when this was discovered at the beginning of April while it was being stowed. It simply fell overboard and was lost. The bottom of the *Bounty* was protected against worms by copper sheathing. None the less some rot set in in the structure of the ship below the water line. At least this was discovered before they sailed, and one of the main cants had to be cut out and replaced.

As the *Bounty*'s long stay in Tahiti draws to a close with the autumn strengthening of the breadfruit plants and the final breakdown in order and discipline approaches, the other Bligh—the fair weather

commander, not the foul weather commander—begins to emerge
more clearly. His first failing is lack of imagination. He does not
understand his officers and men. He knows that in adversity he must
think of them constantly, watching their diet, seeing that they are
kept as dry and warm as possible, recognising that there is a limit
to their endurance, encouraging and praising them as they near it.
It is not only a point of great pride that he brings them, through
some of the worst weather in the world, 27,000 miles with only one
casualty. It is also essential for the successful conclusion of the
enterprise that he keeps his crew intact. Royal Navy training, his
experience as understudy to Cook, taught him all this many years
ago. Like his other exceptional qualities—his seamanship, his skill
as a navigator—his ability to win through against every adversity
makes him a so-nearly-great commander.

Unimaginativeness is the fatal flaw. Without thinking about it,
he expected discipline and morale to be maintained in his ship
anchored off Tahiti on as high a level as if they were beating their
way round the Horn, struggling day and night to keep their ship
afloat and themselves alive. For more than five months, with all
the seductive delights of one of the most beautiful islands in the
world freely and daily available, he left them if not to their own de-
vices then under the ever-slackening supervision of his officers
in whom he had no confidence—while he spent most of his time
enjoying life with the royal family, studying the people, the flora
and fauna, and watching his garden grow.

Bligh at Tahiti was like a rider, with a long way to go and many
dangers ahead, who hacks along enjoying the scenery, and then
suddenly thrusts in the spurs, shouts abuse and whips his horse into
a brief gallop. That bluff Yorkshireman James Cook was not the
most imaginative of commanders, but an instinctive understanding
of the sailor's mind would have warned him to keep his company
of simple, rough ratings and petty officers and inexperienced
'young gentlemen' on the go and fully occupied during this long
slack period. He would have kept his eye on them all right. The
Bounty would have been off every week or two, and at the end of
five months they would have charted every bay, measured every
hill, of all the Society Islands. Cook would have allowed women on
board and turned a blind eye to the promiscuous carryings-on. That
was a lower-deck prerogative. But he would have had them off and
ashore when he went exploring, and his men would have appreci-

ated them and the other delights of Tahiti the more when they got back. Nor would the *Bounty* have had leaky boats on board when she sailed from Oparre.

Bligh at Tahiti deputed responsibility to his officers and cursed them when he discovered they had failed him—as they did, time and again. But they were failing a commander who himself had failed in leadership when a leader's qualities are put to the severest test, when things seem to be going smoothly. A basic tenet of leadership which Bligh never learned is that you never delegate responsibility. You depute and supervise and it is your responsibility if your subordinates fail you. He was too unimaginative and too proud to recognise that his officers were letting him down because he was letting them down.

The quality of the *Bounty*'s officers had once been high. With some of them he had sailed before, others he had known or had been recommended to him; with all of them he had sailed 27,000 miles for nearly a year when they arrived at Tahiti. Moreover, he had found few faults with them at sea, and never when things were going badly for them.

Bligh quite failed to anticipate how his company would react to the severity and austerity of life at sea again after five dissolute, hedonistic months at Tahiti. His imagination failed him again. Moreover, they would within a few weeks be facing a test which would demand as much skill and endurance as doubling the Horn— the passage through the notorious Endeavour Straits between the northern tip of Australia and New Guinea; and then the long hard slog across the Indian Ocean after it, all with the additional responsibility of preserving through storm and drought their delicate cargo of plants.

On 27 February Bligh wrote that 'the plants are in a very fine state and Mr Nelson thinks they will be perfectly established in the pots in the course of a month'; and in the early days of March he began to give serious attention to the state of the ship. The sailmakers were ordered to repair the sails and awnings, the cooper prepared the casks for watering, the carpenter's crew busied themselves with repairs, the armourer was at his forge. Caulking and cleaning below decks took on a more purposeful air; hogs salted down, twenty-five live ones penned in the waist with seventeen goats; green plantains, breadfruit, coconuts and other fruit stowed below and on deck.

Still under the strict surveillance of Peckover, the crew completed their personal trading. They were allowed only enough to fill their sea chests—no more. Bligh was not going to hazard the efficient working of the ship by having piles of personal food and mementoes all over the place. He had seen some ships returning from long voyages with their decks piled high with trophies and stocks of foodstuffs, monkeys and caged pets. That was not how the *Bounty* was going to be. She was crowded enough already with the breadfruit plants on board.

The last days at Oparre were chaotic, crowded and moving. Word had travelled for many miles around that the great ship and the white men were at last leaving. The natives gathered in hundreds from curiosity, for what they could get and what they could offer, and mixed with the domestic 'families' on the upper decks. There was chanting and dancing, eating and drinking and love making, all on a glorious scale. Men queued at the forge and now the armourer worked even longer hours to carry out last repairs to broken tools or to turn pieces of iron into more tools and trinkets. For the women it was considered a prestigious triumph to conceive a half-European child, and they were as open in their appetites as their sentiments, lamenting the imminent severance of long friendships.

Amidst what Bligh described as 'a vast excess of grief', Tynah and Queen Ideeah, their parents and children and relatives, their chiefs and retinue of servants, conducted a prolonged farewell and a bout of gift-exchanging. For the last nights they remained on board, adding to the crowds who lay on deck or slept below.

The last preparations for departure, on shore and on board, were carried out amongst jostling throngs of natives and their children. Somehow the delicate and strenuous task of ferrying the plants to the ship was completed without a casualty—well over one thousand breadfruit in tubs and pots and boxes, and samples of other plants too. Below decks aft the *Bounty* took on the appearance of a floating conservatory, just as Sir Joseph Banks had dreamed it would look, while Nelson and Brown fussed over their charges, pruning, watering and settling in the containers.

An atmosphere of impending doom fell over Oparre Bay on the evening of 3 April. The weather had been dark and gloomy all afternoon, with outbreaks of thunder and lightning. Where the life on shore had centred since the move from Matavai, all became empty and silent, the garden and the huts where Christian, Heywood, Peckover and the guard had lived, all deserted. For nights past there had been singing and dancing along the beach. Now, 'no mirth or dancing', Bligh noted. The *Bounty*'s crew had said a last farewell to their *tyos*, both male and female, and the canoes had travelled only shorewards since noon, paddled slowly and with many cries of sadness. Only Tynah, as a special privilege, his sister and brother and the queen, were allowed to remain on board, grateful at least for one more evening with Bligh.

On 4 April anchors were weighed, and with boats towing and two sweeps out from the ship, the *Bounty* made her way through the buoyed channel out of the bay, watched, it seemed, by the entire population of the island.

'May God bless and protect you for ever and ever' (*Yowrah no t'Etua tee evveerah*) were Tynah's last words as he went over the side to his waiting canoe. He had with him Bligh's last load of presents— shirts and hatchets, saws, files, gimlets, knives, fish hooks, looking glasses, nails and a great number of toys. And, most highly prized of all, the gift that might provide him with a better fortune in future wars and certainly secure his status among the chiefs of all the nearby islands as well as of Tahiti—two muskets, two pistols and four thousand rounds of ammunition. This once-obscure regent of a part of northern Tahiti was now the richest and most powerful ruler in the whole Pacific.

Tynah had wanted a really rousing send-off, a proper gun salute. Reluctantly Bligh had had to refuse him this honour for fear of damaging his plants. Instead, the crew lined the side of the *Bounty* and gave him and his wife three cheers in true Royal Navy style. From the cutter which took them ashore the royal party gave three answering cheers.

Then the *Bounty* made sail and, set on a west-north-west course, disappeared slowly from sight into the sunset.

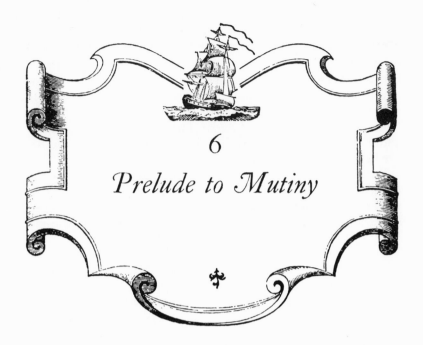

6

Prelude to Mutiny

THE more you look at the three-week-long passage of the *Bounty* from the tranquil waters of Tahiti to Tofua the more curious it becomes. The voyage begins calmly enough, but as the ship proceeds westward, threading through the Society Islands towards the Friendly Islands, a sort of madness seems to overwhelm the ship, culminating in the fury and violence of 28 April.

This is not such a fanciful notion as it may at first appear to be. There is a good deal of reliable evidence on this leg of the voyage. There are Bligh's log and narrative, John Fryer's narrative, and Morrison's account of these last days. In addition much revealing evidence came out at the court martial and from sworn evidence given to Edward Christian and verbal reminiscences by Alex Smith* many years later on Pitcairn Island.

It is not surprising that Bligh himself is the least informative, and the least accurate, guide. It was clearly in his interests to refer to only a few of the minor troubles on board that led to the mutiny, this in order to lend credence to his claim that his officers were worthless; and the log for this period appears to have been written up from notes after he reached Coupang on 14 June. Bligh makes

* An assumed name used when he signed on for the voyage. After the mutiny he reverted to his own name of John Adams.

131

no mention of his worst crises with his officers because it was his contention that the mutiny stemmed from a long-planned conspiracy of which he suspected nothing. The mutineers' sole motive for the attack, according to Bligh, was to return to 'the midst of plenty, on one of the finest islands in the world, where they need not labour, and where the allurements of dissipation are beyond anything that can be conceived'.

Increasingly as the days go by—days characterised by dark, lowering weather, lightning and thunder and tropical downpours—the evidence mounts that Bligh was seized by a form of paranoia which manifested itself in violent outbreaks against his officers in general, and Fletcher Christian in particular.

When these outbreaks had occurred before—and there had been many, though on a small scale—other officers had suffered, especially his *bêtes noir* Purcell and Fryer. But the most victimised had been Christian. 'Whatever fault was found,' reported one witness, 'Mr Christian was sure to bear the brunt of the captain's anger.' The special relationship between the two men, dating back to Christian's first voyage in the *Britannia*, was the reason for the victimisation. This will be discussed at length later. That it existed, at a very passionate level, there can be no doubt. That Bligh's madness infected first Christian—his second-in-command, the man closest to him among all the ship's company—and in a diminished degree his other officers, his warrant officers and the ratings, becomes increasingly evident as we follow events after the *Bounty* clears Matavai Bay at sundown.

The *Bounty* was not the same ship that had arrived off Tahiti the previous October, and would never be the same ship again. Every crew member had been affected by the long relaxed sojourn. They had become soft and lazy. And every crew member suffered from the reaction to seagoing life again with its rigours and discipline. The transition would have been hard under any circumstances. Under Bligh the pressures were powerful indeed.

Let us look first at the commander himself. It is not a characteristic portrait of Bligh that we see between Tahiti and Tofua. It is an unsympathetic caricature. His uneven temper, his parsimony, his relentless demands for perfection, his lack of imagination and self-control, his weakness for publicly humiliating his officers, are seen through an all-revealing lens. It is a portrait of Bligh at the end of his tether. For a man of his temperament, the strains under which he ι ffered were intolerable. They began with the discovery of the state of dissolution and incompetence into which he had allowed his men to decline at Tahiti. It was a nasty awakening from the delights of his own shore life of observing, recording, botanising, living with the royal family. His anger was inflamed by guilt, a guilt that he could not acknowledge to himself. (It was not his fault. William Bligh had no faults.) Soon his outbursts of temper and abuse became hysterical in tone and then had even less effect on his officers.

The *Bounty* needed an iron hand all right. But the pressure should have been applied evenly and with justice, not with abuse, empty threats and histrionics, followed by a sudden return to the familiar taciturnity as if nothing had happened—as indeed it had not in his mind for these outbursts seem at once to have been expunged from his memory. It was all too typical of the man. 'Which of the young gentlemen will dine with me tonight? Mr Christian, may I have the honour . . . ?'

Now let us look at his first victim. The sudden change in Christian's life when the *Bounty* sailed was just as violent as Bligh's. Ashore his duties had been negligible. There were a few thefts from the encampment, and the blistering rows with Bligh that followed them. There was that unpleasant day when it appeared that he might become guiltily involved in the escape of the three deserters. It blew over. The humiliations he suffered publicly from Bligh were more serious, and they left deep scars. But for the most part he lived an agreeable and idle life with Isabella and his man *tyo*.

For a man of Christian's sensitivity and mercurial temperament, the return to the rigours and responsibilities of shipboard life and of the renewal of close and intimate relations with Bligh in the confined quarters of the *Bounty* was especially hard to bear. His own agonised summary of his state of mind during these weeks, so often repeated at the time, and afterwards, was of course that he was in hell—in hell.

It will soon become clear that other of the *Bounty*'s officers suffered severely from the stresses affecting Bligh and Christian. Nothing and nobody was the same as the ship sailed west at a spanking pace in the easterly trades—129 nautical miles in one twenty-four-hour period, over five knots average—beneath heavy grey clouds.

In spite of the long-drawn-out and emotional farewell, there were few regrets among the men at leaving Tahiti. Only a handful of

them had developed 'strong connections' with the native girls—
some said only Christian, Alex Smith and Quintal had remained
with the same girl for most of the time. For the rest, 'everybody
seemed in high spirits' according to Morrison, talking of home,
predicting the length of their passage to the West Indies and thence
across the Atlantic to England, calculating the wages that would be
owed to them. At first it seemed good to be on the move again.

The hard work and the slim rations, the irascibility of their
commander, soon changed all this. Although Bligh had a glut of
food on board—fresh fruit and vegetables, salt and fresh pork,
besides much of the preserved stock from England—he limited the
men to a ration of pork and six plantains a day. When the plantains
were consumed, yams at a pound a man were issued instead. This
was quite adequate to support life. But officers and men alike felt
the pangs of hunger, especially as they were now living strenuously
and had been accustomed to as much food as they had wanted.
For Bligh combined these lean rations with the necessary duties
of exercising at 'backing and filling, making and shortening sail',
refamiliarising the men with handling the ship under difficult
conditions in readiness for the dangerous passage of the Endeavour
Straits.

Evidence of early contention is fragmentary but clear. Bligh had
reinstituted his daily inspections for cleanliness. Most of his men were
found wanting and had their grog stopped. On 12 April John
Sumner was given twelve lashes for neglect of duty. On another
day during exercises Bligh and Christian fell out about some real
or supposed failure. Bligh cursed him roundly in front of the crew,
as he had so often done before. Christian responded mildly. 'Sir,
your abuse is so bad that I cannot do my duty with any pleasure.'
Bligh lashed out at him again.

On 11 April everyone welcomed the diversion of the discovery
of an uncharted island. Already it was a surprise in this area of the
Pacific to sight an unknown shore, and Bligh closed it with interest,
especially as its associated reefs and keys made it a hazard of which
fellow navigators should be warned. This was Aitutaki, the most
northerly of the Cook Group, and Bligh hove to as close inshore as
he dared and spent two days and nights here, trading with the
natives and recording in detail all that he could learn of the people
and the place. Characteristically, the men were quick off the mark,
and by signs indicated to some native men who came on board that

next time they should bring some women with them. Terms were quickly agreed, but before the contract could be consummated the *Bounty* was away again, steering west-south-west for the Friendly Islands.

Bligh had planned one more halt before making for the Endeavour Straits and Coupang in Dutch Timor. This was to be at Nomuka in the Friendly Islands, a small island some 1,800 miles west of Tahiti, shaped in the form of an equilateral triangle, and measuring about two miles on each side. Unlike Tahiti and so many of the Society Islands, Nomuka was topographically flat and uninteresting. It was, however, well charted and a number of navigators had been here since Tasman discovered it on his remarkable voyage in 1644. Bligh himself had visited the island with Cook in 1777 and had personally charted much of the coastline when he had been entrusted with the responsibilities of reconnoitring the best anchorage in the *Resolution*'s launch. On that occasion he had rejected the southern shore which, though well sheltered, appeared to have no watering facilities, always a primary consideration. He had therefore worked the ship round to the north side, where he found an excellent sandy beach for drawing up the boats.

Like Tasman before him, Cook had suffered from the thieving tendencies of the natives. Flogging seemed to have no effect on them—it was like flogging a ship's mast, Cook noted, and in the end he had resorted to shaving the culprit's hair and holding them up to ridicule. When Cook had left he had all but exhausted the island of its food supplies, as he was later to do at Karakakooa Bay. It had not been a particularly friendly place.

Here Bligh intended to wood and water for the last time in the Pacific. He sighted the outlying islands of the Nomuka Group on 22 April, worked his way carefully through the shoals and anchored in the same bay on the north side as Cook and he had used twelve years earlier.

The events at Nomuka provide an ominous and fateful overture to the violence of a few days later. Everything that happened on this island seems to carry a foretaste of calamity.

The visit began badly. Although Bligh claimed to know the place so well he had difficulties in finding the most convenient and safe anchorage, and this was very unlike him. When he went ashore he gave the chiefs a generous supply of presents and was dissatisfied with the *quid pro quo*—a number of coconuts, of which they already had sufficient. Then the bower anchor disappeared soon after they anchored 'for the want of a little exertion by the mate.'

When Bligh went ashore he saw that the people presented a melancholy sight by contrast with the Tahitians. 'Numerous were the marks of mourning,' he noted. 'Bloody temples, their heads deprived of most of the hair; but what was still worse, almost everyone with the loss of some of their fingers. Several fine boys about six years old had lost both their little fingers, and many men both these and the middle finger of the right hand.' Besides these obscene self-inflicted scars, they were a puny, sickly lot, many with dreadful sores on their bodies, and even the youngsters 'not pretty engaging children as at Otaheite'.

The wooding and watering parties went ashore the next morning, a nasty dark day of spitting rain. Christian had eleven men carrying casks for the collection of water. Will Elphinstone took four men with axes and saws for felling and cutting up the timber. Christian's orders from Bligh were curious. He was to take arms ashore but they were to be left in the boat because he said they would be 'much safer on shore without them'. You are to have nothing to do with the natives, continued Bligh. Nor are the natives to be fired on. Elphinstone's party was not permitted to carry arms at all. The water was to be drawn from a pond a quarter of a mile inland, the best water that could be found; the trees felled 200 yards along the shore from the point in the cove where the boats were to land.

Christian took the launch ashore in the morning and met with trouble from the moment he landed. Hundreds of natives had been attracted by the arrival of the *Bounty* to this line of shore from different parts of the island, and from nearby islands too. Some were hostile, some friendly, many of them just curious, all acquisitive. There were attempts to interfere with Christian's men as they made their way inland. The natives tried to take the casks and became so threatening that Christian decided to ignore Bligh's orders and armed himself and his men with muskets, leaving two of his party to guard the launch.

The harassment continued all the way through the woods to the pond. The natives, armed with clubs and spears, made darting attacks, and when Christian aimed a musket at them, this produced, according to Morrison, 'no other effect than a return of the compliment, by poising their clubs or spears with a menacing look'.

Under conditions of great difficulty and danger, with the natives constantly snatching at their clothes and their arms, Christian managed to bring off two launch-loads of filled casks. He returned to the *Bounty* with the second boat-load and came on board, where Bligh was enjoying his usual practice of entertaining the local chiefs. It had been a tiring and anxious morning, and Christian reported on the situation to his captain.

CHRISTIAN: I am having great difficulty carrying out my duties, sir.

BLIGH: You damned cowardly rascal! Are you afraid of a set of natives while you have arms to defend yourselves?

CHRISTIAN: The arms are no use while your orders prevent them from being used.

Lacking further instructions, Christian continued with his duty, although later Bligh sent Fryer ashore in the large cutter with a reinforcing party.

This is what Fryer wrote about the next stage in the events of that extraordinary day:

'When I came on shore there were only two men at the boat. The rest were up with Mr Christian at the watering place. . . . I landed among a very great number of natives, who behaved very friendly. Among them was a good looking young man and woman that seemed to me to be chiefs. I asked the people in the launch which way I should go to the watering place. They pointed out the way as there were a number of small lanes between the plantations. This man and woman took me by the arm and pointed out the way that I must go, putting their hands to their mouths in signs of drinking. I then gave orders to the people that were in the boat to lay off their oars until I should come back. I had not gone far when I met Matthew Quintal . . . rolling a cask of water down to the boat with a number of the natives about him. I returned to the boat with him and saw the cask hoisted in and then took Quintal to the watering place. I had not gone far when I met this man and woman I saw first at landing. They were very anxious for me to go with them, making signs to eat. I gave the woman a jew's harp and two or three small nails and left them walking before a number of natives.

'Soon after I parted from those friends, Quintal called out, "Mr Fryer, there's a man going to knock you down with his club."

'I turned myself round rather surprised and saw the man brandishing his club over my head. But as soon as he found that I knew his intention he set off into the plantation. I was not armed, even with a stick.'

What a nightmarish scene! The press of numbers, the unpredictability of the natives, the young couple attempting to entice Fryer away while a moment later a warrior attempts to club him from behind. Up at the pond the children keep picking at the men's clothes as they hasten to fill the last of the casks, while at the same time natives half hidden among the trees hurl stones at the party. One native has made off with the cooper's adze, racing away between the trees before anyone can catch him. A warrior with an especially long and lethal spear keeps thrusting it provocatively at Christian.

This is the scene that confronts Fryer when he reaches the pond. 'Let us get the casks back to the launch, empty or full,' he calls out to Christian. Then he feels in his pocket for more nails—'iron currency' the *Bounty*'s men call them—and offers handfuls to the natives nearest to him, indicating that it is payment for help in rolling the casks down through the plantations to the shore.

There is merry hell going on down at the cove too. Native children are in the water all round the cutter, climbing on the oars, trying to get over the gunwale, shrieking and laughing, half in fun, half in hysteria. One of the sailors, fearful that the cutter will drift on shore, has thrown out the grapnel, against Fryer's orders. Quick as a flash, some of the children dive to stir up the sand of the seabed, while others concealed by the dirty water cut the rope and make off with the grapnel. They are even cunning enough to pull on the severed rope under the water so that the theft remains undetected until it is too late.

Amidst the pandemonium on the beach—some teasing, some threatening—Christian managed to hoist the remaining casks into the launch while Fryer, told of the theft by shouts from the cutter, remonstrated with the natives. It is too late, they explained by signs. We are very sorry. The grapnel was taken by natives from another island and the canoe has already departed.

Christian and Fryer then climbed into their boats and put off, thankful to have got away without injury and with the loss of only one grapnel and the adze, although the wooders had also lost an axe.

Bligh was beside himself with fury when he heard of the losses. 'God damn your blood,' he shouted at Christian, 'why did you not fire—you are an officer?' And then he turned on Fryer. The master's attempts to cool Bligh's passion were not successful. When Fryer pointed out that the loss was not very great, Bligh retorted, 'By God, sir, if it is not great to you it is great to me.'

It was a day of equal madness on board the *Bounty* as on shore. The cutter and the launch were hoisted in after they had been cleared of their cargoes, and then Bligh gave a most curious order. Up to this time at Nomuka, and at all the other islands, trading had been controlled by Will Peckover. It had been his chief duty for all the months at Tahiti. Bligh correctly believed that this would prevent possible disputes and accusations of unfairness both among the natives and his own men. It had also prevented the men from accumulating private hordes of food and collecting too many mementoes —always a temptation when their value in England was so high.

Now Bligh told Fryer, at whom he had just been cursing within the hearing of the men, that everyone could buy what they liked— food, shields, spears, clubs, curios of all kinds. To Peckover he said, 'Purchase anything, and don't mind how much you give for it.'

At this surprising concession and new profligacy another sort of pandemonium broke out, a wild and reckless trading. The number of canoes about the *Bounty* had earlier increased to more than one hundred, from the smallest to great ocean-going craft capable of carrying ninety people. These had been warned off with the return of the cutter and the launch. Now it was indicated that they could return, and under the newly indulgent eyes of Bligh and the chiefs whom he had as guests on board, the frenetic bartering began— nails for yams and coconuts, combs for carved shields, mirrors for spears, toys for yams and hogs. Within a short time the decks were so cluttered with new purchases that it was difficult to get about. Below decks it was the same. The *Bounty* looked like a bazaar after a riot. And nobody seemed to care.

As suddenly and unexpectedly as Bligh had released this flood-tide of trading, he brought it to a halt. Turning to his master, he yelled, 'Mr Fryer, we'll heave the anchor up and go away.'

The natives were driven off the chaotic decks back to their canoes, the ship's company stood to their stations, the anchor was raised, two men loosened the fore topsail, the fore topmast staysail was hoisted, and they proceeded slowly out to sea.

From the forecastle, Fryer heard Bligh calling out urgently again, 'Hand the arms up! Hand the arms up!'

Imagining that the ship was being attacked, Fryer hurried aft. 'What is the matter, sir?' he asked.

'Why don't you come to assist me?' Bligh demanded angrily.

'I didn't know that you wanted any assistance. Only hearing you call for the arms I imagined that something must be the matter.'

Bligh repeated wildly, 'Get the arms up, sir. I'll keep these fellows and see if I can't get the grapnel.'

Suddenly Christian and Fryer understood what Bligh was about. He was not, after all, going to let them get away with it. He was going to try Cook's old stratagem and hold the chiefs on board as a ransom for the grapnel, something that could be replaced in minutes from the ship's stores.

And so the *Bounty*'s crew took on another new guise—from armed labourers on shore, to busy traders on board, and now to a formidable fighting force armed with muskets, bayonets fixed, cutlasses and pistols. It was a bewildering change of scene, and an alarming one for the chiefs.

Bligh had five of them in all. One of these, a handsome chief named Nageetee, he ordered ashore—and how gladly he left!—with the news that the others would be detained on board the *Bounty* until the grapnel was restored. This led to great lamentation on shore and among the canoeists who had been warned to keep astern of the ship, and also among the prisoners, who had so recently been flattering themselves that they were honoured guests. All cried and began the horrible practice of inflicting wounds on themselves, beating about their eyes with their fists.

The next turn in this series of events was for Bligh to muster all his officers and men, who were still under arms, and deliver to them a scorching indictment of their inefficiency and cowardice. 'You are all a parcel of lubberly rascals,' he shouted at them from the quarter-deck. 'I'll trim you all, do you hear.'

It had been a strenuous and sometimes a dangerous day for many of them and things seemed to be getting out of hand. What had happened to their captain? He appeared to have lost all control of himself. They experienced a mixture of fear and resentment. It almost seemed as if he was taunting them like this in order to provoke further violence. Then they saw him advance with a pistol in his hand towards Will McKoy, never a favourite of his. He pointed it at his head and called out so that all could hear, 'I will shoot you if you do not pay attention.'

Bligh turned on them all threateningly again. 'With four more men, and all of us armed only with broomsticks, I could disarm the lot of you.'

No one attempted to deny this. Nor did there seem to be any answer. For a moment it appeared as if Bligh might take up his own challenge. Instead he took the more orthodox method of disarming them by ordering them to stand down, all but two who were to act as guards over the unfortunate chiefs, to whom he now turned his attention. With the guards in support, he drove them down to the mess deck, gave them a pile of coconuts and completed their humiliation and distress by ordering them to peel them for his dinner.

This long and exhausting day was drawing to a close. The *Bounty* was under way, slowly moving out to sea, and the men were examining and counting their new acquisitions and discussing among themselves how much each would be worth back home. All but one of the canoes had fallen far astern. This was a large one, full of women, whose cries of anguish could clearly be heard as they inflicted more wounds on themselves, tearing at their heads and faces and shoulders with sharks' teeth.

At sundown there was still no sign of the grapnel, and Bligh suddenly wearied of the whole business. It was clear that it was irretrievable, and what did he want with four native chiefs on board? Did he not have enough worries already? He went below, dismissed the guard, and brought the chiefs up on deck, indicating that they were released and offered the big canoe alongside to take them off.

The chiefs were beside themselves with relief and gratitude. In floods of tears they embraced Bligh in turn, and Bligh presented each with a hatchet and saw, several large toys, some nails, knives and gimlets. It was a moving yet horrifying moment when the canoe came alongside. Now in a fever of masochistic relief, the women had redoubled their self-inflicted blows so that their faces were scarcely visible beneath the blood that poured from their head wounds.

There are two conflicting reports on the manner of the chiefs' departure. Bligh was convinced that he had friends for life. They showed such gratitude and expressed such warm thanks for his goodness 'that it affected us all. I told them', continued Bligh, 'that all English people were their friends.'

Morrison interpreted the scene differently. 'They only smothered their resentment,' he reported, 'seeing that they could not revenge the insult.' He thought that if a weak-manned ship ever came to Nomuka after this, the islanders would 'remember this day's transactions and make them suffer for it'.

As the shore fell slowly astern in the darkness, they could still hear the awful noise of the natives beating themselves. This steady thudding sound of canoe paddles against skulls was a percussion overture to the crescendo now only thirty-six hours away.

During the night the *Bounty* steered a northerly course towards Tofua but made little progress in the light winds. Nomuka was still in sight astern, and more of the Friendly Islands could be made out, Tokulu, Tougua and Mataku to starboard. Bligh was not seen on deck during the morning, and the *Bounty* was at peace, like a patient suspended between one nervous breakdown and the next.

The captain remained below until noon, when he was seen emerging from the hatchway and making his way to his own personal pile of coconuts on deck, close to the rail between the guns on the quarterdeck. Suddenly he was seen to swing round and call for the master. 'Mr Fryer,' he said accusingly, 'don't you think these coconuts have shrunk since last night?'

Fryer looked at them carefully. 'Sir, they are not so high as they were last night,' he admitted, 'but I think the pile may have been flattened by the men walking over them during the night.' This could well have been the case as there was no alternative for anyone passing along this side of the deck.

Bligh remained convinced that he was the victim of a robbery and ordered the ship's company to be mustered and the master-at-arms to have brought up on deck every coconut stowed below. This took some time, for everyone had traded for a supply, at twenty nuts for a nail, at Nomuka; and it was not easy to place them in individual piles on decks already crowded with stacks of fruit and vegetables, caged hogs and goats and chickens. Every one of the *Bounty*'s company stood beside his pile as if on inspection parade, some bewildered, some angry, all apprehensive at this fresh demonstration of their captain's eccentric behaviour.

Christian was the first to bear the brunt of Bligh's attack, which was delivered in staccato shouts. 'Damn your blood, you have stolen my coconuts,' Bligh addressed him.

'I was thirsty,' Christian answered, at once confessing to his crime. 'I thought it of no consequence. I took one only, and I am sure no one touched another.'

This did not satisfy Bligh. 'You lie, you scoundrel,' he went on, shaking his fist in Christian's face. 'You have stolen one half.'

Christian shrank before this tirade. 'Why do you treat me thus, Captain Bligh?' he asked. 'I hope you do not think me so mean as to be guilty of stealing half your coconuts.'

'Yes, you damned hound, I do. You must have stolen half of them or you could give a better account of them.'

Then he turned from Christian and confronted the rest of his officers and men, shrieking and waving his fists in the air, accusing them indiscriminately of theft. Turning on Edward Young, a formidable figure at any time, now glowering resentfully at his captain, Bligh demanded, 'How many nuts did you buy, Mr Young?' Young told him. 'And how many did you eat?'

'I do not know, sir. I have not counted how many remain.'

Bligh turned to the next man, repeating his questions, moving on again, until every one of the ship's company had been interrogated. The men were let off more lightly, and it was again clear that it was the officers who were the first objects of Bligh's fury. 'Mr Samuel,' he went on, addressing his clerk in more moderate tones. 'The people may take their nuts below. Those belonging to the officers will be stowed aft and no one will touch them.'

He swung on the assembled company, his voice and his fury rising in unison again. 'There never was such a set of damned thieving rascals under any man's command before. God damn you, you scoundrels, you are all thieves alike and combine with the men to rob me. I suppose you will steal my yams next. But I'll sweat you for it, you rascals. I'll look after you for a bit longer for my own good, but I'll make half of you jump overboard before you get through Endeavour Straits. You may all go to hell!'

He turned again to Samuel standing at his side, and in a loud voice so that all could hear, 'Stop these villains' grog, Mr Samuel, and give them but half a pound of yams tomorrow. If they go on stealing, I'll reduce the allowance to a quarter-pound.' At that, he turned abruptly away and went down to his cabin.

With quick blows Bligh had struck at any seaman's two most

sensitive areas, his stomach and his possessions. They were dangerous injuries, too. Far from home, in the cramped and public conditions of shipboard life, a sailor's private property is sacrosanct. Many
a shipboard affray has sprung from robbery from a sea chest or
hammock. In the eyes of the *Bounty*'s officers Bligh was committing
mass robbery not only of their coconuts but of their grog and the
food to which they were entitled. No wonder, then, as Morrison
observed, 'the officers then got together and were heard to murmur
much at their treatment'. Fearful that more inroads might be made
on the food they had bought for themselves at Nomuka, on which
they might now have to depend for their subsistence, officers and
men alike began hiding their supplies about the ship.

Bligh had not yet finished with Christian for that day. At four
o'clock in the afternoon, in light winds from the east and off the
island of Ogodoo, Bligh came up on deck again to decide whether
to continue on his northerly course or turn west to keep Tofua on
his starboard quarter. Christian was on deck, too, and when Bligh
spotted him he reopened his attack, calling him a thief and a scoundrel.

When Christian could get away from his tormentor, he came
forward. Purcell saw him coming and noticed that tears were
coursing down his cheeks. In spite of all that he had suffered, it
was the first time any of them had seen him brought to this condition.
'No, he was no milksop,' one of the sailors commented later.

'What is the matter, Mr Christian?' Purcell asked.

'Can you ask me, and hear the treatment I receive?'

'Am I not as badly treated as you?' Purcell suggested. There was
a measure of truth in this. Purcell had been one of Bligh's most
long-suffering victims, though he had never had as much to bear
as Christian. Purcell was one of those men who bridle easily and are
over-conscious of their rights.

'You have something to protect you, and can speak again,' he
said, referring to Purcell's privileges as a warrant officer. 'But if I
should speak to him as you do, he would probably break me, turn
me before the mast, and perhaps flog me. If he did,' Christian
continued in a desperate voice, 'it would be the death of us both,
for I am sure I should take him in my arms and jump overboard
with him'.

Purcell tried to console him. 'Never mind, it is but for a short
time longer.'

'I am sure the ship will be a hell going through the Endeavour Straits,' said Christian.

There were others close enough about these two officers as they talked to overhear what they said. One heard Christian say, 'I would rather die ten thousand deaths than bear this treatment any longer. I always do my duty as an officer and as a man ought to do, yet I receive this scandalous usage.' Another heard confirmation of his desperation: 'Flesh and blood cannot bear this treatment any longer.'

How seriously were these threats taken by Christian's shipmates? By a small number—and certainly by Purcell—they were taken very seriously. Unless Christian too had gone mad, why else did he now start giving away to his friends the mementoes and curios he had bought at Nomuka? A number of people heard about this, and benefited. Then there were his letters and papers. His friend Stewart was among those who heard the story that after Bligh's last outburst, Christian had been seen tearing them up and throwing them overboard.

As the evening advanced, more rumours circulated through the hot decks—it was a particularly hot night, humid, oppressive—that the second-in-command was contemplating suicide or desertion. He could take it no longer. There was real concern among many of the ratings when they heard. They were genuinely fond of Christian, who was easy on discipline and made them laugh. When things were at their worst, Christian helped to make life endurable. They loved his antics, the way he treated them as if he was one of them. Bligh's vendetta against him only sharpened their affection for him. What would it be like without him?

Christian absorbed the brunt of the captain's unpredictable temper, and, at least until the arrival of the *Bounty* at Nomuka, he had acted as a stabilising and restraining influence between the force of authority and the oppressed lower deck—for that, as always, was how they judged their status.

In the confined quarters of the *Bounty* news travelled fast, and word of Christian's despair, of his plans to desert ship, had reached a number of ears by sundown. After the events of the past few days, and after the extraordinary scenes on the quarterdeck that morning, both officers and men were expecting a climax. Never in the sixteen months since the *Bounty* had left England, even during those fearful weeks off Cape Horn, had such a feeling of impending doom been experienced in the ship.

There was not a man on board, from the youngest 'young gentle-man' to the oldest veteran, who expected soft treatment at sea under any captain. Many had suffered under harder men than Bligh and served in ships where flogging took place much more frequently than in the *Bounty*. Nor did flogging in itself create disaffection: flogging was just one of the accepted unpleasant aspects of life at sea, like weevils in the bread or a squall off a lee shore. The restless-ness now stirring in the *Bounty* stemmed from two causes. First there was the widespread resentment at the recent injustices and deprivations. This was easily recognisable and easy to understand. Less tangible was the fear for the future. The notorious dangers of the Endeavour Straits, to which Bligh was frequently referring, and of the Great Barrier Reef—its shoals, its hidden coral reefs, its rocks and islets, unpredictable winds and currents—all stoked up the fires of anxiety in the men's minds. It was a hazardous enough business under any circumstances. Under a commander who, that very day, had threatened to throw overboard half his officers before they reached the straits, who seemed to have lost control of his senses as well as of his officers, the prospect was fearful indeed.

As the light faded the mood on board the *Bounty* grew into one of mixed confusion and despair and deep anxiety not only about their passage of the Endeavour Straits—that was still some weeks away —but of the next day and what new disturbances were in store for them. With the coming of darkness a volcanic eruption on a nearby island—they had seen its smoke as far distant as Nomuka and it had never since been out of sight—brightened into a flickering flaming torch that lit up the rising smoke above it and illuminated the surrounding sea.

At about 7.30 p.m. the skies cleared and for ten minutes, before the ocean closed over it, the thin three-day-old moon was visible beyond the *Bounty*'s bowsprit.

Christian was in his berth going through his possessions when John Smith, Bligh's servant, brought him a message. The captain desired his company at supper. This had happened before and after a row, many times before. But after today's events, Christian had assumed that all intercourse between them had ceased, surely for ever. In any case, he was completing arrangements that would result in his never seeing Bligh face to face again. It was all over. Within a few hours he would have quit the *Bounty*, would be drifting among these islands awaiting the opportunity of being seen and picked up by a native canoe. And he had provisions for a day or two. He might die of thirst or exposure, or be torn apart by a shark. If that was to be his fate, by his reckoning in his present state of mind, it was a less frightful one than the hell of the *Bounty*.

'Tell Mr Bligh that I am indisposed, Jack, and give him my compliments.'

None of the other midshipmen had believed that even Bligh would have the effrontery to invite Christian to his table on that evening, not after all that had just happened. They had made an agreement among themselves that, if any of their number should be invited instead, they would refuse.

Having failed with Christian, Bligh sent Smith to the 'young gentlemen's' mess. Would any of them care to sup with their captain? In turn they all refused. Then Tom Hayward, ever ready to toady, told the servant that he would be glad to accept. As he left, the boos and hisses of his fellow midshipmen followed him aft.

Purcell had been one of the first to hear of Christian's plan to desert ship that night. Trusting him as an ally, and needing his aid, Christian approached him during the evening for some planks, rope and nails. Purcell was glad to help, and several others heard later that Christian had lashed the planks to the two masts stowed in the launch to make an escape raft, working at speed and unseen inside the boat. Confirmation of Christian's plans came from an unexpected quarter. As part of his duty routine earlier in the day when he was watch-keeper, Christian had secretly ordered a small hog to be killed and roasted for the youngsters in his mess. When supper time came, it could not be found and they had to do without it. But before going back on deck, young Tinkler, Fryer's brother-in-law, reaching for his hat behind a sea chest, felt a clothes bag instead. He pulled it out and found that it belonged to Christian. Inside was the cooked hog and a breadfruit—supplies, as he realised later, for the would-be deserter's voyage on his raft.

Bligh's supper invitation to Christian and the other midshipmen was not the captain's only surprise peace overture of the evening. Fryer was taking the first night watch—8 p.m. until midnight. He was one of those who had heard nothing of Christian's desertion plans, though his own relations with Bligh were as bad as ever. The days when they messed together with drunken Huggan were mercifully distant in his memory. Seldom since then had the captain and his master been on speaking terms except for official business. To Fryer's astonishment, when Bligh came up on deck, as he always did before turning in, he began chatting cordially to him.

In reply Fryer commented conversationally, 'There is a fair breeze springing up, sir, and we had a new moon earlier. That bodes well for our arrival off the coast of New Holland.'

'Yes, Mr Fryer,' Bligh answered. 'It will be lucky for us to arrive on that coast with a good moon.'

Bligh, it is recorded, then gave instructions for the night and returned to his cabin. He hung up his uniform, donned his nightshirt and nightcap, and after completing his log—an invariable last duty—retired to his bunk. The predicted 'fair breeze' did not spring up while he was awake—he would have felt it at once if it had.

When William Bligh fell asleep with, one imagines, no presentiment of the fate in store for him a few hours hence, the *Bounty* was still wallowing gently in the warm Pacific seas in Latitude 19°45′S., Longitude 175°05′W., just thirty miles south of Tofua, one of the Friendly Islands.

7

'The eyes of famine'

Bligh's log 14 June 1789

❧

A<small>T</small> 7 a.m., one and a half hours after he had been dragged from
his cabin, Bligh continued to watch keenly for the chance
that could lead to a counter-mutiny. Although there were frequent
outbursts of cursing and shouting not one of the mutineers relaxed
their guard for a moment, nor showed further signs that they
might succumb to an alcoholic orgy.

The small cutter in which Christian intended to cast adrift Bligh,
his clerk and the two midshipmen was at last got into the water.
It at once began to sink. Someone called out to the men in it to
bail faster. It was no good. One might as well throw Bligh and
his cronies straight into the water as into this jolly boat.

Christian reluctantly gave orders for the large cutter to be hoisted
out instead, a long and complicated operation demanding the
attention of ten men as the boat's thwarts had been unshipped and
it took twenty minutes to fix them. It took almost as long to get the
boat into the water.

When the large cutter was at last alongside there was one man
in it, blind Michael Byrn. No one knew how he got there, and it
was some time before he was even noticed, the attention of the
mutineers and loyalists alike having been diverted by an unexpected
development.

It was 7.15 a.m., the sun was well clear of the eastern horizon, baking hot the decks. It was going to be another warm, steamy day. The mutiny, which up to this time had been mainly chaotic and riotous, had assumed a more clearly defined shape. To the surprise of those who had expected an alcoholic orgy the refreshment interlude had brought this about. Before, apart from the obvious ringleaders, it had not been easy to identify all the mutineers. The committed loyalists could not pick out all the committed mutineers. Absent below decks were Fryer, Peckover, the botanist Nelson and Bligh's servant Smith—all obvious Bligh men—guarded by the arch-mutineers Quintal and Sumner. Now it suddenly became clear that at least twenty of the crew, and probably more, were not only loyal to Bligh but were determined to leave the ship with him.

This greatly complicated Christian's problem. No longer was it a matter of casting adrift Bligh and the three others in the small cutter. This was mutiny on an entirely different scale, a scale for which he was unprepared. Who would have guessed that anyone would choose to be cast adrift in an open boat in the middle of the Pacific rather than remain on board the *Bounty*? It was now horribly clear to him that he had seriously miscalculated the mood of the men.

This unforeseen situation caused Christian new and agonised indecision. If he kept behind by force those who wanted to leave there would be the constant threat of a counter-mutiny. He would have to remain on his guard day and night. The loyalty even of some of those who had taken up arms was already in doubt—Isaac Martin for instance, who had refreshed Bligh with fruit and had given other signs of friendliness. And Young? What about his old friend Ned Young, who had inspired the plot and was still nowhere to be seen?

If Christian lost all those who wanted to accompany Bligh, the *Bounty* would be a greatly weakened ship with hardly enough crew to man and sail her. Moreover, the loyalists would have to be given the launch for there was scarcely room for ten men in the large cutter. Already vehement demands were being made for the launch. Cole and Purcell, both valuable men, both Bligh men, were marching boldly aft to the quarterdeck.

'You must give us the launch, Christian,' Cole demanded. Christian did not reply, he did not even seem to hear. Three times Cole repeated his request.

Bligh broke in, 'For God's sake, Mr Cole,' he cried, 'do all that lays in your power.' Cole was already doing what he could.

Purcell, too, spoke in an agonised voice: 'I have done nothing that I am ashamed or afraid of,' he said. 'I want to see my native country. You cannot turn us adrift in the cutter, Mr Christian. Let us have the launch and not make a sacrifice of us.'

Christian was not surprised by Purcell's reaction to the mutiny. Self-righteous Purcell, a difficult, weak man, always at loggerheads with Bligh, who despised him. But Purcell lacked the will and courage to turn against him now the chips were down.

Young chose this moment to reappear momentarily. It was a mystery where he had been hiding. Christian felt a profound sense of relief that he had someone else to turn to as well as a powerful new ally. Young had a musket with fixed bayonet. He resolved Christian's dilemma by indicating assent to Cole's demand.

'Hoist out the launch, Mr Cole,' said Christian.

With these words Christian began a new and purposeful phase in the mutiny. Cole went forward, and for the third time on that busy morning the elaborate procedure for getting a boat into the water was put in hand. This time there was less shouting and less delay.

The launch, the biggest boat carried by the *Bounty*, stood in a chock on the deck forward, and being twenty-three feet long overall came back as far as the fore hatchway, projecting slightly over it. It was a well made boat, with copper fastenings, six feet nine inches in breadth and two feet nine inches in depth. It could, of course, be rowed, and two masts could be stepped. There were six seats athwartships for the oarsmen, and a five-foot-long seat on each side in the stern quarters. There was no decking. Fifteen men would be the launch's normal maximum capacity.

As soon as the launch was hoisted out, the men who had chosen to follow Bligh either hastened below to collect their personal possessions and any supplies they could lay their hands on, or asked others to do so for them. Purcell ordered one of his carpenter's crew, Thomas McIntosh, to get a bucket of nails and a cross-cut and whip saw, and himself got his clothes chest and put into it several personal articles.

Purcell next demanded his tool chest from Christian, a vitally important piece of equipment in any ship, which Churchill had cannily purloined and got to the quarterdeck. Christian at first refused, and then against Churchill's protests yielded to Purcell's pleas. It was by no means Christian's only ambivalent act during the mutiny; and each filled his followers with uncertainty and fear, for this was no time for weakness and indecisiveness in their leader.

The launch was in the water, and some of the men were already in it, receiving and stowing away oars, sails, twine, lines, a dozen hammocks, bags and boxes of clothes, rope and canvas—all with frantic speed, as if the ship were about to go down. With every additional item the launch sank lower. Midshipman Heywood helped Purcell in his struggle to get his precious chest into the boat. And still the *Bounty* disgorged her contents into the cluttered bottom of the launch.

Christian was trying to stem the flow of goods and was waving his bayonet threateningly and calling out, 'Carry nothing away!' No one took much notice. Churchill was being more noisy and violent and effectual. Most of the mutineers were showing signs of their heavy draughts of rum. At one point Churchill climbed into the launch and began to retrieve Purcell's tool chest. Quintal leaning over the rail above shouted encouragement: 'Damn them, if we let them have these things, they will build a vessel in a month.' One of the loyalists tried to stop Churchill. Churchill struggled with him, got the lid of the chest open and grabbed from inside some of the largest and most useful tools, tossing them amid cheers and cries of protest to Quintal above.

But Bligh's men were winning other bloodless engagements for possession of survival material. Morrison (though no one was still certain which side he was on) had got hold of a towline and grapnel and had dropped them down into the launch; and Cole, after wrapping some clothes and personal treasure inside his bedding and stowing them in the launch, busied himself for the common good. 'Help me with a cask from the hold,' he ordered Morrison. And no sooner was this in the launch then he was up on the quarterdeck after a compass, undismayed by the armed opposition.

Quintal had quit his guard duties below and was now watching Bligh. When he saw the bo'sun trying to get the compass from the binnacle he exclaimed, 'I'll be damned if you have it! What do you want with a compass with the land in sight?'

Cole protested boldly. 'Quintal, it is very hard you'll not let us have a compass when there are nine more in the store room.' He turned for support. Able seamen Burkett was the only man near.

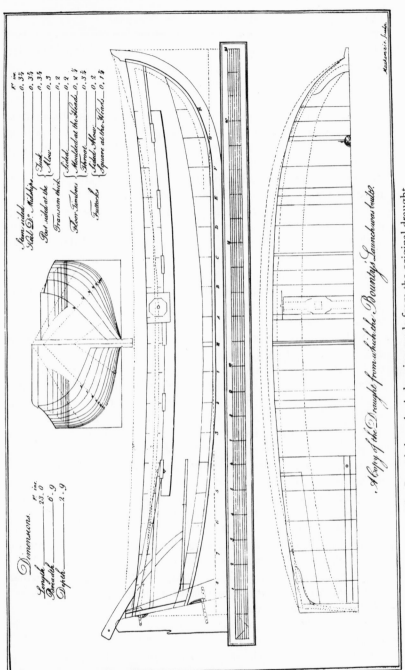

The *Bounty's* launch. A drawing made from the original draught

He looked ferocious and was armed to the teeth. To Cole's surprise he spoke up for him. 'Quintal,' he said, 'let Mr Cole have it.' Cole hastened forward with the precious compass under his arm before anyone could stop him.

Most of the *Bounty*'s crew were now hurrying, the loyalists to stow everything they might need to keep themselves alive, the most aggressive mutineers to prevent them. Tom Hayward, released to collect his personal gear, came up the hatchway with his fuzee—his flintlock—as well as his bag. Quintal, ever alert, snatched away the firearm. 'Damn your eyes if you'll have that!'

Bligh's clerk was economical in his personal possessions. Just a few shirts and stockings in a pillow case. He was more concerned with his master's belongings, his box of surveys and drawings for the past fifteen years at sea, his timekeeper, his log and journals and commission. Samuel got on deck with them, where Churchill intercepted him and seized all but the last three. To Bligh's vehement protests he replied savagely, 'Damn your eyes, you are well off to get what you have!'

Amidst all this tumult and conflict and hurrying to and fro and up and down the hatchways, while the launch sank lower and lower in the water, two men remained outside the main stream of the mutiny. Incredibly, the shark was still attracting the attention of Charles Norman, who remained leaning over the stern rail as if nothing had happened on board the *Bounty* since dawn. The other member of the crew who remained inactive, cut off by his blindness and an accident of chance, was the fiddler, Michael Byrn. He was still in the rejected large cutter, still forgotten by everyone, without even his fiddle. In his fear and bewilderment he was crying. At length he was seen by Cole. 'I do not know why he was crying,' he said. 'I suppose for no other reason than he was blind and could not see what was happening.'

But there Byrn remained during all the last stages of the mutiny quite helpless. Fryer was the only other loyalist who remembered seeing him. He overheard him calling out to no one in particular.

'If I go into the boat they will leave me when they get ashore as I cannot see to follow them.'

It was just after eight o'clock and the launch had been in the water for half an hour. After three hours of noise and wrangling it was time to be off. The most ardent loyalist had long since recognised that there was no chance of re-taking the ship, and the more

vocal mutineers were constantly uttering threats to use their weapons
—'Blow the bugger's brains out!'

From the head of the gangway the launch could be seen to be
in a chaotic condition with sails and oars, bundles and chests and
lengths of rope and line lying across and between the seats just as
they had been thrown in. Half a dozen loyalists were already on board,
some attempting to create order, others taking in and trying to
stow more cargo, from gourds to bundles of clothes, bottles of wine
and yet another sea chest. Protests that no more could be carried
from those whose luggage was safely stowed were overwhelmed
by appeals from those who had only what they stood up in.

Purcell was in the launch examining his tool chest again and
counting his losses. He looked over the side and saw how deep in
the water they already were. There would be many wanting to come
for whom there would be no room. Already in any sort of a sea
the launch would at once be swamped. Several loyalists were on the
gangway, ready to come down at the word. He saw Isaac Martin
pushing his way through, unseen by the mutineers, clutching a bag
now instead of the musket he had been holding since Purcell had
first seen him. So the American had changed his mind! He was a
loyalist after all!

'What are you doing here?' Purcell demanded as soon as he was
in the launch.

Martin, innocently: 'I am going in the boat with you.'

'If we ever get to England I'll endeavour to hang you myself,'
Purcell shouted at him, so loudly that his voice reached Quintal
and Churchill above. Fearing that this might encourage the less
partisan of their number to follow him, the two mutineers brought
their muskets to bear on Martin and ordered him out. Between the
devil and the deep blue sea, Martin climbed obediently up the gangway again, ignored his own musket which he had left on deck,
and walked forward alone to the bows to contemplate his unhappy
situation.

On the quarterdeck the anguish and argument had reached the
inevitable point of decision and crisis. Peckover, Nelson and Samuel
had been brought up from their quarters with Fryer and were
standing with Hayward and Hallett under guard.

Christian was still standing beside Bligh, as he had been now for
almost three hours. His agony of mind was reflected so clearly in
his dark face that even the most distressed and frightened men who

saw him at this time remembered it long after. Several of those present, including Bligh himself, considered that he might take his own life at any moment.

Christian turned to the two midshipmen and the clerk. 'You are to go into the launch now,' he told them.

'Why, Mr Christian, what harm did I ever do you that you should be so hard on me? I hope you won't insist on it,' Hayward begged.

Hallett echoed Hayward's plea. 'I hope not, sir.'

Christian did not reply. Nor did he look at them. After this one order he again remained silent and preoccupied.

Matthew Thompson, a thin, dark figure, was on guard over the arms chest and at first refused to allow Hallett and Hayward below to collect their gear. He relented when Hayward said they had Christian's permission. There was no sign of life on the orlop deck, where by contrast with the upper deck the *Bounty* was like a ghost ship. Neither of the midshipmen had seen it like this since they had left Tahiti. But there was one member of the crew still here after all. Hayward caught a glimpse of him sitting on his sea chest, arms folded, in stunned retreat from the din above. It was young Heywood, once one of the captain's favourites. 'Hurry and get into the boat,' Hayward called to him as he hurried to his own berth. There was no time to await a reply.

His clothes were all that Hayward was allowed to take with him. Back on the quarterdeck he begged Christian in vain to be allowed to take his instruments and charts.

'Go to the launch, Mr Hayward,' said Christian, who had now emerged from his period of contemplation.

The two midshipmen realised the futility of further argument. Hallett, the younger by six years, was visibly agitated as he went forward; it was altogether too much for Hayward, who succumbed to tears of anguish.

While Hayward and Hallett were below, Bligh's wrists had been untied, and soon he was being hustled to the head of the gangway by Burkett, Quintal, Sumner, Millward and McKoy, with Christian leading the way. Young Tom Ellison, tireless as any schoolboy since the beginning of the mutiny, was relishing the part of pirate, but now began to overplay it. Wielding his bayonet dangerously he attempted to break through Bligh's escort, crying, 'Damn him, I'll be sentry over him!' The others merely nudged him aside.

Captain Bligh determined to make one last effort to end this long nightmare. Before the party reached the head of the gangway he halted. He appeared utterly exhausted. Christian turned towards him, wary of a counter-plot even at this late stage. 'Come, Captain Bligh,' he said, 'your officers and men are now in the boat and you must go with them.'

This was not in fact true. Fryer, Cole and Peckover among others were still on deck.

'If you attempt to make the least resistance,' continued Christian, 'you will instantly be put to death.'

Bligh was looking earnestly into Christian's eyes, entreating him to relent. 'Consider what you are about, Mr Christian,' he said. 'For God's sake drop it. I'll give my bond never to think of it again if you'll desist.'

Christian still made no reply.

'I have a wife and four children in England,' Bligh pleaded, 'and you have danced my children on your knee.'

'It is too late. I have been in hell.'

'It is not too late,' said Bligh.

Whatever hell Christian had been in it could be no worse than the torment he was suffering now. Yet there was still a hard, implacable note in his voice when he answered. 'No, Captain Bligh, if you had any honour, things would not have come to this, and if you had had any regard for your wife and your family you should have thought of them before and not behaved so much like a villain.'

Still they had not yet done with one another. Amid the growing impatience of mutineers and loyalists alike, they continued their duologue, one of the strangest that has ever taken place between a ship's captain and his second-in-command.

'Can there be no other method?' Bligh demanded at one point.

Cole broke in, repeating the plea, and Christian turned on him. 'No, I have been in hell this fortnight past. It is too late. I am determined to suffer it no longer. You know, Mr Cole, that Captain Bligh has treated me like a dog all the voyage. I have been in hell.'

'I know it very well, Mr Christian,' answered the bo'sun. 'We all know it. But drop it, for God's sake.'

For a second it seemed to some of the mutineers—especially Quintal and Churchill—that there was a real danger of Christian weakening. He had already offered to give them a tow towards the nearest island.

Fryer, too, was pleading with Christian again, desperately pro-
posing that Bligh should be put in irons instead of in the launch,
Christian to be the new commander. This was the sort of compromise that Quintal and Churchill most feared and they shouted Fryer
down and closed about Bligh as if to preserve their prize.

Another figure had appeared among the guards, the mutiny's
éminence grise, Edward Young, musket in hand. He seemed to
emerge from nowhere whenever events reached a really critical
point. Bligh had not seen him when he had come on deck briefly
before, and had thought that all the midshipmen were with him
except Christian himself. Bligh looked at him accusingly. 'This is a
serious affair, Mr Young,' he warned.

'Yes, sir,' said Young, 'it is a serious matter to be starved. I hope
this day you get a belly full.'

These were the first words that anyone had heard him speak since
the outbreak, and they were the last, too.

Quintal and Skinner acted as guards at the head of the gangway.
They were less concerned with who left the *Bounty*—the more of the
buggers who went the better as far as they were concerned—than
with what they took with them, and that meant only personal possessions. As a result the launch was now ludicrously overloaded with
more than twenty on board.

When Bligh and Christian—the deposed, the rebel—came to the
gangway and looked down their reactions were the same, though
for different reasons. Bligh saw that they would not survive a day
with that number on board; Christian that he could not work the
ship, certainly not in any sort of an emergency, with the men left
to him. More serious, the entire carpenter's crew was in the launch.

Christian, energised by the presence of Young, made some
quick decisions. He wanted no trouble-makers, but he did want
skilled men. He would have Joseph Coleman the armourer, and
McIntosh and Norman of the carpenter's crew, but not the carpenter
himself. Bligh could have Purcell, tiresome grumbler that he was.
And Fryer, too, who was still under guard on deck.

Christian called by name the three men he wanted who were
sitting with their bundles of clothes in the confusion of the boat.
Bligh added his own voice, suddenly reassuring and hearty. 'You
can't all go in the boat, my lads. Don't overload her. Some of you
must stay in the ship. Never fear, my lads, I'll do you justice if ever
I reach England.'

The three men climbed obediently up the gangway, like youngsters deprived of an outing. Fryer, for his part, was trying to persuade Christian not to put him in the boat, claiming that the mutineers would need him to sail the ship.

'We can do very well without you, Mr Fryer.'

Bligh broke in, this time in contradiction to his protagonist and asserting his authority for the last time. 'You are to remain on board, Mr Fryer.'

Nobody seemed to want the ship's master—a nuisance, a trouble-maker, even a danger. But Christian had the last word, backed by a threatening cutlass. 'By God, sir, go into the boat or I'll run you through.'

That left only Bligh. He knew that any further pleas would be wasted. But he turned to Christian and asked him one more question. 'Do you consider,' he asked, 'this treatment a proper return for all the friendship I have given you in the past?'

Christian was visibly upset and uncertain how to answer, if answer there was. What was there to say to his old friend, his new implacable enemy? Their relationship, once so deep and so passionate, had been shattered, though only God knew how and why. Everything had changed since those slack, sensuous months at Tahiti. Now all was confusion and misery and bitterness. And the destruction of what had once been a wonderful friendship was—at this very moment—dividing the *Bounty*, and as a consequence none of their shipmates could escape. The price was as high as that. Soon half would be placed in desperate hazard, the other half would become desperate fugitives for the rest of their lives.

In Christian's voice and in the words he spoke he showed again how deeply disturbed he was. Already he wanted to reverse this tide of events and go back three hours in time. But, as he had exclaimed a number of times already, it was too late. 'That—Captain Bligh—that is the thing—I am in hell—I am in hell!'

Bligh knew that there was no more to be said. He walked down the gangway in dignified silence and stepped unaided into the launch, where a place had been cleared for him in the stern. He was followed a few moments later by one of the mutineers carrying Christian's own sextant and nautical tables. Bligh looked up at Christian standing at the rail above. He knew that he had been responsible for this compassionate act.

Christian said, 'There, Captain Bligh, this is sufficient for every purpose. You know the sextant to be a good one.' They were the last words he spoke to his captain.

Their other serious need was for firearms. There was no weapon of any kind in the launch. 'Mr Christian, send me down some muskets, for God's sake,' Bligh cried out.

The mutineers had been momentarily subdued during the captain's disembarkation; but on hearing this demand the wilder elements—Quintal, Ellison, Smith, Skinner, McKoy among them—gave vent again to the curses and threats they had been uttering before.

'Blow the bugger's brains out!' And one wag yelled, 'What do you want with firearms on the Friendly Islands?'

Cole gave orders for the launch to be cast off, though they kept a line to the *Bounty* for the promised tow. As they drifted astern some last messages were called from the *Bounty*'s quarterdeck. Charles Norman, forcibly detained, his shark long since forgotten, was rolling his head and his eyes in the curious way he had when under stress. He was in tears, as were several others. 'I wish I could go with you to see my wife and family!' he cried. 'Remember me to them, Mr Hallett.'

Coleman was leaning over the rail, the big heart he had had tattooed on Tahiti showing on one of his bare arms. 'Don't forget I have had no hand in this,' he called out desperately. 'If you ever get to England, remember me to a Mr Green at Greenwich.'

Morrison, at his side, had a less specific message. 'If anyone asks for me, tell them I am somewhere south of the line.'

Another tearful voice came from an unexpected quarter, from the large cutter alongside which had not yet been hoisted in. It was Michael Byrn, who had listened from his helpless blind world to all the last stages of the mutiny. 'I am sorry I cannot leave to come with you.'

A voice was heard to reply: 'We must not part with our fiddler.' It was impossible to tell whether it came from the launch or the ship, but no one took any steps to claim him.

The launch rubbed along the *Bounty*'s hull, slipping by degrees towards the stern quarter, for another fifteen minutes. Bligh and Cole were trying to create some sort of order in the boat, which was in such a state that they could not even unship the oars. During this time there was a constant trade between the ship and the boat, just as if the launch was a native canoe and they were again engaged in the bartering they had enjoyed so often off Polynesian shores.

William Bligh as a junior Post-Captain, 1790.
Fletcher Christian: an artist's impression based on contemporary descriptions. Drawn by Larry Learmonth. (© Richard Hough 1972)

H.M. Ships *Resolution* and *Discovery* at anchor in Karakakooa Bay. Drawn by Thomas Edgar, master of the *Discovery*

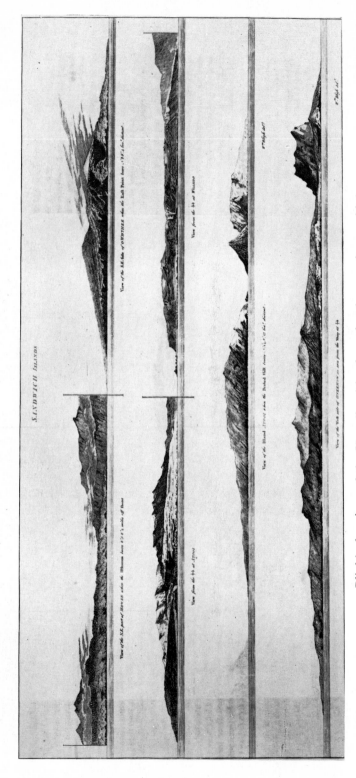

Bligh's drawings of the Hawaiian islands made when serving as ship's master in H.M.S. *Resolution* under Captain James Cook. From volume II of *A Voyage to the South Pacific Ocean* (1784)

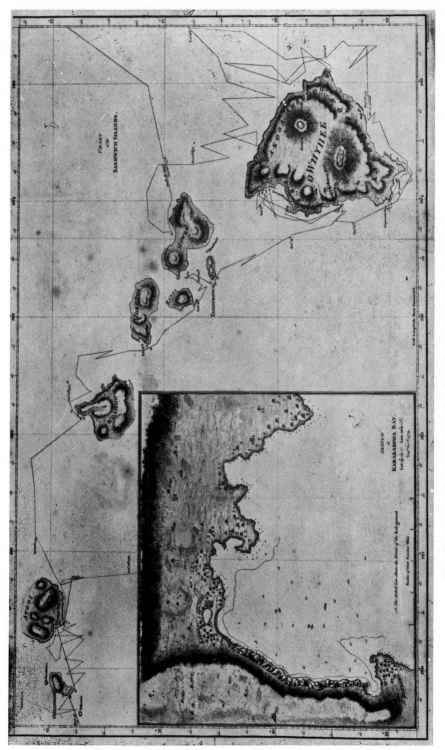

Bligh's chart of the Hawaiian islands and sketch of Karakakooa Bay

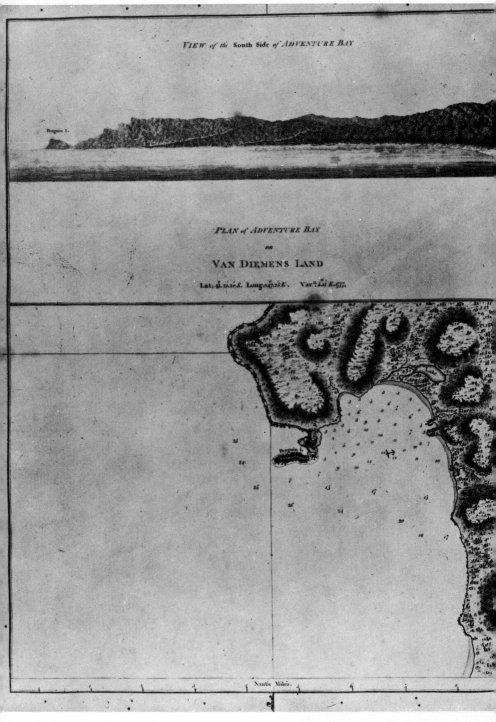

Adventure Bay, Tasmania, from Bligh's sketch when sailing with Cook
in 1777

Matavai Bay, from a contemporary sketch

Overleaf: Bligh and his loyalists cast adrift in the *Bounty*'s launch

Nomuka. A highly stylised drawing from Dalrymple's *Voyages and Discoveries in the South Pacific*, published sixty years before the *Bounty's* arrival

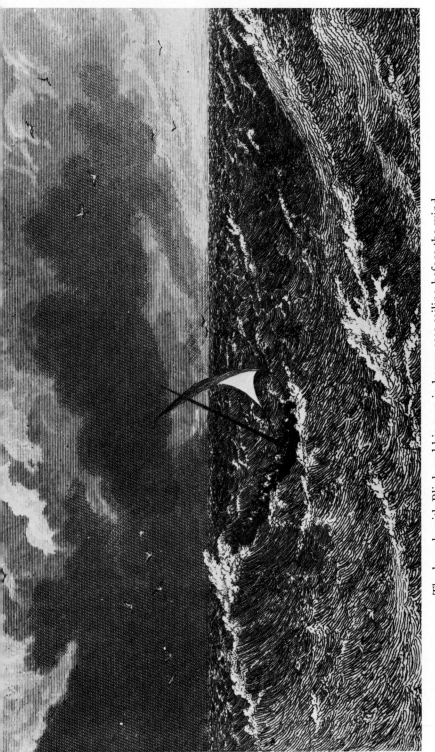

The launch with Bligh and his men in heavy seas sailing before the wind on a westerly course towards Australia

'My beloved Betsy.' Elizabeth Bligh

William Bligh as a discredited and unpopular figure in 1794 after completing his second and successful breadfruit voyage. Drawn by George Dance. Reproduced by permission of the National Portrait Gallery

Peter Heywood's sketch of H.M.S. *Pandora* foundering with some of the manacled mutineers still on board

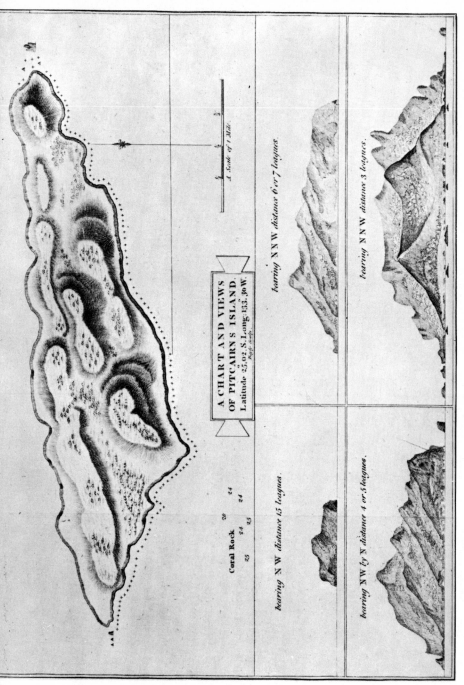

A CHART AND VIEWS
OF PITCAIRN'S ISLAND.
Latitude 25.02. S. Long: 133.30 W.

A Scale of 1 Mile.

Coral Rock

bearing N W distance 15 leagues.

bearing N W ½ N distance 4 or 5 leagues.

bearing N N W distance 6 or 7 leagues.

bearing N N W distance 3 leagues.

The page from Hawkesworth's *Voyages* which attracted Christian to the
uninhabited island of Pitcairn

Landing in Bounty Bay

Jack Adams's house

Jack Adams in 1825, patriarch of Pitcairn, four years before his death at the age of sixty-two

Thursday (later Friday) October Christian, son of Fletcher and Isabella Christian. Drawn in 1825

Bligh's last mutiny—the Rum Rebellion. Johnston's soldiers arresting
Bligh, 26 January 1808

In a last effort to get some more provisions and some arms before it was too late, Cole offered his bosun's call and his watch. Churchill produced four cutlasses and lowered them over the port quarter at the end of a line, thereby arousing Millward and Skinner, two of the drunkest and most belligerent men, to more obscene threats.

Others went below and reappeared ten minutes later with some twenty-six pound chunks of pork which they had salted down at Tahiti. Morrison began throwing them over the rail, and Norton, the beefy quartermaster (and the *Bounty*'s heaviest and most awkward seamen), attempted to catch them. Some of the pork fell into the sea and sank before anyone could retrieve it. 'Damn your clumsy eyes!' cursed Cole, pushing him aside and taking over the duty himself.

The *Bounty*'s mutineers found themselves dividing into two camps during these last minutes, when attachments and individual fears alike were clarified and men's emotions were stripped of cover. While the cursing on the quarterdeck of the *Bounty* continued as fiercely as ever, several more of the mutineers showed signs of willingness to help, almost as if to ingratiate themselves with the loyalists in case there might after all be a day of reckoning. Two more gourds of water were lowered; and Burkett called out to Peckover, 'Can I get you anything?'

'I have only what I stand up in,' the gunner replied, indicating his shirt and trousers. 'Please fetch me my clothes and a pocket book.'

Mills went off ostentatiously, with Burkett tagging along behind, as if two must be needed for this chore. This only inflamed further the extreme element so that one gesture of charity brought forth another torrent of derision and threats. At one point Skinner, in ugly mood, had to be forcibly restrained from firing his musket into the boat. 'Hold it back, Dick—hold it back!'

The drunken, violent party continued to predominate, in noise and numbers, and those in the launch became increasingly anxious. Cole veered the boat dead astern, where it was at least safe from the *Bounty*'s guns, and he suggested to Bligh that they should cut the line and forego the tow.

Others in the boat were noting facts for the record, as Burkett, Martin and Churchill had feared they would be doing. They were counting and identifying the mutineers. With nineteen loyalists in the boat, including the captain, there should be twenty-four left on board, and Byrn in the cutter. Byrn was no mutineer, nor were Coleman, McIntosh and Norman. But there were only seventeen on deck, Christian the one officer. After his two brief appearances, Young was nowhere to be seen. His part in the affair was already something of a mystery. Heywood and Stewart, both non-mutineers who had not been allowed to return on deck when they had gone below for their clothes, were absent too. And another missing mutineer was Matthew Thompson, seen to be armed earlier.

It was nearly ten o'clock, the sun was already very hot. What little wind there had been earlier had died to almost nothing, and there was only a gentle swell as if to nurse for a while the deep-laden boat. Bligh and Cole were getting the men to the oars. The cries from the *Bounty*'s quarterdeck were more aggressive than ever, and they would all be relieved to get beyond the range of the four-pounders.

The men dipped the oars when Cole cut the line and the gap at once began to widen and the taunts and threats—'You'll never reach the shore!' 'See if you can live on a quarter pound of yams a day!'—grew fainter.

Christian's voice was heard, too. After all his earlier cries of anger and anguish it was curious to hear him as the practical new commander of the *Bounty* calling for the top gallant sails to be loosed. It was like eavesdropping on a world they would know no more. Only one man was seen to respond to Christian's order, the tireless Ellison, who nipped eagerly up the shrouds.

The *Bounty* steadied on a west-north-west course, hardly moving through the water. The launch was travelling at twice her speed, with two men at each of the six oars, steering an opposite east-south-east course in order to get clear as quickly as possible.

When they were out of range of the *Bounty*'s guns Bligh ordered the men to ship oars and get the foremast stepped. It took time to dismantle Christian's discarded raft—how many of their number beside Purcell recognised it for what it was or guessed its purpose?

Rowing and sailing (though the wind offered almost no help until 4 p.m.) the launch changed course to north-east. Some thirty miles distant was Tofua, the island which had offered them such pretty bright lights the night before. It was out of sight from sea level, but they had no need yet to draw on Bligh's genius as a navigator for the volcano's eternal smoke scored the sky and marked their destination.

If the sea remained as calm as it was now, they had a good chance of making Tofua. But after Tofua? The nearest European settlement was thousands of miles away; their launch was no longer than four men stretched out; the distance between gunwale and the water less than the length of a man's hand; and they had food and drink for no longer than one week.

As the *Bounty* bore away slowly to the north-west, and Cole and Fryer restored some sort of order in the launch, Bligh sat still and silent in the stern contemplating their situation. He was experiencing a sense of deep relief, a feeling close to exaltation. The noise and the fury were over, the die cast. The silence and peace were wonderful. And, as always, he was reassured with the comforting knowledge that he had done no wrong, committed no error of judgement, performed throughout according to the highest standards of the service: in short, a victim of villainy and circumstances beyond his control. His ship, as he wrote in his log shortly after, had been in the most perfect order, his plants flourishing, everyone in the most perfect state of health. Even now, after this appalling calamity, 'I felt an inward happiness which prevented any depression of my spirits. Conscious of my own integrity . . . I found my mind most wonderfully supported, and began to conceive hopes . . . to be able to recount to my King and Country my misfortune.'

And what had brought about this misfortune? A long laid plot. It had all begun nearly three months before, in Oparre Bay, with the cutting of the cable. He had thought at the time that the natives had been guilty of this outrage. Now he knew without any doubt that they had been innocent, that 'it was certainly done by some of these people to strand the ship'. How could he have known at the time? he asked himself. 'With such deep laid plans of villainy and my mind free of any suspicions, is it not wonderful I have been got the better of?' Now it was suddenly all clear to him. Christian and his fellow pirates never intended to leave the paradise on earth with 'its allurements of dissipation'.

Everything in Bligh's mind was arranged to conform to this explanation. The *Bounty* was returning to Tahiti. She was steering in the opposite direction now only as a blind. Why else had the mutineers many times cried out exultantly 'Huzza for Otaheite!' He committed this to his log as a comforting fact though he was the only one to hear these cries.

Bligh's reaction to the catastrophe which had overwhelmed him proves also his resilience and peerless courage in the face of seemingly hopeless odds, and his determination to recover something from the ruins of his plans, his reputation and his career. Even as he was consoling himself that he was the innocent victim of a vile plot, he was preparing to recoup his fortunes. First he must make his way to England, then he must clear his name, regain the favours of his patron, exact revenge on those who had injured him, and complete the breadfruit mission. Nothing less than this would satisfy him.

To plan a programme on this scale within a short time of being cast adrift on a hostile ocean thousands of miles from civilisation, required superhuman self confidence. Not for one moment did Bligh allow himself to believe that he could fail. God, and right, were on his side.

For the present he was not going to divulge his plans to anyone in the launch. It was enough for them to think that they would land and settle on Tofua or another of the Friendly Islands to await rescue. If they were to endure the dangers and privations of an open boat voyage of thousands of miles it must seem to be of their own choosing. He had no doubt that it would soon become their choice.

The volcanic island of Tofua is five miles long and four miles wide, an inhospitable place at any time, and always liable to violent eruption. The present eruption was a mild one, more like a slow leak in the earth's skin. The island had a fearsome reputation among the natives of the Friendly Islands. Its volcano was regarded as one of the entrances to the underworld of spirits after death, its god a chief's son who drowned himself and was transformed into a great man-eating shark. In spite of these drawbacks, it was inhabited in 1789 and was often visited by the people of the neighbouring islands. Most of the shoreline is steep black volcanic cliff. Only on the south-east side of the island are there good landing beaches.

Through the hot afternoon, with six men at the oars, the launch made slow progress towards the smudge of smoke on the horizon. Once a particularly large shark made an attack on the oars: the Tofuans would have regarded this as a supernatural ill-omen from the island's god. Bligh's men had no trouble in beating it off, but to them it was a salutary reminder of their likely fate if the boat were swamped.

When an easterly breeze got up at four o'clock, they put on better speed and soon they could make out the craggy south-west coastline of the island, the mountains rising to 1,500 feet beyond it.

It was already dark when they closed the shore, and hearing only the thunder of the rollers beating on the rocks, Bligh decided to stand off through the night with two men at the oars. To warm and give his men cheer, Bligh served them all with half a pint of grog, about one-half of their total supplies. It was the last generous ration of rum, or of anything else, they were to enjoy for seven weeks.

Tofua appeared no more promising in the morning, without signs of cultivation, or water. Lacking the knowledge that there were convenient landing places in the south-east, Bligh took the launch along the west coast of the island and at length discovered a small cove on which the surf beat fiercely. With the boat held by a grapnel some twenty yards from the shore, Samuel and a small party climbed over the side and waded to the rocky shore to reconnoitre the hinterland for supplies. They climbed the steep cliff a hundred yards from the sea and returned at noon with only a few quarts of fresh water from pools in the rocks.

The afternoon was a little more promising. Bligh worked the launch south, and this time they spotted some coconut trees high on the cliff-tops. Again a small party of brave swimmers got ashore through the surf with ropes, climbed the cliffs and collected twenty coconuts which were hauled out to the boat with the ropes. That night, back at their old station where they were sheltered from the rising seas, they each had a coconut for supper and made themselves as comfortable as they could in the bottom of the boat.

Bligh had never believed that eruptive Tofua could offer them more than temporary comfort. But this island of ill-repute was not to let them off so lightly. The wind was too high to allow them to get safely to sea on the morning of 30 April. So Bligh, rather than lie without occupation through the day, determined to lead another shore party in the hope of collecting some provisions before they left. After issuing a morsel of bread and a teaspoon of rum to every man, he scrambled over the side with Nelson, Samuel and a supporting party, taking with him for arms half their cutlasses, and, for safety in case it was swamped in the boat, his precious log.

This time they found some lengths of vine hanging down the cliffs, clearly provided to assist any climbers and the first proof of the island's being inhabited. Bligh led the way boldly to the cliff-top and struck inland. Sure enough, there were some huts, a plantain cultivation nearby, though still no sign of natives.

Now Tofua offered its modest attractions in turn. After the plantains, a cave was discovered, deep-set at the head of the cove, and after that some kindling to light a fire which helped to protect them from the mosquitoes. Bligh decided to allow half his men to sleep ashore in the cave to give them a break from the discomforts on board and to allow more room for the others. On the following morning, some natives at last appeared. They were friendly and helpful, anxious to please and to trade—buttons torn from the sailors' jackets for plantains and breadfruit. More natives arrived, this time by canoe. They, too, seemed friendly.

Bligh explained that their ship had been wrecked and that they were the only survivors. The natives showed no signs of either joy or sympathy at this news; but towards evening, Bligh wrote in his log in the cave, 'I saw with peculiar pleasure that we had increased our stock of provisions, and that at sundown the natives left us in quiet possession of the cove.'

Now confident that this island after all might supply them with the provisions they would need to survive the long open boat voyage—of which his men still knew nothing—Bligh again sent parties inland to trade and collect fruit and anything else that might support them. More canoes began to appear, evidence again of the speed at which news travelled among the Polynesians. Some were from other islands. One or two of the faces were even familiar. Two chiefs who appeared on the beach offered the ominous information that they knew that Bligh had been on Nomuka. If they had heard these tidings, they must know of his treatment of the chiefs there. Bligh at once made them presents, not on the old lavish scale but as lavish as he could now afford—an old shirt, a knife apiece.

The first familiar signs of hostility began to creep into the conversation and to manifest themselves in the pressure of numbers on the beach which only two days earlier had appeared so deserted.

'How is Captain Cook?' The inevitable question. 'How is Captain Clerke?' Like the rest, they had long memories here. Then with special interest, 'How was your ship lost? By storm?'

Out of the corner of his eye, Bligh saw a party of natives moving towards the line securing the launch to the shore. Another chief approached Bligh, who had now gathered his force at the cave mouth. This time Bligh recognised the face immediately. It was handsome Nageetee. How had these Nomukans reached Tofua so rapidly? And why had they come? Did they have some premonition of the mutiny, of Bligh's fate, and of the fact that he would seek succour on this volcanic island?

Nageetee seemed especially solicitous and anxious to learn of Bligh's health. Yet it was more like a concealed threat than a genuine enquiry.

The natives had now seized the line and were attempting to drag the launch ashore. Bligh saw the need for action. His party had two of the cutlasses, one in Samuel's hand, the other in his. These were their only weapons and they were outnumbered by more than ten to one by natives armed with spears and stones.

Bligh rushed at one of the chiefs, holding his cutlass over him and demanding that his men should leave go of the line. The chief gave the required order and the natives retreated. For the present they were safe. But for how long?

By noon the situation on the beach had formed a pattern with which Bligh was only too familiar: crowds about him and his shore party, a few showing signs of a continuing friendship which was even more alarming than the predominating evidence of growing numbers and growing hostility among the rest. Trading continued, but it seemed now more like a ritual prelude to violence. Breadfruit, even some spears, were offered to Bligh. He quickly accepted both. Several chiefs came up close to Bligh and Nelson, suggesting that they should sit down on the beach, perhaps for a friendly chat. The alarming invitation was refused.

A strong body of natives lined the shore, ostentatiously separating the two parties of white men, chanting and knocking together their stones in a threatening chorus. Bligh gathered his men about him, ordering them to show no signs of fear, and keeping up a show of normalcy by serving them, from the accumulated supplies, their midday meal, a breadfruit and coconut each.

'We will await sundown,' Bligh told them. 'They may leave us then as they did before.'

In the early part of the afternoon it became evident that the natives had no intention of departing, and the signs of hostility increased. Fires were lighted about the beach as proof that they were settling down for a long siege. With a superb show of insouciance, Bligh settled down in the cave to write up his log, describing his immediate circumstances so that the world might know one day how he had died. When he had finished, he closed the book and gave it to Will Peckover. 'Get it to the boat if you can,' he told him, 'and tell Mr Fryer to keep the boat well in on the beach when he sees us breaking out.'

Peckover walked boldly down the beach, pushing his way through the crowd, holding the book under his arm. This object was judged by the natives to be something of special value and they made lunges at him in an attempt to seize it. But Peckover broke through successfully, waded out to the boat and delivered the message and the log.

Several chiefs now came up to Bligh's cave, where the men were gathering together their possessions in preparation for their push.

'Will you not stay the night?' asked one.

'No, I always sleep in my boat,' answered Bligh. 'But in the morning let us do more trading.'

'You will not sleep on shore,' said another chief, and this time it was a statement which suggested he would not leave it either.

'*Mattee!*' (We will kill you!)

Bligh seized one of their number by the arm, holding his cutlass in his other hand as a sign that he would be killed if an attack were made. Everyone who witnessed this gesture recognised its meaning.

Then Bligh led his party in a line down from the cave, across the beach 'in a silent kind of horror', as he described this moment.

It was like a repeat of that nightmare scene in Karakakooa Bay just ten years earlier. Between Bligh's party and the launch there were two hundred warriors, beating their stones, bent on their destruction. Bligh walked straight towards them as if they were urchins at a street corner. His commanding presence, something fearful in his demeanour, served to hold back the massed natives during the time it took for his men to wade out through the surf.

'Remain with me.' Bligh had Purcell by his side, the man he despised above all his other officers in the *Bounty*.

When the rest of the shore party had scrambled safely into the launch, two events occurred simultaneously on shore which at last signalled the inevitable explosion of hate and fury. The chief in Bligh's grip broke free and raced off into the crowd, and another chief raised his hands as an order for an all-out attack. Bligh and Purcell both saw this signal and ran into the sea, struggling through the waves towards the launch.

Bligh's wonderful courage was inspiring every one of his eighteen men. Not one panicked. Six were at the oars, ready to row for their lives as soon as their captain was on board. Fryer was at the launch's stern, closest to the beach, holding the line securing the boat to the shore. A party of natives were hauling on the other end to pull the launch onto the rocks. It was a diabolical tug-of-war which Fryer could not hope to win, so he suddenly let go and the natives fell in a ludicrous heap.

John Norton, the *Bounty*'s hefty quartermaster, chose this moment to show gallantry to match his captain's and leaped into the surf to tackle the natives single-handed and weaponless, and to free the line. Fryer and others called to him, 'Come back to the boat!' But the cries were lost in the sounds of the sudden release of the natives' fury, and Norton struggled on alone. In a second, and like Captain Cook and the marines in Karakakooa Bay, he had been hurled to the ground and was beaten to death with stones. Five dark figures struggled for the possession of his trousers as he died.

Fryer helped to haul his captain into the launch. The stones were flying thick and fast, many of them wounding the men. Other natives had waded into the surf, some seizing the stern, others Purcell's legs as he attempted to climb over it. This tug-o'-war was short-lived, too, Purcell kicking free and struggling over the counter, helped by Bligh and Fryer. Bligh drew his knife and severed the line, then slashed at the natives' arms until they released their grip.

At the other end of the launch the crew were hauling frantically on the grapnel line, which was still held fast, while the oarsmen pulled for all their worth. Even their combined strength could not have broken the grapnel. But it was as if the god of Tofua had relented at last and interceded to preserve them, for as the flying stones became an annihilating barrage and hastily manned canoes closed about them, one of the flukes of the grapnel broke. They were free at last.

The fleeing launch was no match for the natives that pursued them out of the cove. Again and again their canoes closed on it, releasing salvoes of stones like broadsides from nippy frigates against a wallowing merchantman. Peckover at one of the oars was struck an awful blow on the cheek but kept rowing gallantly, while Bligh and Fryer stood up, urging the men on and catching some of the missiles. These they threw back as hard as they could go—though 'we were very much inferior to them', Bligh acknowledged. One canoe, manned by a dozen warriors, closed the launch. 'Come back for the man you have left behind!' they taunted. And then from a few yards again began to hurl stones.

Soon the Englishmen must all be stunned or dead, and the launch overwhelmed. Bligh realised this and remembered a wily plan which had succeeded before. 'Throw over your clothes!' he ordered his men; and himself picked the breadfruit and plantains from the bottom of the launch and hurled them over the side, too, as an additional bait.

The trick worked wonderfully. It was like throwing raw meat to a pack of wolves. At once the natives put aside their paddles and dived into the water, struggling to be the first to reach these prizes.

Darkness was falling, the sea was rising, the Tofuan coastline fading into the distance. Bligh ordered the foremast to be stepped, the lugsail set. The launch put on speed, the nightmare was over, and they began tacking south into the rising wind.

'Poor man,' wrote Bligh in his log of Norton. 'This was his second voyage with me as quartermaster, and his worthy character made me feel his loss very severely. He has left an aged parent I am told he supported.'

But the horrible death of John Norton proved a blessing to his shipmates for he had been the weight of two men. Now the launch moved more swiftly through the water, now the freeboard had marginally increased so that they would have to bail less in bad weather. His absence meant five per cent more food for every man, five per cent more room in the packed little craft. Never had there been a more noble act of self-immolation.

What was to be their plan of action now? It was almost dark, the sea was choppy and they were taking in water as they worked south down the western shore of the island. Every man was depressed, frightened and nursing his wounds and bruises. Bligh told them they were heading for Tongatabu, an island he had visited with Cook. Here, he said, they were sure of a welcome and of acquiring all the supplies they needed. He had friends among the chiefs of the island, he added.

Cole said, 'I believe, sir, that we shall be treated the same as at Tofua.'

'Oh no,' Bligh replied reassuringly, 'they are quite a different kind of native at Tongatabu.'

'Did you have any trouble with the natives when you were at the island?' Fryer asked—knowing well what the answer would be.

'We had to confine some of them for theft,' Bligh admitted.

'In that case, sir,' Fryer answered, 'they will make us account for this as the natives have done for confining their chiefs at Nomuka.'

'What would you do, then, Mr Fryer?' Bligh asked innocently.

'Sir, providence may land us on some friendly shore if we make a fair wind instead of working to windward.'

'And you, Mr Cole?'

'Sir, I would rather trust to providence and live even on an ounce of bread a day than go to Tongatabu, for I believe the natives would take everything we have then cut us to pieces.'

There was a murmur of agreement all round the launch. Then Peckover spoke up. 'Could we not make Timor, sir?'

Everyone knew that Will Peckover had sailed that way with Cook, and past Timor. Here there was a long-established Dutch settlement where they could be sure of a friendly reception and a passage back to Europe. This was to have been their route in the *Bounty*. But if the Endeavour Straits was a feared hazard in that vessel, with its charts and navigational aids and a full crew, it was infinitely more dangerous in this little launch without a single map to guide them. Moreover, as Bligh at once pointed out, Timor was 1,200 leagues, some 3,600 miles, distant.

The only nearer European settlement might be at Botany Bay on the coast of New Holland. Six months before the *Bounty* had left Spithead, Captain Arthur Phillip had commanded a convict expedition of no fewer than eleven vessels bound for this remote bay. Like Bligh's own breadfruit expedition, this too had been the inspiration of Sir Joseph Banks who had once visited Botany Bay with Cook and had deemed it ideal as a convict settlement. But Bligh had no knowledge of the fate of the expedition. They might all have been shipwrecked, or turned back, or if they had arrived they might all by now have starved or been killed by the natives, or have risen up against their guards. Bligh did not fancy the idea of Botany Bay, and this possible alternative was never discussed.

Peckover's suggestion found instant and excited response from the men in the launch. At the prospect of friendly European faces, relief from their ordeal, and a berth back to England, the pain of their injuries and all thought of the dimensions of the undertaking that lay ahead, were at once forgotten; and there was, as Fryer recorded, 'a great deal of cheerfulness'. It was as if in a few days they would be walking up the quay at Coupang to a warm welcome and a warm meal—and thence up the gangway of an East Indiaman bound for their homeland.

Bligh recognised the dangers in this euphoric mood, and began to warn them of the reality of what lay ahead. In a twenty-three-foot open launch they would face storms and the hazards of shipwreck. They might die insane from the heat and thirst. The food would be rationed severely on an eight-week basis. They had on board 150 pounds of biscuit in bags, some of it already spoiled by sea water, twenty pounds of pork, a few coconuts and breadfruit, the last mouldy. For drink, they had twenty-eight gallons of water, five quarts of rum and three bottles of wine. That was all.

Bligh had had the ration all worked out for some time in preparation for this moment. 'Well, my lads, can you live on two ounces of bread and a gill [quarter pint] of water a day? For this is all you will receive.'

There was a chorus of agreement. Bligh was still not satisfied and asked each man individually by name if he was prepared to face these stringent rations. 'Aye, sir!' 'Aye!' There was not a voice of dissent.

Now Bligh addressed them all again. 'That you have all agreed to abide by these rations is a sacred promise you will never forget?'

Again: 'Aye, sir!'

The decision he wanted had been reached by a more satisfactory route than he could have hoped for. The suggestion of Timor had not even been his.

Fryer was at the tiller. 'Shall I put the helm up, sir?'

'Yes, in God's name put up the helm, Mr Fryer.'

The launch swung round and scudded before the wind at a fine pace as if joyously in tune with the unanimity of her crew. 'Let us give thanks for our miraculous preservation,' Bligh began the prayers on that night of decision. 'Oh Lord, we have faith that you will continue to offer us your gracious support. . . .'

The skill, courage and endurance of the launch's crew were put to severe test within hours of their decision to run out of the Pacific Ocean before the wind. A gale blew up in the night, and a blood-red sun at dawn told of worse to come. By the middle of the morning they were being driven before a full easterly gale and were taking in so much water that they had to bail for their lives. Bligh had set only a reefed lug foresail. This threatened to tear to shreds when they were poised on the summits of the huge waves; and a second later as the launch plunged into the trough it hung limp on its yard.

By noon Bligh reckoned that they had already sailed nearly ninety miles from Tofua, and he served a teaspoonful of rum to each man and a quarter of a bruised breadfruit. Later in the day he realised that there would have to be sacrifices if they were to avoid being swamped. Every man was allowed one change of clothes and no more. The rest went over the side with all their private possessions, some rope and spare sails. This lightened the boat considerably and simplified the arduous task of bailing.

The boat was behaving wonderfully, and this maintained a feeling of self-confidence even when in a mountainous sea it seemed impossible that they would not be overwhelmed. Every man was continuously soaked for forty-eight hours. This, Bligh believed, was the worst part of their ordeal. At night, if they dozed off for a short time, they awoke so numbed that it was a long and painful business to get their limbs moving again.

Even during their worst sufferings, from storms, downpours of rain and later in extreme heat, Bligh continued to plot their progress, recording the distance covered by regularly estimating their speed (with a line and counting off the seconds) and making observations at noon whenever the sun could be seen. When the sea was very rough the only way he could do this was by standing in the centre of the boat, a man on each side holding him steady.

Their survival clearly depended on plotting their position and progress towards Australia. But this was not enough for Bligh. So deeply trained was he in the traditions of the navigator that he continued also to record in his log all the new and unrecorded land he discovered.

We can see him in his seat in the stern of the launch, his jacket protectingly over his head and shoulders, hunched over his book writing:

'The first island seen bore South 4 leagues close to which lies a high rock. The next island bore S.S.W. 5 leagues, the next bore S.S.W.4 leagues . . .'; and drawing a rough accompanying chart which he will later perfect so that it forms a tolerable guide even for anyone sailing these seas today.

He had heard from the natives of Nomuka of a group of islands to the north-west which they called 'Fidgee'. Today Bligh is recognised as 'the real discoverer of the islands of Fiji', the first European to sail through them, recording no fewer than twenty-three islands in all. It is evident from his chart that he sailed first through the Lau Group and then west-north-west between the Windward and Leeward Groups, with Viti Levu on his port quarter, the most extensive of the Fiji Islands, and Vanua Levu to starboard, of which he sighted only the south-western coastline.

Bligh regrets that his is such a superficial survey. 'Being constantly wet it is with the utmost difficulty I can open a book to write, and I am sensible that I can do no more than point out where these lands are to be found, and to give an idea of their extent.' This is the nearest to an apologetic statement that Bligh ever made in his life.

On the evening of 6 May, without any warning, the launch struck the now notorious reef north-west of Vatuera Channel, finding no break and at length passing over it where there was only four feet of water. They passed close inshore of several of these rich and attractive islands, seeing clearly the full fresh water streams pouring down the cliffs from the mountains while they eked out their half gill of stale water, and eating their two ounces of mouldy bread within full sight of growing plantains, yams and bananas. It was hard to bear, but there were no protests from the crew. The islands were obviously inhabited, and in their weak condition and without firearms, the risks of being seized were too great.

How right they were! On every one of these Fijian islands sentinels kept watch from high vantage points for strange or defenceless craft. 'Such were lawful prey,' one authority has written, ' "those with salt water in their eyes", being doomed by the ancient law to the bamboo knives, the heated stone ovens and the cannibal maw.'

On the following morning the launch must have been spotted from the island of Waia, for two sailing canoes put off and began to gain on them rapidly. Six men were ordered to the oars and the launch put on speed, bearing away to the north-west clear from the island. The pursuit lasted for more than three hours. One of the canoes gave up quite soon, but the second continued to gain on them. The spirit of the launch's crew was shown by Lawrence Lebogue, the sailmaker and the *Bounty*'s oldest man—'a bit of a character'. He was at one of the oars, pulling for all his worth, with Bligh urging them all on.

'Heave away, lads,' Bligh called out, 'if they come up with us they will cut us all to pieces.'

'God damn my eyes, sir,' Lebogue responded forthrightly, 'you are frightening us out of our wits. Let them come and be damned— we'll fight them for as long as we can. It's a fine thing, by God, for you to be the first to be frightened.'

Fryer intervened before he went too far. 'You old scoundrel,' he told him, 'if you speak another word I will come and heave you overboard.'

Soon after three in the afternoon the second canoe gave up the chase and the men shipped oars with relief.

In less than an hour they began to suffer a new ordeal, one which recurred time and again during the voyage. The rain came down, heavily and continuously, chilling them through more completely than the sea water during the gale. During the night 'we experienced cold and shiverings scarcely to be conceived'. There were only two remedies, which Bligh resorted to on every morning after these soakings. First he ordered his men to strip, rinse their clothes thoroughly in sea water, squeeze them out and put them on again. The result was surprisingly warming and refreshing. Then he gave them a teaspoonful of rum, which worked wonders.

To counter the constant invasion of spray and sea water, Bligh fitted a pair of shrouds to each mast and rigged lengths of canvas round the boat as a makeshift weathercloth. Its effect was to raise the height of the boat above the water a further nine inches. He also put the crew on two watches so that they divided their time equally between lying in the bottom, and on the seats. Both situations were wet and uncomfortable but the routine of changing watches every four hours seemed to give a measure of order to their lives, prevented disputes about room, and prevented the more lethargic from lying curled up motionless, perhaps for days on end, as they had in the past.

There were consolations for this long period of wet weather. They were no longer thirsty. Every man drank as much fresh water as he needed, and by spreading a sail they were able to collect thirty-four gallons in one night, an indication of how heavy the rain was. And, miserable though it made them, this spell of weather probably saved their lives. As Bligh wrote, 'I consider the general run of cloudy and wet weather to be a providential blessing to us. Hot weather would have caused us to have died raving mad with thirst, yet now although we sleep covered with rain or sea we do not suffer this dreadful calamity.' Two weeks later they endured a brief spell of the clear burning hot weather he had dreaded and at once began to experience 'a languor and faintness which gives an indifference to life'. The miserable rain was indeed a life-saver.

As the launch continued on its westerly course from Fiji, through recurrent storms, gales and downpours of tropical rain, and as the men weakened day by day, Bligh resorted to a variety of makeshift methods to preserve their health and spirit. The great thing was to prevent them from succumbing to this state of 'indifference to life' which at one time the heat induced. Somehow or other, he had to keep their minds alert. He had them make a sort of patchwork union jack out of a bundle of old signal flags which had been thrown into the boat. This took many days' work and because it was intended to identify them when they reached a port was in itself a harbinger of their eventual relief.

He recounted all that he had heard about Australia and Timor, drew them maps—as far as he could remember—to show their course and their destination. He reminisced about his early voyages, and encouraged them to do the same about theirs. They threw out fishing lines, and these, as always at sea, were a subject of endless speculation, though they never brought a fish on board.

In the evenings Bligh would lead his men in songs, rousing the weak or reluctant until all were singing in one great chorus, the brave but unlovely sound reaching far out over the lonely surrounding sea. Later, when their throats were parched and their voices cracked, the chorus sounded fainter and even less melodious. It did not matter—there was no one else to hear them.

Bligh also encouraged his men to prolong their meals as far as the miniscule rations allowed. An elaborate ritual grew up around the simple process of consuming a few ounces of food each day. Most of the men dipped their bread in sea water to give it some sort of a taste, and then ate it very slowly, savouring every morsel. Bligh himself always broke it into small pieces and mixed it in with his water ration in a coconut shell, using a spoon, and, as he said, 'taking care never to take but a piece at a time so that I am as long at dinner as at a more plentiful meal'.

The daily bread ration of two ounces was split into three parts and served at 8 a.m., noon and at sunset. Bligh did not serve the precious pork regularly, and kept it as a surprise. This added interest

The original of Bligh's log, and the gourd, the measuring cup and
bullet weight used on the open boat voyage

and even excitement, to every day's eating. When it appeared and
and was weighed out with tender and elaborate care at half an ounce
a head, there was all the greater jubilation.

On the fifth day after leaving Tofua Bligh devised a pair of scales.
It was a brilliant stroke of extemporization. The making of the
scales alone made a distraction. Now every meal was preceded by
another time-consuming ritual which held everyone's fascinated
attention. The scales were made from a pair of coconut shells. For
weights, Bligh used some pistol balls which someone chanced to
find in a corner of the boat. Twenty-four of these weighed just one
pound; thus the weight of one ball exactly represented one man's
bread ration for a day, and divided in three parts the ration for one
meal.

After twenty-one days at sea Bligh made one of his regular checks
on his stocks and discovered that there was enough bread on the
present allowance for only another twenty-nine days instead of
thirty-four. He was satisfied that none had been stolen for he kept
it in Purcell's commandeered tool chest, the key to the lock always
with him. He could explain this loss only because of rottenness,
or from fallen crumbs when the pieces were broken. At the time of
this discovery he was also beginning to have doubts about Timor.

Might there not be difficulties in finding the settlement? He had only an approximate idea in his memory of its position on the coast. He determined to allow for the need to continue their journey to Java—and this, allowing for possible contrary winds or becalmings, might require a total of six more weeks at sea.

Yet already, after three weeks, they were all showing signs of weakness. 'Our appearances were horrible,' wrote Bligh, 'and I could look no way but I caught the eye of some one in distress.' To add to their woes they were suffering acute pain from constipation. It was a terrible decision to take, but Bligh hardened his heart again, and that evening he made the announcement to his men. From the next day, he told them, there would be no bread at sundown—a one third cut in their basic food. As consolation he promised to reinstate the evening allowance if they continued to make fair progress. That night he wrote in his log that it had been 'like robbing them of life'.

As a token that providence might finally favour them, booby and noddy birds were sighted, a sure sign that land was not too far distant. The boobies, so named for their seemingly idiot habit of perching on a ship's rigging quite unafraid of man, circled the launch, sometimes plunging into the sea about them. At noon the next day one of the men caught a noddy in his hand and killed it. It was the first bonus to their rations since they had been at sea, and was handed to Bligh in excited anticipation.

Bligh, who described this noddy as the size of a small pigeon, divided it, entrails, bones and all, into eighteen equal parts and, in accordance with naval tradition, allocated the parts by 'Who shall have this?' One man stood with his back to the launch's company while another man pointed in turn to the spread-out parts calling 'Who shall have this?' The first man answered each time with a name until all the bird had gone.

There were other brief moments of hope and happiness on the long passage west towards the Great Barrier Reef. On 24 May, after suffering fifteen days of cold and wet, the sun came out, its warmth acting as a soothing balm to their emaciated and rash-scarred skin. All hands stripped off shirts and trousers, now almost threadbare from their frequent rinsing and squeezing out, hung them to dry and basked naked in the heat. On 26 May another bird was caught, this time a booby, the size of a duck. Bligh reserved the blood for those in the weakest condition, among them Ledward and that once tough old mariner, Lebogue. The next day they ate fish for the first time, even though lines had been out day and night. It was a second-hand catch, however, from the stuffed maw of a third booby which had recently fed well.

Then, towards the end of May, they sighted more evidence that they were approaching land—many birds, branches of trees floating past the launch. Even after they had reached the coast of Australia they still faced some 1,300 miles to Timor, and the worst hazards of their voyage. But Bligh had given them hope of a respite ashore, and perhaps some addition to their supplies. From their overcrowded world of wetness, pain and complaint, an island on which they might build a fire and search for mussels among the rocks seemed like heaven itself.

Exactly one month to the day, to the hour, after he had been cast adrift in the launch, Bligh caught his first glimpse of Australia. With no more than a sextant, an old quadrant and a book of tables— lacking even a timepiece—Bligh brought the launch to within fifty miles of the Great Barrier Reef on the afternoon of 27 May. As confirmation that the mountains of northern Queensland were close at hand he had already noted, like any canny mariner, that 'the clouds kept fixed in the west.' That night after their supper of just one gill of water there was excited speculation among even the weakest on board.

At midnight Fryer relieved Peckover as watch-keeper. An hour later he heard a sound he had not heard for three weeks. Turning to the helmsman he asked:

'Don't you hear a noise like the roaring of the sea against rocks?'

'Yes, sir, I think I do.'

Fryer got up and, stepping between the lying bodies in the bottom of the boat, reached the mainmast, standing against it for better height and steadiness. After a moment he caught a glimpse of a long white stain on the sea ahead and called back, 'Port the helm.' Then he immediately lowered the mainsail with the help from others on his watch.

Bligh was woken up. The breakers were perilously near now, not more than a quarter mile away. Fryer had already got some of the stronger men to the oars and they pulled as hard as they could to bring the boat clear. To everyone's relief they were for the present beyond sight and sound of the reef, and they waited expectantly for the dawn.

At daylight they hoisted sail again and brought the launch towards the reef, catching their first sight of land, an island within the reef, three hours later.

Cook was the only European who had sailed and charted these waters. That was nineteen years ago. He had had his troubles. The *Endeavour* had run on to a reef and had only just escaped destruction. It had been a dangerous, anxious time for the great navigator. But he had reported gaps through the 1,500-mile-long reef through which a sailing ship could enter into the island-studded calm water beyond.

To penetrate this reef in a launch which could not sail close to the wind, manned by a crew in the last stages of weakness, was a hazardous business indeed. The wind was from the south-east, and fresh at that, yet in order to discover a passage they had to sail parallel with and close in to the reef. One touch of that razor-sharp coral, as Cook had discovered to his cost, could rip open the bottom of an ocean-going ship. Their little launch could be torn to splinters within seconds.

It was galling to see beyond the spray and the curling breakers the still waters and the inviting islands and yet be unable to reach them. 'If we could get there all our dangers would be over,' someone said to Fryer.

A few minutes later Fryer himself spotted a possible gap. He was standing at the stern, steadying himself with the foresail tack.

'Do you see anything?' Bligh shouted above the thunder of the surf.

'Yes, sir, I can see a place where there are no breakers.'

Bligh confirmed the discovery and the helmsman was ordered to steer towards it. At first it looked too narrow to allow them through safely. Then as they ventured nearer it seemed to open up before their eyes. With the wind behind them, and assisted by a fast current, the launch shot through the gap—now known as Bligh Boat Entrance—and into the calm, serene waters beyond.

Bligh bore in towards the mainland on a north-westerly course, and late in the afternoon ran in to a fine sandy beach on an island just off Cape Direction. Appropriately, and inevitably, he named it Restoration Island, both for the anniversary on this day of the

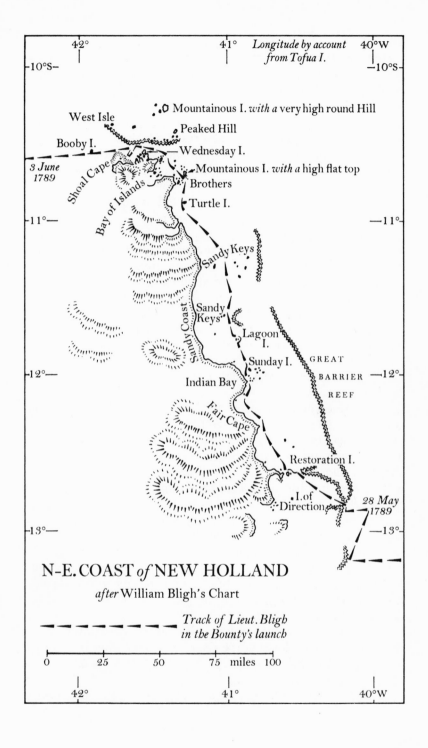

42°   41°   40°W

−10°S−   −10°S−

Mountainous I. *with a* very high round Hill

West Isle   Peaked Hill

Booby I.   Wednesday I.

Shoal Cape   Mountainous I. *with a* high flat top

*3 June
1789*   Brothers

Bay of Islands   Turtle I.

−11°—   —11°

Sandy Keys

Sandy
Keys

Sandy Coast   Lagoon
I.

−12°—   Sunday I.   GREAT   −12°

Indian Bay   BARRIER

REEF

Fair Cape

Restoration I.

I. of
Direction   *28 May
1789*

−13°—   −13°

N–E. COAST *of* NEW HOLLAND

after William Bligh's Chart

– – – – – – – – – –   *Track of Lieut. Bligh
in the Bounty's launch*

0   25   50   75 miles 100

42°   41°   40°W

restoration to the throne of King Charles II in 1660, and to commemorate their own salvation.

When the moment came for the crew to step ashore, many of them could scarcely make their way through the water to the beach. 'We were,' remarked Fryer, 'like so many drunken men.' Cramped and tossed about for so long, starved almost to death, some could not for a while enjoy the delight of standing up on solid ground without assistance. Fryer said that he was 'so weak that when I first landed my head was so light that I fell down'. Others crawled to the nearest rocks, and tore at the oysters.

At Restoration Island the men's speed of recovery was matched by the rapidity with which they reverted to their old ways. For a while it was as if the mutiny had never occurred, that the open boat voyage was already a forgotten nightmare. Within twenty-four hours, when their bellies had been filled with oyster soup, bread, salt pork and spring water and berries picked from the bushes; when they could lie in groups in the shade of bushes close to a big fire that kept away the flies; then the grumblers began to grumble, the slackers to slack, the restless to plead that they should continue their voyage at once—and Bligh himself to hector and nag, curse and then threaten.

It was true enough that, as Bligh observed, 'these unthankful people were no sooner saved from perishing with want and fatigue than they had forgot the mercies they had received'. But this state of affairs was not brought about by the men alone. These were, after all, ordinary enough seamen, all selected or approved by Bligh, with whom they had now served for some eighteen months—not 'the villains', 'the pirates', the mutineers of the *Bounty*.

The first complaint came, as usual, from Fryer, who grumbled when Bligh cut off the bread ration for their second big oyster-stew feast, and according to Bligh 'created disorder among those who were weak enough to listen to him'. His only ally for the present appeared to be Purcell again. But there were others who thought it was already time for them to be on their way and they also spread disaffection among the men.

On the second day Bligh ordered his men off to search for oysters and himself settled down in the shade of some bushes to write up his log, which included a thorough account of the fauna and flora— such as it was—the tides and topography, of this commonplace little island, communicating with no one except Midshipman Hallett who brought him berries from time to time. It was a repetition in miniature of the situation in Tahiti, with Bligh absenting himself as far as possible from the activities of his men, appearing only occasionally and then to upbraid them for slackness and theft. On the morning of 30 May he was convinced that someone had been at the remaining pork, but failed to discover the culprit.

By now everyone was in a bad temper, and Bligh was picking on many of the men in turn to find fault and abuse them. There were several reasons for this ill-humour. Besides the reaction to their ordeal, most were suffering from stomach pains from the unaccustomed food, especially the berries, which the less restrained gorged in great quantities. To this was added the discomfort of their continued constipation, 'most of us having had no evacuation since we left the ship'. And they were anxious again for their safety. Although there were no natives on the island there was no doubt that they could reach it because there were cinders of old fires and old weapons about the rocks, and one party had discovered a couple of crude wigwams. Later, natives in great numbers were sighted on the mainland waving their spears threateningly.

That evening they embarked again in the launch and left Restoration Island for fear of being attacked, and to search for another temporary home that might also be richer in oysters.

At Sunday Island, named for the day of the week they landed on it, matters got worse and there was almost another mutiny. Besides those perennial trouble-makers, Fryer and Purcell, Fryer's brother-in-law young Robert Tinkler, Robert Lamb the butcher, George Simpson, Tom Hall the cook and the surviving quartermaster Peter Linkletter, all formed into an anti-Bligh group. Again the dispute was over food. Bligh sent out parties in different directions about the island. Some grumbled and said they were too weak or too ill to search for oysters, among them the master's mate Elphinstone, a firm Bligh ally and for this reason alone always a target for Fryer's nagging. Fryer at length went off with his party, muttering that it was every man for himself and there was no one too sick for the duty. When he returned to the boat later, carrying a bag of clams and oysters and some dog fish, he heard the sound of raised voices. His crony Purcell had arrived back first and Bligh was cursing him, while the carpenter was answering obscenity with obscenity.

It seemed that Bligh was attempting to take Purcell's bag from him, claiming that all the food gathered was common food in his charge. Purcell resisted this hotly. It was against all his previous instructions. Bligh cursed him for a damned scoundrel. 'If I had not brought you here you would all have perished.'

'Yes, sir,' Purcell replied, 'if it had not been for you we should not have been here.'

Bligh was evidently too slow to catch the note of sarcasm. 'What's that you say, sir?'

When Purcell repeated his words, Bligh again called him a scoundrel.

'I am not a scoundrel, sir, I am as good a man as you.'

This was too much for Bligh who determined, as he wrote later, 'to strike a final blow'. He meant this literally too, for he seized his cutlass, slicing the air above Purcell's head, and ordering him to fetch another cutlass to defend himself.

Purcell flinched back, appalled at this prospect. 'No, sir, you are an officer,' he said.

Fryer judged that things had gone far enough and now stepped between the men. 'No fighting here,' he told them firmly. 'Mr Cole, please arrest both these men.'

Everyone had gathered round to watch this interesting contest, and among them all only David Nelson appeared to be actively supporting the captain.

Bligh, still holding the cutlass, turned furiously on Fryer, calling him a scoundrel, too. 'If, sir, you interfere with me in the course of my duty and a disturbance arises, you will certainly be the first person I shall put to death.'

This silenced the master, and silenced the muttering crowd at the same time. Bligh ordered the parties away again on a further search, and when they obeyed reluctantly he knew that he had ended any risk of rebellion for the time being.

The disaffection of his men was not Bligh's only worry. He was now haunted by the fear of attack from the natives who had certainly followed their progress up the coast and had witnessed their landing on this second island. It was almost as if these Queensland aborigines, like the Friendly Islands' natives, had foreknowledge of their arrival and route and had planted threatening evidence of their proximity. Besides the wigwams and scars of old fires at Sunday Island, they found a canoe lying abandoned upside down in the sand. Bligh estimated it as thirty-three feet long and capable of carrying some twenty men. They were being closely watched by the natives on the shore—stark naked, they were, with short bushy hair, carrying spears and some unidentifiable smaller weapon. On the afternoon of 31 May Bligh climbed to the highest point of the island, noted a safer islet to the north, and determined to leave just before dark in the hope of throwing off their pursuers.

Their stay at this third island was a fiasco and seemed to justify those who had pressed for some days that they should waste no more time and continue their voyage. Bligh still hoped to add more usefully to their stores, which so far amounted to only a few clams and oysters which he had dried—enough for only two days at sea. At this islet he hoped to procure some turtles, fish, perhaps some birds and more molluscs, too. He could then embark for Timor with a reduced risk of starving to death.

The failure to kill more than a few noddy birds and a handful of clams at this islet, brought about by the undisciplined behaviour of his men, was almost more than Bligh could bear. By making too much noise, the turtling party succeeded only in driving them away before any could be caught. Then one of the bird-hunting party, Robert Lamb, who had been a constant trouble, went ahead and frightened the birds they found in a cove. Bligh gave him a good beating when he heard. Later the man boasted that he had eaten on the quiet no fewer than nine boobies raw.

It was Fryer's carelessness which finally decided Bligh to leave this ill-fated spot. Bligh ordered a fire round which they should all gather for warmth and protection against the flies at night. It had to be a small and well-controlled one for fear of the natives. But Fryer decided to make one of his own, away from the rest of the party. During the night it got out of hand, a spark caught the dry grass, and in seconds the islet became a blazing beacon in the darkness.

Fear further inflamed Bligh's anger at his master—a villain, a rebel and a fool all at once. 'It only rested with the natives to come after us and we must inevitably have fallen a sacrifice,' Bligh wrote before issuing orders for the launch to sail at dawn.

When they were at sea again a remarkable change came over the men, as if it was only when confined within the launch, with all its attendant shared hardships and dangers, that they were capable of working harmoniously and loyally together. At once the grumbling

ceased and Bligh again became undisputed commander. Bligh himself behaved as if all their disputes ashore had never occurred, and
now looked back to the time among the islands as a success.

'I have been just six days on the coast of New Holland,' he
summarised this intermission in their voyage, 'in the course of
which it is to be observed oysters with a few clams have been the
only supply we met with besides water. Indeed it was all I could
expect, but equal to this perhaps we have benefited by having no
fatigue in the boat and good rest at night. With these advantages
every one has certainly prolonged his life, and poor as the supply
has been I am very sensible of the great good it has done, and has
relieved my mind from many a distressing thought.'

Although they were back on rations little better than before—
just a few dried oysters or clams to add to their bread allowance—
for a time everyone was full of confidence and good spirits.

On the evening of 2 June, with a fresh favourable south-east
breeze, they had reached the Adolphus Channel, and Cape York,
the northernmost tip of the continent, was only a few hours away.
Bligh hove to for the night with the grapnel, and in a last attempt
to augment their supplies sent a party ashore to an island. They
found only the remains of freshly dead turtles (sure sign that, even
here, the natives were still about) and the launch continued its
passage just before dawn.

Ahead of them was the feared Endeavour Straits, and they would
need daylight to negotiate the hazards of uncharted reefs and unpredictable currents. On his port beam Bligh noted a bay of islands,
and so named it, continuing on a north-westerly course. In fact,
as he discovered later, the bay had been the opening to the Endeavour
Straits. Bligh was already well north of Cape York, and it was not
until noon that he ordered the helm to be put over. For the first time
since they had reached the Great Barrier Reef, the launch turned on
to a south-westerly course, to take them through a far narrower and
even more dangerous route than the Endeavour Straits, the Prince
of Wales Channel.

From this time until sunset Bligh negotiated shoal water, rocks,
sand banks, and reefs. It was a nightmare passage, with the lookout
calling from the bows and Bligh issuing sharp orders to the helmsman. Yet for all the risks of immediate destruction, like the peerless
navigator he was he took note of the position and bearing of as
many of the hazards as he could to add to the knowledge of these

seas gathered earlier by Cook. And today it is possible to plot with absolute precision the launch's route from inside the Great Barrier Reef clear into the Arafura Sea.

By eight o'clock in the evening they were free from the worst dangers and the open sea lay ahead. It had a tonic effect on all hands, and Bligh noted with surprise their cheerful and optimistic spirit. 'It seemed as if everyone had only embarked with me to proceed to Timor, and were in a vessel equally calculated for their safety and convenience.'

This bright optimism was short-lived. The worst eight days of the whole voyage were ahead of them. The strength they had gained from their few sustaining meals among the islands could not be expected to last for long. Their reserves of strength were infinitely less than they had been when, after six months of good living, they had first been cast adrift. Most of the men did not realise how awful they looked. They had become accustomed to the sight of their own emaciated limbs, their sores, and the gaunt appearance of their shipmates. Bligh saw them as they really were, and was filled with the gravest doubts that many would survive this last leg. Nor could he quite keep from his mind the awful idea that they might be reduced to cannibalism. There had, after all, been cases of this in the past in open boats, when lots had been drawn for the final sacrifice. He rejected it before he seriously considered such a development. 'I do not believe,' he wrote, 'that among us such a thing could happen, but death from famine would be received as from any violent disease.' After reaching this comforting conclusion he served them all with six dried oysters and a twenty-fourth of a pound of bread for dinner, and in the evening gave prayers for their deliverance.

Four days later Bligh was noting graver signs. The men were becoming lethargic and slept for much of the time. They had to be awakened for their bite of food, and some were slipping fast, among them the surgeon and old Lebogue. On 10 June he considered that more than half of them were showing signs of 'an approaching end to their distresses'. He did not yield an ounce on the rations though there still remained enough for another fifteen days and there were already signs of land ahead and they were making good time across the Arafura Sea.

Strict economy had now become an obsession with Bligh. He had determined to reach civilisation with only one survivor rather than serve a fraction more bread. Fryer and Purcell, but no one else, later accused Bligh of taking more than his fair share of the supplies. He certainly wrote in his log at this time that he felt 'no extreme hunger or thirst', and 'my allowance satisfies me, knowing I can have no more'. We can be sure, however, that Bligh did not cheat; to do so would have been utterly against his character. No matter what happened on shore, at sea in the launch he was consumed by his determination to reach civilisation and the means to reach this end.

By the following day, 11 June, everyone was at the last extremity. Their imminent end seemed to bring about a new unity of spirit. Those strong enough to do so had complained and grumbled and pleaded for an increase in their allowance during the previous days. This happened no more. Never had their prospects seemed lower nor their goodwill towards one another higher. There was even a special tenderness in the way they helped Ledward and Lebogue to sip their special allowance of wine in the evenings.

Bligh looked at their swollen legs, their 'hollow and ghastly countenances', observed their extreme weakness, and wondered what had come over them. Cole regarded his captain and observed, 'I really think, sir, that you look worse than anyone in the boat.'

This brought Bligh back to reality. He laughed and returned him 'a better compliment'.

Yet, though Bligh might appear at least as bad as anyone, he was the only one among them who still remained confident that the boat would reach its destination. At noon he calculated that they were less than one hundred miles from the eastern extremity of Timor. When he passed this information to his men they showed 'a universal joy and satisfaction'.

The coast of Timor was sighted soon after 3 a.m. on 12 June, when even the weakest among them rose from the bottom of the launch and broke into hoarse cheers of relief; then, led by Bligh, knelt down in prayers of thankfulness for their merciful deliverance. At daylight they sailed close inshore, noting the rich and agreeable landscape, the plantations and scattered huts. No sign of a Dutch settlement, or of a possible landing place, appeared during that day, and when night fell Bligh hove to for fear of missing their destination.

It was not until the early hours of 14 June that they learned for sure that their ordeal was over and relief at hand. Word had gone ahead of them, and the commander of the fort at Coupang fired two cannon as a signal. With the makeshift union jack hoisted and the men at the oars, the launch was pulled towards the harbour entrance with a vigour that surprised them all.

They sighted two square-rigged vessels and a cutter at anchor; then as the greyness faded from the sky, they observed other sights they had missed for many months—a jetty, buildings, the fort itself, horses and carts and white people, strangers, dressed in the European style, among the gatherings of brown Malaysians. The world they had never expected to see again was spread out before them like a vision at dawn after a long nightmare.

There was a European sailor on the jetty looking down in astonishment at the packed boat. He waved, and when he spoke it was in English, as if he had been sent all this way to greet and give praise and do honour to his countrymen on their deliverance after the longest and most remarkable open boat voyage in history. (He had in fact come ashore from one of the square-riggers, which happened to be from England; but the timing was like a miracle to Bligh and his men.)

What this anonymous English sailor saw is best described by Bligh himself, even though he was one of their number.

'For anyone to conceive the picture of such poor miserable beings, let him fancy that . . . he is in the moment of giving relief to eighteen men whose ghastly countenances, but from the known cause, would be equally liable to affright as demand pity; let him view their limbs full of sores and their bodies nothing but skin and bones habited in rags, and at last let him conceive he sees the tears of joy and gratitude flowing o'er their cheeks at their benefactors.'

Some alone, some supporting the weakest among them, the eighteen men disembarked from the launch for the last time and made their way slowly—'scarce able to walk' remarked Fryer—to a nearby house; where, with marvellous appropriateness, they were served with tea and bread and butter for breakfast.

8

'The great rock'

At midday on 28 April 1789 the *Bounty* was a ship without a commander, its company divided according to their reactions to the violent events of the morning and the parts they had played in them. Some were simply stunned by the sudden breakdown in order and the appalling consequences of what they had done. Others were cast into a deep sense of guilt and gloom; and others again—Churchill, Quintal, McKoy and Thompson among them—were still buoyed up with the excitement of the release from discipline and the heady prospect of a return to idleness and dissipation. Byrn was still bewildered by it all. Coleman, Norman, McIntosh and Stewart who had all been forcibly detained were sunk in despair.

Fear was the dominant emotion, even among those still enjoying their grog-induced Dutch courage. It was difficult for them to encompass the enormity of the crime they had committed, or witnessed, the most heinous in the service. As the reality of the events of the morning sank into their minds the fear gathered strength, affecting even the spirited and inebriated Tom Ellison and that ruthless sailor, 'Reckless Jack' Adams.

Christian himself, who had long since regretted his impetuosity and was already haunted by the last sight of the packed, wallowing launch slowly disappearing towards the north, was cast down into a state of acute melancholy and distress. Last night he had wanted only to escape. A conspiracy of events had prevented him from succeeding. Next, inspired by Young and (innocently) also by Stewart, he had brought about an insurrection against his tormentor, planned at first only to dispose of him, and three others whose continued presence on board the ship Christian had judged to be dangerous. Four lives to be sacrificed. Itself an agonising consideration.

Then events had got out of hand, until to his horror he found himself sentencing to likely death almost half the ship's company, all men he knew intimately, many of them with families and many his friends—the steady, reliable gunner Peckover, fat John Norton, the butt of so many jokes, old Lebogue, Will Cole the bo'sun. If they drowned or died violently at the hands of the natives—and one or the other seemed inevitable—the guilt was Christian's and his alone. If any survived to bring news of this day to England, his beloved brothers, the entire Christian family, would be dishonoured, and the name Fletcher Christian remembered with loathing and shame for ever. He would have to live with these morbid speculations, probably never learning what happened to Bligh and his men, for the rest of his life. The price for his own escape from hell had been too high.

The state of paralysis which overcame the *Bounty* after the mutiny was broken when the wind rose in the afternoon. Someone had to take command of the ship. Surely it would be Christian himself? But when one of the men approached him he denied that he was their new captain. 'I have no right to command you and I will act in any station I am assigned to.'

Christian had his wits about him and was already emerging from the gloom he had suffered earlier in the day. 'Christian was always cheerful,' reported Adams, not altogether accurately some time later, 'and his example was of the greatest service in exciting his companions to labour.' His resilience, the speed at which he could snap out of his moods of dark introspection, had often been noted among his shipmates in the past. He had never so far been down for long. These men, the guilty and the non-guilty, were his responsibility now and he must rise to the needs of command. But he was not going to propose himself. Others must do it. They did so, eagerly and unanimously.

But from this time it was observed that Christian went everywhere with a loaded pistol sticking ostentatiously out of his pocket.

Christian now acted briskly. If they were to survive there must be discipline and order again. He applied both with a firmness that created surprise and anxiety among some of the sailors who innocently believed that they had mutinied for freedom and licence. Christian passed over Edward Young and Peter Heywood as second-in-command and second watch-keeper, judging the first to be too slack, the second too inexperienced. Instead he ordered George Stewart, a non-mutineer and a severe taskmaster, to take command of the second watch. McIntosh took over Purcell's duties as carpenter, Mills was made the gunner, Morrison bo'sun and storekeeper. Churchill retained his position as master-at-arms. Christian completely trusted him and gave him back the keys to the arms chests. He expected no trouble from the loyalists but he was taking no chances with any possible future uprising and ordered a permanent armed guard over the chests with Churchill sleeping on them in his cabin at night.

All these arrangements Christian settled at once. Just as he had made the appointment of the *Bounty*'s new captain a democratic decision in order to protect himself against future trouble, so on that first evening he consulted his men about their long-term plans.

'Where will you sail to now, lads? Remember that if the launch reaches a port there will be an immediate search for us. And they will come to look for us anyway later when the ship does not return.'

'Carry us wherever you think proper, sir,' one man spoke; and there appeared to be general agreement with him. Tahiti, the mutineers knew, was out of the question. It would be the first place that any searching vessel would make for.

Christian had already given serious thought to the matter and had judged that a number of his men had no intention of settling for the rest of their lives on a Pacific island. Some of the less active mutineers and those who had been forced to stay on board would want to reach England again even if they had to place their lives at the mercy of a court martial. For the present he thought that the sooner he was rid of these men the better.

For himself and the hard core of his collaborators there were no alternatives to a future as hunted criminals. They needed a remote island, defences against a possible attack, land, women, livestock, and a roof over their heads. Christian told his men that he had chosen as a possible home the island of Tubai, some three hundred miles south of Tahiti, noted but not landed on by Cook whose description of it among Bligh's books seemed to match their needs. It was far from the likely route of any traffic or searching vessels, and had a single harbour with difficult access. Cook had written of the natives that 'their countenances express some degree of natural ferocity'; but they could hardly be worse than those of the Friendly Islands.

In marked contrast to the launch, and for the first time for seventeen months, there was no reading of prayers on the *Bounty* that night.

On the long voyage east, beating against the trade winds for more than four weeks, the discipline on board the *Bounty* was certainly no less severe than under Bligh, even though they knew where they were with Christian; and on two watches instead of three life was more rigorous than they had experienced for a long time. He even ordered them into uniform, which the seamen had never worn before. He was convinced, he said, that 'nothing had more effect on the minds of the Indians than uniformity of dress', and that from the beginning they must establish their superiority over them. Using the *Bounty*'s stock of spare studding sails, the ship's company settled down to cut out and sew these uniforms, a task which kept them busy for most of the passage to Tubai.

Everything was made shipshape on board. After the litter of the mutiny had been cleared away, the piles of fruit which had covered the decks under Bligh's regime were tidied up. Down in the great cabin Nelson's conservatory was partly dismantled and the once-cherished plants which he and Bligh had cultivated and brooded over as if they were their own children were brought up on deck and hurled into the sea—all but a few of them which Christian ordered preserved in case there were none at Tubai. Christian then moved into Bligh's cabin, as befitted his new rank. With a complement of only twenty-five instead of forty-four they all enjoyed less cramped conditions than before.

The personal possessions of Bligh and the loyalists, their sea chests, their mementoes, books and clothes—all were brought up on deck, divided into twenty-five lots which were then drawn for by the men and stowed in neat marked heaps in the great cabin among the surviving plants. This was typical of the orderliness Christian insisted on—and no one was inclined 'to dispute the superiority of Mr Christian'. 'Mr Christian' it was among all of them, right to the end.

Tubai was sighted just one month after the day of the mutiny. It is a typical volcanic Polynesian island, some five miles long by three wide, entirely encompassed by a coral reef except—as Cook had reported—for one narrow gap on the north-west side which leads into a bay in the lagoon within. Christian hoisted out the large cutter and ordered its crew to lead them in, sounding all the way.

Their troubles began almost at once. It was twelve years since the natives had first seen a European vessel, Cook's *Resolution*,

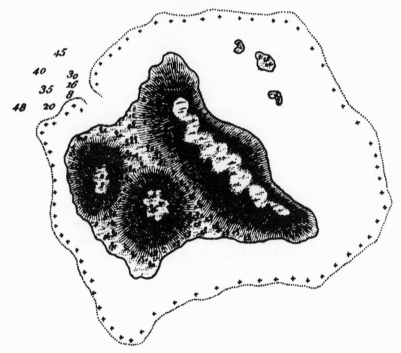

TOOBOUAI Island
Lat. 23°. 25 *S*.
Long. 210. 37 *E*.

Cook's chart of Tubai, printed in his journal, and used by Christian in his efforts to colonise the island after the mutiny

which had not paused to anchor. Polynesians have long memories, and all the inhabitants who were old enough recalled the prizes they had come so tantalisingly close to acquiring on that occasion. Now dozens of canoes were launched from the beach and came out towards the *Bounty*, each with one or two natives standing and blowing conch shells, making an idiotic and seemingly purposeless noise, like an animal's yowl of boredom. Soon the decks were thick with natives, scrounging and thieving for all they were worth, encouraged by the small number of crew and the wealth of goods below decks. Christian had great difficulty in getting rid of them without using violence, and it was obvious that they would be back, and in greater strength.

The next morning's assault was planned and executed with great cunning. First eighteen nubile young women, escorted by five men, came out to the ship. They were the pick of the Tubaian girls, 'all young and handsome', they were described, 'having fine long hair which reached to their waists in waving ringlets', all well versed in seduction. While they were busy at work, the men got below and began filching everything they could lay their hands on.

Christian was on his guard and knew that this was a mere diversion. The main attack soon developed—no fewer than fifty canoes cutting through the smooth waters, all manned by warriors with spears and carrying cords to secure any prisoners. The baying of their conch shells filled the lagoon with an insane and now threatening chorus.

Christian had ordered the *Bounty*'s four-pounders to be loaded with grape-shot. He waited until the attackers were within point-blank range, and then gave the order to fire, with barrels at maximum depression, straight down into the packed canoes.

The result was devastating. The men screamed and fled, joined by the girls and the pillagers. A dozen had died in the attack and many more had been wounded.

Christian named their anchorage Bloody Bay. Later he went ashore with an armed escort to survey the island. He had not changed his mind about the place, in spite of the catastrophic start, and remained convinced that he could dominate these people, or that they could learn to live together in peace. The island did not appear to be overcrowded—in fact everyone had fled from their homes in fear and taken refuge in the hills. The land was ripe for cultivation. Fruit grew in abundance, though there was no livestock.

And, above all, in the unlikely event of a searching ship arriving
at the island, it would be an easy place to defend, just as he had
hoped it would be from Cook's description and map. Already he
was siting the position for the fort, secure against attack from the
sea, defended by the *Bounty*'s guns which they would bring ashore
before destroying the vessel. Here, he believed, they could create
the ideal island settlement.

All that they needed were native men to serve them and help
them against any island uprising, some livestock for breeding and
for meat, and women. All appeared to be unavailable here. 'We
lacked women,' said Adams later, 'and, remembering Tahiti, where
all of us had made intimate friendships, we decided to return there,
so that we could each obtain one.'

There was no doubt about Adams's order of priority. He was
thinking of his own Jenny (Teehuteatuaonoa). Only one or two of
the others had made lasting attachments at Tahiti, McIntosh his
Mary, and Christian, of course, his Isabella. But all preferred the
idea of finding their wives at that other island.

The *Bounty* sailed again into Matavai Bay on 6 June 1789. By
now Christian had realised the cardinal mistake he had made in
not disposing earlier of his non-mutineers. They knew all his
plans, and no matter how many promises they made nor how good
their intentions, if they were allowed to remain at Tahiti the news
that the *Bounty* was at Tubai would leak out sooner or later. The
only way to avoid this risk was to prohitibit shore leave to all the
ship's company and forbid them under the threat of the most savage
punishment—several dozen lashes, even keel-hauling—from talking
to the natives about their plans. Like it or not, they must now all
stick together on the Tubai enterprise.

There was enormous excitement among the natives when the
Bounty was sighted, but at Tahiti Christian could watch the canoes
coming out to meet them with complete equanimity. He had an
ingenious and elaborate story ready for them, built up on Bligh's
earlier tale that Cook was still alive, a sort of roaming plenipoten-
tiary of King George of 'Pretanee' with responsibilities all over the
Pacific.

We met Captain Cook, Christian told the chiefs in his halting
Tahitian, and Captain Bligh had gone on board with some of his
men, taking with them the ship's launch and all but a few of his
plants. Cook and Bligh had then sailed off together to Whytootackee,

a settlement in New Holland which Cook had been sent to establish by orders of the king. As soon as possible, Christian continued glibly, Bligh would come back to Tahiti with more gifts for his old friends.

All this made believable and welcome listening to the Matavaians, and when Christian told them that their beloved Cook would like food and stores for his new settlement, they fell to with a will, bringing out the best of all that was needed—no fewer than 460 live hogs, fifty goats, chickens, the bull and cow originally left at Tahiti by Cook ten years earlier, and, for good measure, some dogs and cats. Soon the *Bounty* began to look more like Noah's Ark than an armed brig in the service of King George III.

They had less success with the natives, who showed disappointing reluctance to leave their families and homes for Whytootackee. Finally only Jenny, Mary, Sarah and Isabella, who still regarded themselves as the wives of Adams, McIntosh, Quintal and Christian, agreed to remain on board, to help create the first ever Anglo-Tahitian settlement together with seventeen men and boys and a young girl. Some of these were stowaways, including a restless traveller from the neighbouring island of Bora-Bora, a chief named Hitihiti who, sixteen years earlier, had ranged the Pacific with Cook, from New Zealand to the Marquesas Islands and the Antarctic. He could not resist the temptation of another voyage.

But also among this company from Tahiti were seven women who, at the last minute, were tricked into remaining on board when the ship sailed.

This shipload of livestock, fruit and plants, of stowaways, children and English mutineers and their reluctant as well as willing Euro-pean and Tahitian passengers, sailed out of Matavai Bay and south towards Tubai on 16 June 1789. The passage was a stormy one and there were scenes of pandemonium and distress above and below decks—'hogs and goats trampling over each other for want of room', wrote Morrison. But the only casualties were the bull, who lurched and fell and broke his old legs (surely the first English bull to succumb to a Pacific storm), and four hogs and a goat, before the *Bounty* slipped through the break in Tubai's reef and anchored in the lagoon again a week later.

The proceedings on this remote tropical island now assume a

more unreal tone than ever. Christian, already arch-mutineer and
self-confessed murderer, now takes upon himself the twin duties
of colonial administrator and military governor of this new fragment
of the British Empire. His rule is absolute. When Matthew Quintal
and his friend John Sumner go ashore for the night without leave,
he orders them to the quarterdeck and, in front of the rest of the
crew, holds a pistol to Quintal's head and barks out, 'I'll let you
know who is master.' He claps them both in irons until they think
better of their ways.

Then, conforming to colonising practice, Christian himself leads
his mixed party ashore and starts work on the fort without further
delay. It is to be a magnificent and grandiose affair, nearly one
hundred yards long on each of its sides, with earth walls eighteen
feet thick at the base, surrounded by a twenty-foot-deep moat, and
entered by way of a drawbridge. On each of the four corners one
of the *Bounty*'s four-pounders is to be mounted, and the ship's
swivel guns strategically placed along the top of the walls.

Within this fort they will be secure from native uprisings and
attack from the sea alike. And, in patriotic style, and in memory
of the old country, it is to be named Fort George. Above it, even
while it is under construction, the union jack flies bravely.

Other settlers are put to work clearing and tilling the land and
planting crops. Everywhere there is a sense of purpose and optimism;
spirits are high, for there is nothing to equal the zeal of homemakers.

A halt to the promising start of this new settlement was brought
about by two forces, one from within, one from without. Fear for the
future was behind both. The Tubaians, submissive after their
earlier bloody defeat, became increasingly anxious and restless. They
watched from afar the moat being dug and told one another that
they were to be exterminated and this was to be their mass grave.
The hogs, which Christian had ordered to be let loose on the island,
created havoc among the natives' crops; and they regarded this as
calculated vandalism.

But the most serious conflicts stemmed from the colonists'
continuing shortage of women. Whatever other consequences to the
mutiny toughs like Churchill, Sumner and Millward had expected,
a shortage of women in their lives was not among them. They
became increasingly reckless in their efforts to persuade some of the
local girls to join them and several times on these hunting expeditions the men were ambushed, stripped of their clothes and beaten.

Like any good colonial governor, Christian tried to maintain peaceful relations and sent conciliatory gifts to the chiefs with his demands to return stolen goods. But he had no experience or training in civil administration and failed to understand the cataclysmic effect their arrival was having on the settled life of the islanders. Tubai was a tightly organised, delicately balanced agricultural community. The presence of these white men with their magical weapons of death and their insatiable appetites posed a constant threat to their lives, their women and their future food supplies. They occupied a large area of ground where land was life. And their presence had an unsettling effect on the balance of power between the island's three chiefs. A favour to one was an insult to the other two. An insult to one suggested special favours to the others. Under ordinary circumstances the rivalries provided a healthy outlet for the natives' aggressive tendencies, short of warfare. Christian and his men disrupted all this. Real violence was inevitable, and the wounding, abduction and killings culminated in a minor colonial war—muskets against spears—in which sixty-six natives were killed and many more wounded, the Englishmen suffering only two injuries.

And so it went on, with scuffles and fights every day. By early September Christian's brave plans to create a mixed white-dominated society were shattered. They were too busy dealing with uprisings to complete the fort. Worst of all, he was now facing a mutiny of his own. Some of the men who were still without women were demanding that they should be allowed to seize them. Christian answered that this would do them no good and would lead to murder—they must get them by peaceful means. The men said no, demanded grog from the ship's stores before they would continue the debate, and when this, too, was refused, some hotheads broke the lock to the spirits store and helped themselves.

Christian saw his power and control over this violent minority fast slipping, and realised, too, that his own life was in increasing danger, and not only from the natives. Wisely he temporised, then gathered his men about him for a discussion on their future and a free vote. Sixteen out of twenty-five voted to quit Tubai and return to Tahiti where the women were compliant and the men friendlier. Christian accepted the decision gracefully. 'Gentlemen,' he said, 'I will carry you and land you wherever you please. I desire no one to stay with me. But I have one favour to request—that you will grant me the ship, tie the foresail and give me a few gallons of water, and leave me to run before the wind, and I shall land upon the first island the ship drives. After what I have done I cannot remain at Tahiti. I will live nowhere where I may be apprehended and brought home to be a disgrace to my family.'

The tone of this speech, its emotional overtones, its frankness, are all typical of the man. He has attempted to rule and has failed. His great enterprise has failed too. They do not need him any longer, and most of them prefer to risk life on Tahiti, the only friendly island in the Pacific, they were beginning to believe.

This speech had an immediate and equally emotional response from other of his men. His old friend Young was the first to speak up. 'We shall never leave you, Mr Christian!' he called out. Other voices joined his. 'We will never leave you!' Eight in all.

With their plans completed, the men put them into immediate effect. Everything that had been brought ashore was taken back to the *Bounty*, and Christian also had Brown collect some of the finest fruit plants and saplings he could find—bananas, breadfruit, yams, plantains, sugar cane, oranges—and stow them in the great cabin, until it began to look as it had in Bligh's time. They might never see fruit like this again.

The Tahitians were embarked, together with two local natives who had linked their fortunes so closely with the white men that they feared for their future on the island. On 18 September anchors were weighed and to the immense relief of all the island's inhabitants and most of their uninvited guests, the *Bounty* put to sea and disappeared to the north.

Christian never knew how close to discovery they had been at Tubai. A month before they left the island, the brig *Mercury* sighted Tubai in the evening and closed it at night, passing within two miles and observing the lights on shore. In daylight she could not have failed to spot the *Bounty* at anchor.

Nor did Christian know—or could have credited the possibility if word had reached him—that Bligh had by now reached Timor safely and had already despatched reports of the mutiny to India, the other Dutch settlements and to Governor Phillip in Botany Bay, with a detailed description of every one of those who had remained on board the *Bounty* so that 'the pirates' might be identified and apprehended. In a few days' time the Admiralty in London, too, would have news of the mutiny.

The *Bounty* arrived off Tahiti for the third and last time on 22 September 1789. There had been no further disagreement among the crew. Christian was to have the ship and the eight hard-core mutineers who had agreed to stick with him: Young, Mills, Quintal, McKoy, Adams and Williams, the American Isaac Martin and Nelson's late assistant, William Brown. With the help of the two Tubaian natives, who had no wish to land at Tahiti and had sworn everlasting loyalty to Christian, and some more men they hoped to persuade to accompany them from Tahiti, Christian reckoned that he could work the *Bounty* safely. Isabella, Mary, Jenny and Susan would of course remain with their *tyos*. The other men would find their own women.

Midshipmen Stewart and Heywood, Byrn, Coleman, Norman and McIntosh, who had taken no part in the mutiny, felt safe enough to set up home at Matavai. Here they would remain until they could take passage on board a passing vessel, or were picked up by a searching British ship. Besides these six men, Morrison, Churchill, Burkett, Sumner, Millward, Hillbrand, Muspratt, young Tom Ellison, Skinner and Mat Thompson preferred to risk discovery at Tahiti.

None of these men at present wished to travel further. They were weary of roaming the Pacific in the *Bounty*, and unwilling to face again the hostility and violence of islands like Nomuka and Tubai.

With the personal possessions of Bligh's party already divided between them, it remained only to make a similar division of the ship's common goods—the liquor and wine, including Banks's high quality maturing wine from Tenerife, the cooking utensils, the tools, the twine and cable, and most important of all, the contents of the arms chests.

Christian went ashore with the first of the Tahiti party in the cutter which was loaded to the gunwales with their possessions and arms. He was anxious to be away quickly. He was filled with a feeling of restlessness and unease, trusting neither his companions nor the Matavai chiefs who must now soon learn the truth about Bligh and the mutiny either from his shipmates or the natives who had been abducted to Tubai and were now returning to their homes. At this critical moment anything might happen. Even his old friends

Stewart and Heywood, faced with the imminent loss of their only immediate means of escape to freedom, might suddenly change their minds and attempt to retake the ship.

The news that met him on shore only increased his anxiety. A great ship like the *Bounty* had been here and had only recently left. The ship's master, Captain John Henry Cox, and his crew had been puzzled by Tynah's tale of the *Bounty* returning under a new captain ('Titreano' he had called Christian) and leaving again loaded with livestock for a place called Whytootackee, where Captain Cook had built a new settlement. Christian knew that it would not take the Admiralty long to put two and two together from this garbled story after the *Mercury* returned home.

Besides, as Captain Cox had explained to Tynah, Cook was no longer alive. And Bligh Cook's son indeed! The captain had made it clear that Cook had been dead ten years and to prove it he had presented to Tynah another picture to stand sadly alongside his precious portrait by Webber of Cook. It was a dramatic one that already hung in so many English homes, of the great navigator's assassination by other Polynesians, painted by Zoffany.

Tynah and his chiefs had been furious at the deception that Bligh had perpetrated at their expense for all those months. Now, already grief-stricken that their demi-god would never visit them again, came the news of the mutiny, of the casting adrift of Bligh and nearly half those they had known. All this on top of the *Mercury*'s visit, the *Bounty*'s unexpected return—twice over—the myth of the Whytootackee expedition, the events at Tubai. The effect of these shocks on a volatile people was unpredictable and Christian determined not to wait to witness the reaction.

Christian had wanted to fill some of his casks with water. But he thought that even this was too risky. The only chief he talked to was Wyettoa, Hayward's old male *tyo*, who made no attempt to conceal his fury; but not, as Christian first expected because he had set his old friend adrift, but because Christian had only cast adrift and not killed Bligh, his sworn enemy.

The last picture the world had of Fletcher Christian for more than eighteen years was of him standing on the black volcanic sandy beach of Matavai Bay, the cutter drawn up ready to take him to the *Bounty* anchored a half-mile out. He is in earnest discussion with

Stewart and young Heywood, advising them, giving them both hope
and warning. They might not be here for as long as they had expected. A ship would certainly come. 'When it does, give yourselves
up at once. Do not attempt to hide. You are both innocent,'
Christian told them. 'No harm can come to you, for you took no
part in the mutiny.'

Then he took his family friend, Peter Heywood, aside, asking
him to deliver messages to his own family. Christian recapitulated
in detail all the events connected with what he called 'that unfortunate disaster' as he wanted his family to know them: how Stewart
had called him to relieve the watch at 4 a.m., how when he went on
deck his brain was on fire. 'Tom Hayward was asleep, John Hallett
not yet on duty, and it was then that the idea of taking the ship
first entered my head. I alone was responsible for this act,' Christian
emphasised. 'This is what you must say.' He was determined that
no one else should be implicated in the incitement to mutiny. It
was his mutiny, his alone.

Then he said something which Heywood never divulged to anyone.

Christian now shook hands with his old friends and waded out
to the waiting cutter.

Everyone except Stewart and Heywood believed that the *Bounty*
would remain at anchor for two more days to take on wood and
water, and on that evening there were numbers of natives on board
—twenty-six in all—supping and drinking with the seven remaining
mutineers. When darkness fell and while the festivities continued
below in the forecastle, Christian and Young silently cut the anchor
cables, hoisted sail and stood out past the reef. It was the only way
they could be sure of having enough women this time. Without
them Christian knew that their settlement, wherever it might be,
was doomed before it began.

When the natives came up on deck at daybreak they were alarmed
to discover that they were at sea. Christian attempted to reassure
them. 'I am visiting another part of the island,' he lied. As the day
advanced they became increasingly suspicious and distressed. One
of the young women, more determined and courageous than the
rest, dived overboard and struck out strongly for the distant reef.
None of the others dared to follow her.

Christian and Young took stock of their spoils. In all they had

eighteen women, only four of whom were on board of their own
free will, and six men. Two of the men were the Tubaians, the other
four were unwilling victims of Christian's trick. All were regarded
by the Englishmen as manservants—slaves really—to help with the
heavy work of building their houses and tilling the soil, and for the
present to help sail the ship. All passed muster for this role.

Unfortunately the same could not be said for all the women.
These included six who had somehow been included in the previous
evening's festivities and who were past their best childbearing years.
They were very promptly dealt with. Later in the day when the
Bounty was passing Moorea—but not so close that any who wanted
might be tempted to swim ashore—and a canoe put out from the
island, Christian had the six surplus women, 'who were rather ancient', taken off. The eight remaining kidnapped women, 'who were
much afflicted at being torn from their friends and relations' (as
Jenny* described them at the time) watched them leave the ship
with envy and longing—if only they were old and fat too!

As the *Bounty* set sail on her last voyage, Christian conducted the
important business of pairing off the women. The white men were
of course given a range of choice. Christian retained his beloved
Isabella, Quintal his Sarah. Adams yielded, without ill-feeling, his
Jenny to Isaac Martin, and took the handsome Paurai from Tahiti
in her place.

All this pairing resulted in only one of the natives having a wife
of his own. This was how it worked out:

White mutineers	females
Fletcher Christian	Isabella†
Edward Young	Susan
John Williams	Pashotu
Matthew Quintal	Sarah
John Adams	Paurai
William McKoy	Mary‡
Isaac Martin	Jenny
John Mills	Vahineatua
William Brown	Teatuahitea

* See below, page 313, for an explanation of this Tahitian woman's account of
the following events.
† Tahitian name, Mauatua, and sometimes affectionately called 'Mainmast' for
her tall, straight figure. See also below, p. 235.
‡ She brought her infant daughter by a Tahitian man.

Polynesian natives		females
Talaloo ⎤		Nancy
Timoa ⎬ from Tahiti		Mareva
Nehow ⎟		Mareva
Menalee ⎦		Mareva
Oho ⎱ from Tubai		Tinafanaea
Tetaheite ⎰		Tinafanaea

This, then, was the multi-racial party which sailed westwards from Tahiti in late September 1789 in search of a home. Many worse-equipped colonising expeditions had set out with lower expectations of success than this one. They had ample provisions, adequate arms, a well-found ship, seeds and plants and even a botanist to look after them. They had a thousand of the most beautiful islands in the world to choose from. They had, above all, the most pressing need to succeed. There was no turning back for this company, or at least for the dominant white males among them.

For this reason there might not, after all, be as many as a thousand islands for them to choose from. Their experiences at Tofua and Tahiti had underlined their vulnerability. The island they must soon find must be remote, harbourless, and at least only sparsely inhabited. The last requirement was the most important. Not only had they suffered enough at the hands of the Polynesians. An inhabited island meant communications, for parties of Polynesians were always restlessly voyaging from one island to another with gossip, and the word of a white settlement would travel at the speed of their great ocean sailing twin-hulled canoes.

'Leave me to run before the wind'—and this is just what Christian now did, with no special destination in mind. It was the most convenient course to take, for beating against the trades with a crew of eight and some inexperienced native assistance would have been a difficult business. In any case, they were as likely to find the perfect island to the west as to the east of Tahiti.

They would not, however, be landing 'upon the first island the ship drives', as Christian had romantically predicted. This island was Rarotonga in the Cook Group, some 700 miles west of Tahiti, one of the most spectacularly beautiful Polynesian islands —with the distinction of having been discovered by a fugitive mutineer.

Tales of great ships manned by white men sailing without women had for many years spread about the Pacific. The legends of their coming, of the wonderful iron tools and weapons they brought with them, travelled from kingdom to kingdom. There were no more enduring legends than those surrounding Cook. These had reached Rarotonga soon after the *Endeavour*'s first visit to Tahiti. As a result, prayers were offered on Rarotonga for his appearance there, too. 'O, great Tangaroa,' ran one of these prayers, 'send your large ship to our land. Send us a propitious gale to bring the far-famed Cookees to our island, to give us nails, and iron and axes. Let us see these outriggerless canoes. . . .'

Now it seemed their prayers were to be answered. Early in October 1789 the *Bounty* hove into sight and anchored inside the reef. Canoes put out from the shore and there was some excited bartering of iron goods for chickens, coconuts and bananas. Only one or two of the islanders managed to get on board. One of these was a chief who made off with a box containing the root of a plant. Later this flourished and provided Rarotonga with its first oranges. Another native managed to get below decks and, after the *Bounty* had left, recounted the extraordinary sights he had seen: the great ship, he reported, was really a floating island; hidden below there were plantations of taro, of sugar cane and breadfruit and bananas and other fruit, all wonderfully watered by two streams.

If, for the Rarotongans, it was a brief and disappointing visit after all the legends of the Cookees, the story of the *Bounty*'s arrival was long remembered on the island. And the myth of the floating plantations, as a result of one native's glimpse of the great cabin's crowded plants at a time when by chance the ship's pumps were being worked, became embellished by time.

This densely inhabited island was no place for the mutineers' settlement, and every minute they remained there increased the risk of some of the women escaping. Christian therefore weighed and disappeared west over the horizon after a few hours. The *Bounty* continued before the wind through other islands of the Cook Group, searching for one that met their needs, always finding them inhabited or otherwise unsuitable. At one island, which Jenny called Purutea, a canoe came out with hogs and coconuts for trade and Christian invited the men on board. 'One of the natives,' Jenny recounts, 'was much delighted at beholding the pearl buttons on the jacket of Captain Christian, who, in a very friendly manner, gave the man the jacket.' Proudly the native stood on the *Bounty*'s rail showing his present to his friends in the canoe below. Any of the crew who saw him would naturally jump to the conclusion that the fellow had stolen the garment and was offering proof of his success before joining his friends.

The next moment there was the sound of a shot, and the native toppled overboard, dead, into the water. His body was retrieved and the natives paddled hastily away, crying out their grief.

The shooting was clearly a mistake. But as Christian made a rapid departure, he was more than ever determined that their island must be completely uninhabited, for there would always be misunderstandings and conflicts with an established population.

At one island after another it was the same story. They would approach it with renewed hope, examining it through the glass from a distance to judge its coastline and interior, close it with caution and expectation; then once again they would spot the dark figures on the beach, the canoes putting out; and Christian would order the helm put over and they would run out to sea again.

Christian's naturally cheerful nature, scarred by guilt and introspection, had turned dour. There was now no gaiety on board the *Bounty*. With tempers fraying and water running low, the ship continued its restless voyage before the wind until they had left the waters of eastern Polynesia far behind them and were back among the Friendly Islands. At one time they were within a hundred miles of Tofua where the mutiny had occurred seven months—and so many thousands of miles of sailing—ago.

Here Christian was forced to anchor and collect water and barter for food, and make a final decision about their future. By chance the island he chose was Tongatabu, charted by Bligh himself when he came here with Cook in 1777. It was not the first time that the mutineers had found useful the immaculate charts made by their late captain. At Tongatabu Christian learned that some of the English cattle Cook and Bligh had brought with them and landed for breeding still flourished.

The *Bounty* remained at Tongatabu for two days, trading, wooding and watering. It was all conducted peacefully and without incident. At the end of the time Christian had made up his mind. He had already spent many hours in Bligh's old cabin studying the charts and books for guidance. They must have hope, a certain destination, for their spirits would break if they continued for much longer casting aimlessly about the southern Pacific. He had noticed signs of unrest even among his friends, and he realised the real risk of mutiny, for the second time, in these waters.

Among the books Christian consulted was the first volume of Hawkesworth's *Voyages*, published in 1773. On page 561 he read again of Carteret's voyage:

'We continued our course westward till the evening of 2d July [1767], when we discovered land to the northward of us. Upon approaching it the next day, it appeared like a great rock rising out of the sea: it was not more than five miles in circumference, and seemed to be uninhabited; it was, however, covered with trees, and we saw it at the distance of more than fifteen leagues, and it having been discovered by a young gentleman, son to Major Pitcairn* of the marines . . . we called it Pitcairn's Island.'

This sounded highly promising to Christian. And there were other attractions. When Carteret was there the surf was breaking on the island so violently that they could not make out a landing, though he had thought that in favourable conditions it would be possible to land at one point. He gave the position as latitude 25°2'S, longitude 133°30'W, 'and about a thousand leagues westward of the continent of America'.

Remote, uninhabited, without harbour or anchorage, Pitcairn was the island for which they had been searching for so long. Its only drawback, as far as Christian could calculate, was that it was so distant from Tongatabu—almost three thousand miles east, against the trades all the way. Like the course Bligh had to follow to reach Tahiti from the west, they would have to sail far south to pick up the westerlies, swinging round in a half-circle to meet the easterly trades again.

Young and the others agreed that they should make the attempt and on 15 November the *Bounty* weighed from Tongatabu, made sail and headed south-east.

Two months passed before they sighted their destination—two discouraging months when the women sickened of shipboard life and suffered acutely from the cold in the high latitudes they penetrated. Jenny talked of them all being 'much discouraged', and of strong pleas to return to the mellow, familiar home island of Tahiti.

Never once did they see land—a seemingly endless cold ocean

* He is believed to have given the order to open fire on the Minutemen at Lexington, and lost his life at the Battle of Bunker Hill.

for week after week, until at length Christian put the *Bounty* on to a northerly course and the temperature began to rise again.

Carteret was two hundred miles out in his reckoning, but when 'the great rock' at last broke the line of the horizon ahead of the *Bounty*'s bows on a dark, gusty evening there was no mistaking it—the silhouette matched exactly the careful engraving in Hawkesworth's book. The date was 15 January 1790. Nine months after the mutiny, Christian had found the home for which he had searched for so long.

That night in stormy weather the *Bounty* stood off and on from the iron-bound coastline, and all they could do the next day, and the day after, was to sail as close inshore as they dared in the high winds, while the ship's mixed company studied the contours of the steep valleys, the crests of the hills, and the shoreline for a landing place.

There was no sign of life, only sea birds wheeling about the cliffs. It was thickly wooded, as Carteret had reported, with miro, purau, banyan and tall coconut palms on all but the steepest slopes: two miles long by perhaps one wide—no more—the land rising precipitously by a thousand feet and more on the southern and western sides, and with only a few breaks in the cliffs along the north-eastern coastline. There was little level ground, but the gentler slopes on the eastern side of the island offered the prospect of land for clearing and tilling.

On the morning of 18 January the wind slackened enough for Christian to bring the *Bounty* closer inshore, and the large cutter was hoisted out. Into it scrambled Brown, Jack Williams, Will McKoy and Christian himself, all armed with muskets in case of hidden natives, and supported by three of the Tahitian men. They rowed ashore across what was to become known as Bounty Bay, negotiated the half hidden rocks, were picked up by a breaking roller, and were hurled on to a narrow beach—no more than a dozen yards wide—at the base of a steep cliff.

It was the first time a landing had been made on this island since a Polynesian community had come here many years, perhaps centuries, before. Evidence of this lost settlement was discovered by Christian soon after they scrambled ashore and struggled up the steep cliff of loose red soil 300 feet to a ridge above—old carved bits of timber, stone axes, some charcoal, stone foundations of old dwellings. It was a good omen. Man had proved that he could live here, even if he had later thought better of it; or, more likely, had responded to the nomadic instincts of the Polynesian voyagers.

Certainly no one lived here now. Christian was soon satisfied on this point. Moreover, the soil was rich, the fruit abundant, the beauty of the place peerless, the climate benign. Here, on this level strip of land above the beach, they could build their dwellings behind the thick curtains of the banyans, invisible from the closest examination by searching eyes from the sea, in the unlikely event of any ship finding its way to this remote corner of eastern Polynesia.

On the following day the *Bounty* was brought in closer to the shore in Bounty Bay, and the ship's company, and with them the hogs and goats and fowls, were ferried ashore in the cutter through the surf, crowding that narrow beach and creating confusion.

Like the early days of any pioneer colony, there was dismay as well as confusion, with so much to be done, and most of it make-shift, just to tide them over—a sailcloth for a roof the first nights, an open fire to roast a hog, exhaustion at dusk, petty quarrels, demands for water and no container to be found immediately. These first hours singled out the adaptable, the tidy, the resilient, the industrious, among the twenty-four people of this mixed race community.

They survived all this stoically, and in this new element, after four months of wandering about the ocean, cheerfulness and a sense of relief predominated. Above all, Christian himself was a happy man again. Jack Adams told of his 'joyful expression such as we had not seen on him for a long time past'. Christian looked forward to his new life here with Isabella, creating a happy and fruitful community, for the present reconciled to his loneliness and isolation.

9

Pandora's Box

✢

SOON after his arrival at Coupang, Bligh dined in the house of a Mr Timotheus Wanjon, the second-in-command of this Dutch settlement, the Governor being indisposed. He had no great appetite and left the table as soon as it was polite to do so, retiring to the room which had been made available to him. Above food and drink, it was peace that he wanted. Here, alone for the first time since the night of the mutiny, utterly weary in mind and body, he lay down to rest and give thanks to Almighty God 'who had given us power to support and bear such heavy calamities, and had enabled me at last to be the means of saving eighteen lives.'

As soon as he had rested he took up a pen and began a letter to his wife—'Know then, my own dear Betsy, that I have lost the *Bounty*.' Bligh continued: 'My misfortune, I trust, will be properly considered by all the world. It was a circumstance I could not foresee—I had not sufficient officers and had they granted me marines most likely the affair would never have happened. I had not a spirited and brave fellow about me and the mutineers treated them as such. My conduct has been free of blame, and I showed every one that, tied as I was, I defied every villain to hurt me . . . I know how shocked you will be at this affair, but I request of you, my Dear

Betsy, to think nothing of it. All is now past and we will again look
forward to future happiness.' He ended with blessings to his children
and to 'the little stranger'—the infant who had been born after he
left England. (In fact they were twin girls, Frances and Jane, making
five girls in all so far.)

Bligh knew well enough, in spite of his reassurances to his wife,
that his future in the service was in danger; and that if he was to
survive at all, it would only be with the support of his patron.
Could Bligh ever redeem himself in the eyes of Sir Joseph Banks
after this dashing of his hopes and his loss of face, as well as profits,
among his fellow planters and merchants? As he recovered his
strength, Bligh prepared a complete account of all his troubles for
Banks, and in the accompanying letter wrote:

'In this, you will find, sir, the misfortunes of a man, who pledges
his honour to you, which could not be foreseen or guarded against,
whose conduct will bear the test of the minutest enquiry, and who
only regrets that you should see him so unsuccessful. But although
I have failed in the completion of my undertaking, I had accomplished
the most difficult part of it. . . .'

It would be seen whether Banks derived comfort from the last
sentence.

As to the rest of the survivors, all at first seemed to recover wonderfully under the tender care of the Dutch surgeon and the kindness
of the settlers, even Ledward and old Lebogue. Bligh was given
a large house for himself and his shipmates—a room of his own,
another for Fryer, Ledward, Nelson and Peckover together, the
loft for the other warrant officers and a large outer apartment for
the rest. The house became a shore-based naval establishment, with
strict rules of conduct and allotted areas for recreation—the hall
for the officers, the back *piazza* for the men. It would be pleasant
to report that this was a happy establishment, for goodness knows
Bligh needed a quiet period. This was not to be. From the time the
Bounty's survivors recovered their strength until Bligh at last got
away from them, their life together was filled with petty squabbles.
Fryer and Purcell were again the chief troublemakers, but not the
only ones. Already by 6 July Bligh is reporting in exasperation that
Fryer's 'insolence and contumacy joined with extreme ignorance
is always giving me trouble'. The next day he hears that young

Robert Tinkler is being saucy to Cole, and that Fryer is encouraging his brother-in-law 'to stick a knife into him'.

A ship was not expected at Coupang for some time, certainly not before the arrival of the monsoon. Bligh was therefore determined to be away as soon as possible to Batavia, where there were more frequent ships back to Europe, but could not face the thought of another sea voyage in the launch. He therefore bought, with money he could raise on the strength of his commission and his rank in the Royal Navy, a schooner which he named H.M.S. *Resource*. It was a small vessel only eleven feet longer than the launch, but it was properly decked and was a good deal more comfortable than their earlier boat. He set his men to work to prepare it for sea. Leaving Fryer in charge, he then went off on trips about the country-side with Wanjon and his wife, while David Nelson went botanising.

It was just like Tahiti all over again. His officers were slack and quarrelsome in his absence and Bligh came back and stormed at them and went away again. On 9 July Bligh records: 'The master's insolence and neglect induced me to give him written orders to attend and report to me the progress of the outfit of the *Resource*.' Relations went from bad to worse, and a month later Bligh writes of 'the vicious and troublesome nature of this man which can only be equalled by his ignorance and meanness'.

To Bligh's troubles was added the sudden loss of his friend, David Nelson. This ever-enthusiastic gardener had taken up his local botanising too soon, and when he caught a chill was quickly laid low and died of 'an inflammatory fever' a few days later, deeply lamented by Bligh who had derived from him not only close companionship over nearly two years, but much knowledge of Polynesian dialects and botany.

The *Resource* got away at last from Coupang on 20 August, towing the *Bounty*'s launch and escorted by two armed prahus for protection in these pirate-infested waters. This last voyage of the *Bounty*'s survivors was one of incessant grumbling, misery and contention. Things reached a head at Sourabaya where Bligh put in for supplies and was entertained by the Dutch governor. There was heavy drinking ashore among the crew and one of the Dutch officials was told by Purcell—no doubt the worse for drink—that they had all been so ill-used by Bligh that he would be court-martialled on his return to England, and that he would be hanged or blown live from a cannon's mouth. This story quickly got back to Bligh, who was striving to preserve his status and the good name of the Royal Navy under the difficult circumstances.

Things went from bad to worse. The departure arrangements were for Bligh to be taken out to mid-river in the governor's own boat where the *Resource* would meet him and take him off. At least this would be a dignified departure, with a touch of formality to it— a demonstration of how the navy could put on a show.

But H.M.S. *Resource* failed to arrive at the *rendezvous*. His men had mutinied, in a drunken, half-hearted sort of way. Bligh at length found his way on board his own boat at the dockside. He was by now in a raging temper and released a torrent of abuse at everyone he met. 'Where is Mr Fryer?' he demanded.

The ship's master at last appeared and received the full weight of Bligh's abuse.

'You not only use me ill,' Fryer replied innocently, 'but every man in the vessel, and every man will say the same.'

Others took up the cry. 'Yes, by God, we are used damn ill, nor have we any right to be used so.'

At this, Bligh once again resorted to arms, and seizing a bayonet he put Fryer and Purcell under arrest and returned to the shore with the rest of the men—'for I no longer found my honour or person safe among these people'.

The Dutch governor was asked to carry out an investigation into the men's complaints, and patiently did so over the following days— though one wonders what he made of this angry English lieutenant with his insubordinate officers and men—men who had, on the one hand performed such a remarkable demonstration of survival and navigation, and on the other suffered the loss of their ship as a result of an even more violent earlier mutiny. It must all have puzzled him and led him to consider again how the English were so successful in naval warfare and exploration.

In the end everyone seems to have wearied of the whole business and expressed more or less conditioned apologies and contriteness. There was not, after all, far to go now, and they were all longing for home, especially Bligh himself. Fryer and Purcell were packed into one of the prahus for safety, and H.M.S. *Resource* sailed less-than-proudly out of Sourabaya with her escort on 17 September, arriving without incident at Batavia two weeks later.

The last days together of the *Bounty*'s survivors were no happier than the previous weeks since their arrival at Coupang, though there were no further uprisings. The monsoon had arrived, the climate was wretchedly uncomfortable and unhealthy. Bligh himself caught a bad dose of malaria and Tom Hall died of it. Three more died later—Will Elphinstone, Peter Linkletter the quartermaster, and Bob Lamb the *Bounty*'s butcher.

Here at Batavia Bligh had reluctantly to sell the launch, and the *Resource*, too, for less than a third of the price he had paid for it.

Bligh learned that the next ship for Europe would sail in two weeks, and that there was accommodation on board for only three. He reserved this for himself, his clerk and his servant. Meanwhile, the others reasonably asked, how were they to keep themselves? They might be stranded here for weeks before they, too, could get a berth in a homeward-bound vessel. Bligh was the only person who could help them.

The climate of relations between the loyalists of the mutiny and their commander is shown in a letter Thomas Ledward, a stout supporter of Bligh throughout, who took no part in any of the troubles, and was a highly educated man, wrote home to his uncle:

'The captain denied me, as well as the rest of the gentlemen who had not agents, any money unless I would give him my power of attorney and also my will, in which I was to bequeath to him all my property, this he called by the proper name of security. . . . In case of my death I hope this matter will be clearly pointed out to my relations.'

Ledward at length obtained a berth in the Dutch ship *Welfare*, which did not live up to its name and was lost *en route* with all hands.

We get only one glimpse of Bligh on his passage back to England in the Dutch East Indiaman *Vlydte*, Captain Peter Couvret, and this is from the last pages of his narrative. He is watching the Dutch methods of navigation and sailing, taking a natural professional interest. His comments are not complimentary. Their manner of steering by compass, of correcting the course for leeway and of computing their daily run, he finds crude and primitive. 'It is not difficult,' he writes, 'to conceive the reason why the Dutch are frequently above ten degrees out in their reckoning. Their passages likewise are considerably lengthened by not carrying a sufficient quantity of sail.'

In spite of these shortcomings, the *Vlydte* succeeded in coming up-Channel and leaving Bligh and his companions at Portsmouth on 14 March 1790.

From Portsmouth Bligh hastened to London where he presented himself at the Admiralty to give an account of why he had returned without breadfruit or his ship. Word of the mutiny spread quickly about the capital. The *Gentleman's Magazine* echoed the general feeling that 'the distresses he has undergone entitle him to every reward. In navigating his little skiff through so dangerous a sea, his seamanship appears as matchless as the undertaking seems beyond the verge of probability.'

During April and May 1790 Bligh's name was on everyone's lips. He was received in audience by King George III, was entertained at a series of adulatory dinners and banquets. At the Royalty Theatre a 'fact told in action' spectacular entitled *The Pirates!* drew great crowds. Subtitled 'The Calamities of Captain Bligh', it included an Otaheitan Dance, a sketch called 'The attachment of the OTA-HEITAN WOMEN to, and their Distress at parting from, the BRITISH SAILORS', and 'An exact Representation of the Seizure of Captain BLIGH in the cabin of the BOUNTY, by the pirates'.

Bligh's account of his misfortunes, sent ahead of him from Coupang, had had the desired effect on Sir Joseph Banks, who was already busily engaged in persuading the Lord Commissioners to prepare another breadfruit expedition—again to be commanded by Bligh, if he was willing. As further proof of his confidence in his protégé, he saw to it that the House of Assembly in Jamaica granted Bligh a gratuity of 500 guineas as a token of its appreciation for his efforts.

United with his beloved Betsy and his girls at Lambeth, Bligh spent much of the summer of 1790 writing up his narrative, based on the log he had retained through all his adventures, on subsequent notes, and his memory. Published by the King's bookseller, George Nicol, under the title *A Voyage to the South Sea, undertaken by command of His Majesty, for the Purpose of Conveying the Bread-Fruit Tree to the West Indies,* it was an instant success.

Bligh's name was further kept before the public by the court martial to investigate the loss of his ship, which was convened on board H.M.S. *Royal William* at Spithead on 22 October. This was a brief, token affair to meet naval regulations. Everyone accepted that Bligh was a victim of a plot and was in no way to blame. The real court martial would be the one to judge those accused of causing and supporting the mutiny—and the Admiralty had no doubt that they would be brought to justice, for such a mountainous breach of discipline could not go unpunished.

John Fryer testified that he knew nothing of the mutiny until it broke out, Hayward and Hallett said that they had seen nothing suspicious, sensibly omitting to mention that the reason for this was that they were sound asleep on duty. There was no reference to the desertions on Tahiti, or the rows after the call at Nomuka, or Christian's plan to desert ship—which were known to Hayward and a number of the others too—or of the later mutiny at Sourabaya.

'The *Bounty* was forcibly seized by the said Fletcher Christian,' concluded the findings, 'and Lieutenant William Bligh is honourably acquitted of responsibility for the loss of his ship.'

The only reference to any disturbances on board the *Bounty* were made at a subsequent court martial on the same day in the same ship. Bligh had thought better of bringing charges against his master, whose evidence might be embarrassing if he told all. The wisdom of this decision was borne out by the later publication by Fryer of his own narrative, which included many scurrilous attacks on Bligh. But Bligh had decided to press charges against Purcell, who, along with the other survivors, had now safely returned from Batavia. They were for misconduct, insubordination, 'refractory behaviour'—six charges in all. Minutes of the evidence have been lost, but the verdict was 'That the charges had been in part proved against William Purcell, and did adjudge him to be reprimanded'.

He was lucky to get away so lightly. But Bligh was not disappointed. It was in his interests that the *Bounty* should be shown as a happy, well-disciplined ship until the sudden outbreak of rebellion.

To Bligh events seemed again to be flowing in his favour after all his calamities and sufferings. The loss of his ship had made him a national hero. The promotion he had sought for so long came to him rapidly, and twice over, first to commander and a few weeks later to post-captain. His family life was joyous and serene. A sixth child—yet another daughter—was born on 21 February 1791. And, one month after the satisfactory court martial, a frigate was despatched to the Pacific to search for the *Bounty* and her mutineers.

Within a few weeeks of Bligh's return, an announcement in the *London Chronicle* had underlined the Admiralty's determination to capture Christian and his cronies. 'It is said,' it ran, 'that by the express command of His Majesty two new sloops of war . . . are to be instantly fitted to go in pursuit of the pirates who have taken possession of the *Bounty*. An experienced officer will be appointed to superintend the little command, and the sloops will steer a direct course to Otaheite where, it is conjectured, the mutinous crew have established their *rendezvous*.' There was some delay after this due to the threat of war with Spain, but by October plans had been completed. One ship only was to take part, a twenty-four-gun frigate, the *Pandora*, with a strong party of marines on board. Tom Hayward, promoted to lieutenant, and John Hallett were included among the officers. Their eagerness to settle accounts with Christian and their familiarity with Tahiti and with the ways—as well as the looks—of their old shipmates, were reckoned to be priceless assets in the search.

The commander of the *Pandora* was a truly ferocious martinet (beside whom, it was said, Bligh was a lamb), one Captain Edward Edwards, forty-eight years old, survivor of a mutiny of his own nine years earlier which he had put down with consummate ruthlessness. There was no doubt that he would comb the Polynesian islands until he had rounded up every pirate. After that, the only danger was that Christian and the others might not survive the passage back to the hangman's noose at Spithead.

Finally, Banks's efforts to get away a second breadfruit expedition proved successful, and in March 1791 Bligh was instructed by the Admiralty to select a suitable vessel. This time he took no chances. He insisted on two ships, a brand new West Indiaman, the *Providence*, and a supporting brig, the *Assistant*, under the command of Lieutenant Nathaniel Portlock, who had been master's mate to Bligh in the *Resolution* with Cook. Bligh took endless pains over his other officers, too, choosing only those with the best records. In addition he had on board a lieutenant of marines, two corporals, a drummer and fifteen marine privates.

On 3 August, with the blessings of the King, his patron, and the whole nation, 'Breadfruit Bligh' (as he had come to be nicknamed, by some affectionately, by others ironically) sailed again for Tahiti. There must be no more trouble. He knew that he would not be forgiven for a second time.

The sixteen members of the *Bounty*'s company who had chosen to remain at Tahiti rather than follow Christian to some secret hideout, discovered to their surprise that they were not the first of their countrymen to settle permanently on the island. Not far from Matavai and getting on well with the natives, there was already living one John Brown, an able seaman from the *Mercury*, a dark-skinned, black-haired, heavily built and rather sinister fellow.

Brown, a heavy drinker and violent in his cups, had had an unhappy passage out from England. He was often at odds with his fellow seamen, and once had wounded a messmate in a brawl. Everyone was fed up with him when the brig anchored at Matavai after its passage from Tubai, and the captain put him ashore to cool off. The next day the captain was surprised to receive a letter from the troublesome fellow saying that he would like to remain on the island, and asking for a copy of the Bible, some carpenter's tools, nails and 'other trifling articles'. Delighted to be rid of him once and for all, Captain Cox gave his assent. 'I have no doubt that he will make himself useful to the Otaheitans,' wrote one of the *Mercury*'s officers innocently, 'and be very much caressed by them, especially as it will be out of his power to obtain any spirituous liquors.'

Before the *Mercury* left, Brown pronounced himself 'content with his situation' and was looking forward to a life removed from the temptation of alcohol and violence, and to a period of spiritual reform. This serene existence lasted just one month. At the end of that time the *Bounty*, full of liquor, arrived in Matavai Bay, and sixteen of her company—several of them more violent and quite as liquor-addicted as he was—came ashore to settle more or less permanently.

The members of this English outpost, made up from mutineers, victims of mutiny, a blind fiddler and a voluntary castaway with a conscience, now broke up into groups according to inclination. Some, like George Stewart, settled down to a quiet domestic existence. Stewart was formally married by the priests to a chief's daughter, whom he called Peggy, and later became an especially fond father to their daughter. Peter Heywood busied himself with a study of the Tahitian dialects and compiled a dictionary. Like Stewart, Skinner and McIntosh both had daughters, and Burkett and Millward had sons by their *tyo*s.

Tom McIntosh was also one of the most enthusiastic boat-builders. It was Morrison who conceived the idea of building an ocean-going launch in which to sail away to one of the Dutch East Indies settlements. He had no intention of spending the rest of his life on this island, and as one of those whose loyalties during the mutiny had not been too clearly defined and whose name had not been included by Bligh among those to whom he promised justice 'if ever I reach England', Morrison realised that it would be safer to give himself up as one who had escaped from the real mutineers than be captured by a searching vessel.

Morrison confided his plan to Tom McIntosh, whose carpentry skill would be priceless, and to John Millward. They could not hope to build the vessel in secret, and they gave out that she was for cruising about the island for pleasure and fishing. Seven more joined them when they heard about the project. It was difficult work with inadequate tools and timber that had to be felled and sawn, and a lack of so many metal parts. Coleman succeeded in building a forge and bellows, and this was a great help. Their launch was to be decked and to measure thirty feet overall—a veritable two-masted schooner.

These shipbuilders fell easily into the routine of discipline and watch-keeping, just as they had at Tubai. It comforted them to hoist the British flag on a flagpost and to hold Divine Service on Sundays, Morrison always delivering the address. Their vessel was to be grandly named H.M.S. *Resolution* after Cook's own flagship.

Charley Churchill and Mat Thompson, on the other hand, became politically ambitious and paid the price. This is what happened to these two roughs. At first they settled at Point Venus, leading worthless and indolent lives among the breadfruit and palms, womanising and working their way fast through their share of the *Bounty*'s wine and rum. Others who followed this way of life were Tom Burkett, John Sumner, Will Muspratt and—regrettably—John Brown from the *Mercury*, whose reformation had been so brief.

Trouble was inevitable. Thompson took a fancy to a young girl, and when he could not have her voluntarily, dragged her into the woods and raped her. When her brother heard about this he searched out Thompson and beat him unconscious. Thompson later returned, bruised and furious, to his hut and found it surrounded by natives—men, women and children. He ordered them away, speaking in English and no doubt wildly, and when they did not at once retire, he fired a musket at random among them. The ball killed a father and the infant he was holding and went on to injure a woman in the jaw.

This dissolute gang decided that it would be wiser to move to another part of the island before there was more trouble, and chose the kingdom of Tyarrabboo on the south coast. No one was able to say for sure just what happened there, but the survivors let it be known to the Matavaian colonists that the king of this province had died suddenly and that Churchill had been made sovereign in his place, no doubt by force of arms. Churchill and Thompson fell out, Thompson's musket was stolen—the worst loss that any white man could suffer.

At this point Burkett takes up the sorry story. 'I heard the report of a musket [he recounted], on which I ran up to Churchill's house, but was stopped by Thompson who stood in the door loading his musket. He asked me if I was angry: as I had no arms I saw it was in vain to say "Yes", and therefore said, "No. I hope you don't mean to take advantage of me." He told me, "No—not without you are angry," and then he said, "I have done him." Upon my approach I saw that Churchill was dead, the ball having passed below his shoulder, through his body, entering at his back. I now thought it high time to be off. . . .'

Revenge by the natives for the loss of their white monarch seems to have come swiftly. Seven of them approached Thompson, hailing him as their new king in Churchill's place, and beguiling him with flattery as they got between him and his arms. Then the largest of them hurled himself at Thompson, throwing him to the ground, and the others seized a plank and held it across his chest while the first beat in his skull with a stone. After cutting off his head, they buried his body.

Things settled down at Tyarrabboo after this, and nothing more was heard by the boatbuilders and the others at Matavai of this separatist group, the two little colonies living quite separate lives, although the incorrigible Brown decided to return to Matavai again.

The first anniversary of their settlement passed, the wet season set in again, and Morrison worked on the problem of sails for the *Resolution*. Without any canvas, they had to make do with native mats, sewn together. But the *Resolution* was a success, a fine sea boat, fast and easy to handle.

With the passing of the rainy season on 1 March 1791, the boat was launched again for further trials along the coast. Three weeks later Norman, Ellison, Byrn, McIntosh, Hillbrant and Millward embarked in the schooner, and with Morrison in proud command, sailed round the island to Tyarrabboo to show off their achievement to the others. When they were on shore greeting their old shipmates, whom they had not seen for so long, a runner arrived from Matavai with the news that some had feared and others had expectantly awaited for so long.

A great ship had arrived in the bay, the messenger recounted. Already an armed party had landed in search of them.

Captain Edward Edwards had enjoyed an uneventful and favourable passage from England. Unlike Bligh, he doubled Cape Horn in relatively calm conditions, and from Tierra del Fuego steered north-west towards Easter Island, sighting that lonely, myth-shrouded volcanic island on 4 March 1791. From here he altered course for Tahiti.

Christian and his party were settled into their permanent dwellings on Pitcairn as the *Pandora* neared Polynesia on the first stage of Edwards's hunt for his prey. On 16 March, with the armourers on board 'busily employed in making knives and iron work to trade with the savages' in exchange for news of Christian and the *Bounty*, the look-out sighted what the *Pandora*'s surgeon in his narrative described as 'a lagoon island of about three or four miles extent . . . well wooded, but had no inhabitants'. They named it Ducie's Island, in honour of the peer of that name—a patron of Edwards—and sailed on through the night.

They were passing the most easterly island of the Pitcairn Group, and were closing on the main island. During the night they passed Henderson and Oeno islands, still uninhabited today, although so near is Oeno that the Pitcairners of the twentieth century sometimes take their boats there for an outing and a few days' fishing, rather as Londoners make for Southend and New Yorkers for Coney Island on a fine summer's day. At dawn on 17 March Pitcairn itself was a few hours' sailing to the south of their route, just below the horizon. The *Pandora* sailed on, making a good pace towards Tahiti, where she anchored early in the morning of 23 March.

Never again would Edwards come so close to his prey. The first news he heard when he arrived in Matavai Bay was that the *Bounty* had sailed away, its destination a secret, six months earlier. On board were Fletcher Christian himself and eight more mutineers.

As soon as they heard of the arrival of the *Pandora*, except for a handful of hard-core mutineers who were determined to resist capture by every possible means, the intention of all the English settlers was to give themselves up without delay as a demonstration of their innocence. Their eagerness was so great that it became something of a race to reach the English man-'o-war. The winner was the armourer, Coleman, guiltless of any piracy and known to everyone as a forced detainee. Even before the *Pandora* had dropped anchor, Coleman was in the water swimming out. Peter Heywood was next. He found a canoe and paddled eagerly out and climbed on board. He was met on the quarterdeck by Lieutenant Larkin, the ship's first lieutenant.

'I suppose you know my story, sir?' Heywood began. Receiving no answer, he went on, 'I belong to the *Bounty*.'

Larkin again made no comment and went down to Edwards's cabin to inform him that they already had their second captive. Soon it was three. Stewart came out also by canoe, and the young men, under armed guard, were taken below to the captain's cabin.

Heywood had by now heard that his old friend Tom Hayward was on board, as well as Hallett, both now promoted to lieutenant. So two at least of those cast adrift had miraculously survived. Heywood asked eagerly for Tom Hayward 'supposing he might prove the assertions of our innocence'.

Edwards agreed and ordered Hayward to his cabin. Peter Heywood's hopes were soon dashed, for he 'received us very coolly, and pretended ignorance of our affairs'.

His old messmate's failure to support him was an especially savage blow. Then 'appearances being so much against us', Heywood later recounted, 'we were ordered to be put in irons, and looked upon,—oh infernal words!—as *piratical villains*'.

It had suddenly become horribly clear that Edwards intended to treat them all as guilty of mutiny until they had been proved innocent, and there were to be no exceptions. Dick Skinner was the next to give himself up, and he, too, was consigned below in irons. Only John Brown among the white colonists was spared. Like the natives, he was quick to recognise where the new strength on Tahiti lay, and allied himself with it. You did not argue with Royal Marines and four-pounders. Brown came on board with the latest news of his countrymen's whereabouts, and told Edwards that a number of them had built a schooner and were on board her on the other side of the island. They would not get far if they were pursued, Brown added, as they had few supplies and only a little water.

Lieutenants Corner and Hayward took the ship's pinnace and launch and set off along the coast in search of H.M.S. *Resolution*. It was a curious rounding-up operation. Only Sumner, Millward, Burkett, Muspratt, McIntosh and Hillbrant determined to make a stand. They fled inland and high up into the mountains with their muskets and a good supply of powder and shot.

The rest, under Morrison, put off in their schooner, not with the intention of fleeing from justice—quite the reverse—but to make their own way to the *Pandora* and give themselves up before they could be intercepted. When they caught sight of the two searching boats creeping along close inshore, Morrison crowded on all sail and made out to sea. Their hand-made vessel bowled along at a spanking pace and neither Hayward nor Corner could get near, which was very galling for them. Soon the schooner was over the horizon and the two lieutenants were obliged to put about and return.

On the other hand, Morrison later failed in his attempts to reach the *Pandora* without risking interception by the ship's boats—something he wished to avoid at all costs—and in the end was forced to sail his craft into a bay west of Paparra, some eighteen miles east round the coast from Point Venus, intending to work his way overland with his party and surrender on board the *Pandora* in Matavai Bay.

These movements were being spotted by the natives, all expectant for rewards, and Brown acted as unofficial agent and interpreter, so that Captain Edwards had a clear picture of the situation in order to prepare his next move.

On the following day Edwards despatched Lieutenant Corner with the launch, and then Tom Hayward in support with the pinnace, to Paparra, first to capture the elusive schooner and her crew, and then the mutineers who had made for the mountains. Corner arrived first. By this time his men were exhausted and he ordered them to rest before continuing the hunt.

Meanwhile Morrison and his party were working their way along this same shoreline on foot, heading for Matavai. Suddenly they came across the *Pandora*'s launch at anchor, and there was the crew, and their officer, all sound asleep. Morrison, without hesitation, awakened Lieutenant Corner, and asked to be taken with his men —all innocent, only seeking a passage back to England—to the ship.

Corner agreed to do so, but for the present he had other business. Pleased that he had completed without any trouble the first half of his mission, he left his prisoners in charge of the master's mate, and set off inland in the general direction of the rest of the fugitives.

Soon after this, Tom Hayward arrived in the *Pandora*'s pinnace, with John Brown as guide. We can imagine that this was an uneasy three-way confrontation: on the one side, Brown, volunteer casta-way who had lived for eighteen months with the *Bounty*'s mutineers, and Bligh's midshipman Hayward, who had been cast adrift with his captain; and on the other side James Morrison and his party, all pleading innocence. Hayward treated Morrison and the rest with the same cool contempt that he had shown Peter Heywood and George Stewart, and ordered their hands to be tied and the prisoners to be sent back under armed guard to the *Pandora*. Then Hayward marched boldly inland with Brown and his contingent of marines to help Corner in his search for the last of their quarry.

Both lieutenants had a hard time of it among the steep gorges, the rushing torrents and dense forests of Tahiti's uplands. Assailed by mosquitoes, sodden with sweat, torn by the undergrowth, depressed by the seeming hopelessness of their task, they climbed higher and penetrated more deeply into the mountainous centre of the island. But a good intelligence service was on their side. The natives, now quickly forgetting old loyalties, guided them towards the runaways' hideout.

Hayward's party were the first to get there. It was dark, and they could see nothing but the outline of a hut. There were men inside. Of that they were certain. They could hear them breathing, see the outline of their bodies. But were they white men or natives?

Brown, zealous as ever in his support of a righteous cause, volunteered to find out. Let the *Pandora*'s surgeon take up the tale:

'Creeping up to the place where they were asleep, he [Brown] distinguished them from the natives by feeling their toes: as people unaccustomed to wear shoes are easily discovered from the spread of their toes. Next day Mr Hayward attacked them, but they groun-ded their arms without opposition; their hands were bound behind their back and sent down to the boat under a strong guard.' Thus were all the *Bounty*'s crew on Tahiti apprehended.

This is the last we see of John Brown, the dark figure of the Tahiti round-up. He had served Edwards well, and when he applied to be allowed to sign on as an able seamen in the *Pandora*, the captain gladly agreed. One can only speculate on what tales he spun of his life on Tahiti; but this once drunken troublemaker was later, and rather surprisingly, described by an officer of the *Pandora* as 'a keen, penetrating active fellow, who rendered many eminent services, both in this expedition and the subsequent part of the voyage'. Brown also managed to put it about that he had 'avoided all inter-course and communication with the *Bounty*'s people. . . .' A minor figure in history, Brown, but the fact that we shall never know the truth adds to the curiosity we feel about him.

The *Pandora* remained at Matavai for five weeks after the last pris-oners were secured, refitting and wooding and watering, while Edwards did his utmost to extract from Tynah and his chiefs the likely whereabouts of the *Bounty*. In this he was singularly unsuccess-ful. Christian had told no one his destination for the good reason that he had not known it himself.

The *Pandora*'s armourer, as always, was especially busy. His first task was to build a cell for 'the pirates'. Edwards describes it as if it were some sort of isolation sanatorium 'for their more effectual security, airy and healthy in situation, to separate them from, and to prevent them from having any communication with, or to crowd and incommode, the ship's company'.

It was, in fact, a single round common cell built on the quarter-deck, entered by a scuttle in its roof, well secured by a bolt, and ventilated by two nine-inch-square scuttles. Sentries paced the roof night and day, and armed midshipmen supervised security on every watch. The ship's crew were forbidden communication with the prisoners; only the master-at-arms was allowed to speak to them, and then only on the subject of provisions. Apart from the clothes they were wearing when they were first confined, they had nothing except a hammock each, which, of course, they could not sling.

Inside this black cell every prisoner had his legs in irons, his wrists handcuffed so that movement was almost impossible. One of the prisoners described how Edwards ensured this:

'The first lieutenant in trying the handcuffs, took the method of setting his foot against our breasts and hauling the handcuffs over our hands with all his might, some of which took the skin off with them, and all that could be hauled off by this means were reduced and fitted so close that there was no possibility of turning the hand.'

'Pandora's Box' was the name the prisoners soon gave their cell. 'The heat of the place when it was calm,' wrote Peter Heywood, 'was so intense that the sweat frequently ran in streams to the scuppers, and produced maggots in a short time. The hammocks being dirty when we got them, we found stored with vermin of another kind, which we had no method of eradicating. Our only remedy was to lie naked—these troublesome neighbours and the two necessary tubs which were constantly kept in the place helped to render our situation truly disagreeable.'

They remained in Pandora's Box for the duration of their stay at Tahiti, and for nearly four months longer while the *Pandora* sailed from island to island in the Pacific, searching fruitlessly— and without plan or intelligence—for Christian and the *Bounty*.

While they were in Matavai Bay they were at first allowed to see their *tyo*s and their children, conversation being conducted through the vents. Tough sailors the *Pandora*'s men may have been, but they were not hardened gaolers and were deeply touched by these visits. Stewart's marriage had been a romantic and blissfully happy one. A few years later a missionary who landed on Tahiti was told of its ending. 'A beautiful little girl had been the fruit of their union, and was at the breast when the *Pandora* arrived. The interview was so affecting and afflicting that the officers on board were overwhelmed with anguish, and Stewart himself, unable to bear the heartrending scene, begged that she might not be admitted again on board. She was separated from him by violence and conveyed on shore in a state of despair and grief too big for utterance.' Peggy died of a broken heart two months later.

The *Pandora* weighed from Matavai Bay on 8 May 1791 to begin the search for Christian and the other mutineers. By the middle of August, when she was north of Fiji, Edwards had to admit defeat and set course west for Endeavour Straits and the long passage home.

Now Edwards was no Bligh or Cook. Not only had his search been without plan, but he had by now succeeded in losing one of the ship's boats and its crew, and also H.M.S. *Resolution*, which for a while had sailed with him, manned by a crew from his own ship. He was, in short, as incompetent as he was a wickedly cruel officer. He never even reached as far as the Endeavour Straits in the *Pandora*.

Edwards kept a more northerly course than Bligh had done and approached the Great Barrier Reef at a point where there are few breaks. These were unknown seas and the result was almost a foregone conclusion. In fact Bligh had gone so far as to predict that 'Captain Edwards would never return as he did not know the navigation of Endeavour Straits'. As usual when it came to navigation, Bligh was right. Missing by a few miles the one wide passage later discovered by Flinders, he sailed slap into the reef on the night of 28–29 August, even though he had a boat out reconnoitring ahead.

It took the *Pandora* some eleven hours before she finally broke up. During the first hours there seemed to be some hope of saving her, and the men were kept hard at the pumps. Later, as she filled, preparations were made for abandoning ship. The cannon were sent overboard, the top hamper cleared, rafts prepared, provisions brought up for the long open-boat boyage to Timor—all undertaken with the ship at an ever increasing list and sinking deeper in the water.

The prisoners, tumbled together in one corner of Pandora's Box, became increasingly anxious as the hours passed and no one took any steps to free them. In desperation they at last broke their leg irons, to give themselves at least some chance of swimming if the hatch were ever unlocked so that they could escape. This is how Morrison describes what happened next:

'As soon as Captain Edwards was informed that we had broke our irons he ordered us to be handcuffed and leg ironed again with all the irons that could be mustered, though we begged for mercy. . . . The master-at-arms and corporal were now armed with each a brace of pistols and placed as additional sentinels over us, with orders to fire among us if we made any motion; and the master-at-arms told us that the Captain had said he would either shoot or hang to the yard arms those who should make any further attempt.'

Later, the three non-mutineers, Coleman, Norman and McIntosh, whom Bligh had named as being forcibly detained on board the *Bounty*, were released to work at the pumps. Byrn was also released, and two more—Muspratt and Skinner—had their handcuffs removed. The rest resorted to prayer, calling out in anguish from time to time, and threatened with a ball in their heads by the master-at-arms if they made any attempt to remove their irons again.

In the last panic-stricken minutes before the ship went down, and when the captain had already abandoned ship—he was by no means the last to leave—the master-at-arms dropped the key down to the unfortunate prisoners, and some were able to release themselves before the water poured in, though they were still trapped.

There was only one moment of heroism in this dismal episode in British naval history. At the very last, a Will Moulter, the bo'sun's mate, risked his life by pausing to unbolt the scuttle and throw it aside. The remaining prisoners fought their way out through the narrow gap and plunged into the sea. But four were still manacled, and they all went down—John Sumner, Dick Skinner, Henry Hillbrant, and Peggy's beloved George Stewart.

'Four of the mutineers were lost in the ship,' ran Edwards's bald statement at the court martial many months later. And no one asked him to elaborate. His callousness towards the survivors continued to the end of the voyage. During their period of recovery on a nearby island, the prisoners were kept apart from the others, firmly tied and deliberately deprived of any shade from the tropical sun until, as one of them described their condition, 'our skin flea'd off from head to foot, though we kept ourselves covered in the sand during the heat of the day'.

On the long arduous journey to Timor they were kept bound hand and foot in the bottom of the boats for much of the time and suffered many threats of having their brains blown out by Edwards.

The boats made Coupang on 17 September, when the same Mr Timotheus Wanjon welcomed them and offered the same hospitality that Bligh and his men had enjoyed more than two years earlier. For Lieutenants Hayward and Hallett it was their second disembarkation at this port from an open boat, in rags and half-starved. For the rest of the *Bounty*'s old crew, the reception was less warm. At Edwards's orders they were placed at once in a prison, in stocks. A week later when the Dutch surgeon made a routine visit, the stench and filth were so awful that he refused to enter until the place had been cleaned out by slaves.

This ill-treatment of the prisoners continued all the way back to the Cape of Good Hope where Edwards transferred them to the English man-o'-war H.M.S. *Gorgon*. It says much for their physical and mental resilience that any of them survived. The worst of their ordeal was now over. They were treated humanely on board the

Gorgon, and their conditions had much improved by the time they reached Spithead. There they were removed to another vessel, the *Hector*, to await their court martial. According to Morrison, 'we were treated in a manner that renders the humanity of her captain and officers much honour, and had beds given us and every indulgence that our circumstances would admit or allowed'.

On the day when the ten surviving prisoners sighted their homeland again for the first time for nearly five years, 18 June 1792, Bligh himself was at the other end of the world, back on the island where all his troubles had begun. He had arrived at Tahiti to begin once again to collect his breadfruit plants on 10 April, following the same course from the Cape of Good Hope that he had navigated on his first voyage. At Adventure Bay in Tasmania he noted that at least one of the apple trees he had planted was still alive, so that he could in after years claim to have been the progenitor of that island's apple industry. Soon after he landed in Matavai Bay he observed other evidence—other fruit—of his earlier voyage. 'A woman with a child in her arms eighteen months old, calling herself the wife of McIntosh, late of the *Bounty*, and gone home in the *Pandora*, came to see me today,' wrote Bligh in his log. This was Mary, and her daughter Elizabeth. There were other progeny of his old crew to be seen about the village, the pretty little orphan of George and Peggy Stewart being cared for by her family, the dusky infant sons of Burkett and Millward and Dick Skinner's little daughter.

It is hardly surprising that Bligh took such an interest in every-thing that had happened after he was cast adrift, and there are many references to news of Christian and 'his villains' in the *Providence*'s log. It was not until many years later, when he was a man of over sixty, that he learned how close to Christian's lair he had sailed in reaching Tahiti—almost as close as Edwards himself when he had just missed Pitcairn.

But on this, his final visit to Tahiti, much of the pleasure and interest of the island seemed to be missing. Things were no longer the same, or perhaps this 'paradise on earth' was tainted by past memories. He does not seem to have picked up again his old close and affectionate relationship with Tynah. Other Englishmen who had since called at the island—and no doubt some of the rougher elements among the *Bounty*'s company—had taught the natives uncouth habits. 'Such vile expressions are in the mouth of every Otaheitan,' he wrote, 'and I declare that I would rather forfeit anything than to have been in the list of ships that have touched here since April, 1789'—the date of his own departure.

Even their appearance had changed for the worse. 'The quantity of old clothes left among these people is considerable; they wear such rags as truly disgusts us. It is rare to see a person dressed in a neat piece of cloth which formerly they had in abundance and wore with such elegance. Their general habillments,' he continues, 'are now a dirty shirt and an old coat and waistcoat; they are no longer clean Otaheitans, but in appearance a set of ragamuffins with whom it is necessary to observe great caution.'

Bligh is clearly thankful to be away again, safe with his supply of breadfruit plants—twice as many as before—out into the clean Pacific and back to his favourite occupation of plotting unknown islands and navigating unknown waters. He adds vastly to the knowledge of that treacherous area of reefs and keys, hidden rocks and islets, between the northern tip of the Australian continent and New Guinea.

The *Providence* arrived in the West Indies at the end of January 1793, with the greater part of the breadfruit alive and in good order. The colony's planters and merchants were delighted, and looked forward to a new period of plenty and even greater profits. Speeches were delivered in praise of Bligh, the House of Assembly voted him one thousand guineas, and he received an official address thanking him for his 'exertions and great merit in bringing to so happy a conclusion the beneficent object of our most gracious Sovereign'. Banks in his turn informed the Jamaican assembly that by their generous vote 'in favour of Captain Bligh, you have made a good man happy, and a poor man comparatively rich'.

The black slaves, it seems, regarded with wonder these new plants whose fruit was to nourish them. They were allowed to approach closely the *Providence* at anchor at Port Royal and to inspect the plants put out specially for public exhibition. 'The poor negroes,' remarked one of the *Providence*'s lieutenants, 'were loud in their praises of "de ship da hab de bush", and were constantly paddling round the "floating forest".'

On his arrival in England again on 9 September 1793, Bligh could write with truth and justice in his log that 'This voyage has terminated with success.' But when he wrote these words he was still unaware of two consequences of his voyage and of his long absence from home—both of them bitter and ironical, both somehow typical of the special brand of misfortune, deserved or undeserved, that dogged his whole life.

The first he did not learn for some time: that when his breadfruit matured and multiplied and fruited, the slaves would not eat them, finding them distasteful and insipid, and preferring their own home-grown plantains.

The second intelligence he learned almost as soon as he came ashore: that public and service opinion had turned against him while he had been away, and that there was even downright hostility towards him among the Lords Commissioners of the Admiralty.

When he had returned before after failing in his mission, suffering a mutiny and losing his ship, he had been proclaimed a hero. Three years later, after a triumphantly successful voyage, Lord Chatham the First Lord refused to see him, though he received his junior, Lieutenant Portlock.

What had led to this snub, this 'unaccountable conduct' as he complained of it to Sir Joseph Banks? He was not long in learning who had succeeded in transforming his public image from a deeply wronged, deeply suffering hero, to a paragon of ruthlessness and cruelty.

10

*Pitcairn Island:
'humanizing
the rude savages'*

✣

'ALTHOUGH that man Christian has, in a rash unguarded
moment, been tempted to swerve from his duty to his king
and country, as he is in other respects of an amiable character and
respectable abilities, should he elude the hand of justice, it may be
hoped that he will employ his talents in humanising the rude savages;
so that, at some future period, a British Iliou may blaze forth in the
south with all the characteristic virtues of the English nation, and
complete the prophecy by propagating the Christian knowledge
amongst the infidels. As Christian has taken fourteen [twelve]
beautiful women with him from Otaheite, there is little doubt of his
intention of colonising some undiscovered island.'

Thus wrote George Hamilton, Captain Edward Edwards's
surgeon in the *Pandora*, after that ship had failed to discover Christian and his party in the Pacific. Hamilton knew Christian by
reputation only, but this rosy interpretation of Christian's likely
intentions—so different from that of Hamilton's commander—was
in fact not so very distant from reality. But another eighteen years
were to pass before anyone from the outside world penetrated the
waters of Pitcairn to learn how far he had failed or succeeded in
establishing his Rousseauesque settlement.

Christian's first favourable impressions were confirmed during

233

their early weeks on the island. They could have ranged the Pacific for another four months without discovering a home more perfectly suited to their needs. In many respects Pitcairn is a typical Pacific island, probably formed by the top of a volcano whose base may rest thousands of feet below the sea. In its geology and configuration it might be Tahiti if the sea had risen five or six thousand feet, swallowing all but the highest peaks of that much larger island. The area on the north-east side of Pitcairn, above Bounty Bay, which Christian had chosen as the site of their future village—no other was possible—represents almost all the flat land on the island, a mere ninety acres of a total area of some 1,200 acres. Rolling land accounts for about a third of this total, much of it cultivable. The rest is steeply sloping or inaccessible cliffs, which on the south-eastern side rise almost vertically to a height of over one thousand feet and are capped by volcanic ash. Deep, narrow valleys cut the sides of the hills and cliffs, and their bottoms become fast-flowing streams after heavy rain.

Fairy terns and noddies wheel about the cliffs and the breaking surf, and in 1790, when the island was still thickly wooded, the red-tailed tropic birds and warblers nested in the miro and rata trees. The timber from these trees, hard and good to work, was ideal for building and fencing and for making canoes. And the seas —as they are today—were rich in red snapper, mackerel, grey mullet, rock cod and lobster. The red colluvial soil produced fine vegetables and fruit, and many brilliantly coloured flowers like hibiscus and bougainvillaea.

Besides all these rich advantages, Pitcairn enjoys a mellower climate than Tahiti and almost all the other Polynesian islands. As the traveller Richard Shaw Nichols wrote sixty years later: 'Had it been found in the right quarter of the globe it might have been taken for a bit of primeval paradise. Situated just within the tropics, the climate is delicious—the heat of summer is moderated by the daily sea breezes—the island knows no winter. Contagious diseases, foul atmospheres, direful social convulsions, carking cares are all unknown.' Pitcairn escapes Tahiti's wet season with its oppressive high humidity. Some eighty inches of rainfall a year are spread out evenly; and the temperature in winter rarely falls below sixty-five, or in summer rises above eighty degrees. The skies are often clear blue for days on end, and the horizon is distant and sharp through every point of the compass.

Christian remained in command of the party for the first weeks as if they had still been on shipboard. He had no intention of taking on the responsibility of governing the island; but everyone recognised the need for a strong organising hand until they became settled. After that they would see. Isabella* made herself responsible for the women's affairs while they continued to live half communally on the shore of Bounty Bay and half on the ship. As the daughter of a chief, quite apart from her commanding stature, she had naturally played this part since the reunion with Christian seven months earlier.

The fair weather which had allowed them to make the landing broke the following day, the wind blew hard, holding up the unloading of the *Bounty*'s hold. But on 21 and 22 January it died down again. Christian gave orders for everyone to work throughout the daylight hours to get up from below everything they might need. The urgency of this task was very real. Bounty Bay offers little shelter from the prevailing easterly and north-easterly winds and he feared that the vessel's anchor might drag or the cable might snap, driving her on to inaccessible rocks, or worse still out to sea.

There was so much that they needed. Even after they had got ashore their personal possessions, the provisions, the plants and seeds and the livestock, the remaining wine and liquor, the tools and arms, the ship's forge and the cooking equipment in the galley, the *Bounty* still remained a priceless source of material. The masts and spars, the stocks of cord and rope, the cabin fittings, the ladders and companionways, the rails and the decks—never again were they likely to have the opportunity of acquiring ready-sawn and matured timber on this scale; nor, of almost greater importance, the nails that secured them. Suddenly they began to understand the high scale of value placed on the products of Western civilisation by the Polynesians.

The cutter was not a convenient vessel for these operations. She

---

* There was a certain historical rightness in Isabella's setting up home on a small island. Christian had given his wife this name in honour of his relative Isabella Curwen, who married into the Christian family. She was an heiress of considerable substance, and one wonders what she would have made of her namesake. Among the properties Isabella Curwen conveyed to her husband, John Christian, was the island named after her, and shortened to Belle Island, on Lake Windermere in Westmorland—a miniature Pitcairn less than half its size but quite as beautiful in its English way.

was too valuable to risk being smashed on the rocks, and was used only for taking the men out to the ship and back to the shore at night. The jolly boat was so rotten and leaky that she was not worth preserving except for firewood. So Christian had rafts made from the *Bounty*'s hatches, and with their cargoes lashed down firmly, these were hauled to and from the shore by ropes, where the women unloaded them.

By midday on 23 January, their work was finished and the *Bounty* had been stripped of everything that could be conveyed by these rafts. The topgallant masts had been sent down, and the fore, main and mizzenmasts. All had been sawn up, lashed and sent ashore, where the strong women had dragged them up the beach to the foot of the cliffs and beyond the reach of the tide.

Now the eight white men and the six natives awaited a word from Christian. They were standing about on the forecastle deck, drinking mugs of rum from the last barrel still on board. Quintal and McKoy, notorious for their tippling, had been at it all through the morning as they had worked. On shore, a quarter mile distant, some of the women were dragging the last raft load out of the surf. Others had fires going and were preparing the midday meal.

Christian appeared from below. He was stripped to the waist, and like the other mutineers was almost as brown as the natives themselves. His chest was gleaming with sweat. He called the mutineers about him, and they squatted or sat on the deck. They knew what he was going to say for they had discussed it as they had worked, and at night on shore about the fire before they had settled down in their makeshift tents. Their ship was now no more than a hulk. The decks which a few days before had been littered with stores and alive with penned goats, hogs, and hens, were now cleared and empty. Above, where for so many months they had been able to look up to see the masts and yards and the network of rigging, the grey sails taut and filled, there was now only blue sky.

'Well, lads, are we to run her ashore now?' Christian asked. 'We can do no more with her here.' He knew that there had been much talk already, and that feelings were not unanimous. One or two had favoured keeping the *Bounty* at anchor for a while longer, others were for destroying her at once—without delay, before minds could change, before perhaps the natives might form a conspiracy to sail away with the women: that would be difficult but not impossible.

Christian and Jack Adams favoured a middle course, to run her on shore where she could later be dismantled. This way they would on the one hand waste none of her precious timbers, on the other preserve for a while, and for their comfort, the knowledge that they had not yet, all at once, cut themselves off for ever from the world. With her hull intact, however damaged by the pounding of the Pacific and the rocks of Pitcairn, the *Bounty* would represent at least a symbol of possible escape.

Will Brown also favoured the saving of the *Bounty* for the time being, and spoke up to say so.

Ned Young said, 'Let us leave her anchored where she is and get ashore for dinner.'

But the others argued for getting her ashore while the wind and the tide were favourable; and at length Christian said with the decisive voice of authority, 'We'll break out the anchor now and see where she goes. Ned, is the cutter alongside and ready? We will have to get smartly into her.'

The six natives were watching from a distance, half understanding what was being discussed, but with no voice in decisions. They were not resentful. They knew their place. Perhaps one of them saw Mat Quintal slip quietly into the waist and disappear below. But if he did he said nothing. It was not his business. Their business was for'ard, at the windlass with their masters. All hands were needed to raise the big bower anchor.

They heaved at the windlass, bodies almost horizontal with the deck, the sweat pouring off their backs under the early afternoon sun, Christian urging them on and sometimes lending his own weight and strength. The anchor was just clear of the sea, water dripping from its rusty flukes, when they heard a sound from the shore, cries of alarm above the sound of the pounding surf. The women were standing at the edge of the sea, some half in the water, waving their arms.

Christian quickly blocked the windlass, giving the chocks a couple of hefty blows, and looked round. There was smoke rising from the main hatch, increasing in volume every moment, and he could hear the dread crackling sound of fire at sea.

Everyone was running aft, white men and natives, crying the only word there was to cry—'Fire!' But they were helpless to do anything about it, and it was growing in size fast, whipped up by the onshore wind. All buckets, even the pumps, had been sent ashore the previous day. Already the freed ship was drifting towards the rocks.

'It's no good, lads, into the cutter,' Christian was shouting. The men were gathering on the starboard side, above the cutter, and the first were over the rail on one of the two ropes that hung down the *Bounty*'s side. Only one man was not yet with them. Then he appeared from aft, a lurching figure, fair in complexion, broad-shouldered, of medium height. It was Mat Quintal, drunk as a lord and fresh from his fire-raising, a sly expression on his face, making his way forward. He had earlier concealed a cask of pitch—enough to set fire to a fleet—and ignited it in the carpenter's store.

'Where have you been, you scoundrel?' Christian shouted at him.

For a drunk man, Quintal had his answer ready fast. 'Best to be done with the old ship. Or the indians would have had her and done for us.'

He was quick on his legs, too, when the roar of a sudden new gust of flame sounded behind him. It was like an explosion. He was on the rope and over the side before any of the natives, and before his crony, Will McKoy.

McKoy was lingering. He was not leaving behind the half empty cask of liquor. He staggered across the deck with it for a few yards and then cried out for help. Two answered the call, and between the three of them they had it to the rail and over the side on a rope, lowering it as if it were a frail priceless piece of furniture into the bottom of the cutter.

'Pull away,' Christian called out. Even down here in the water they could feel the heat of the flames, shooting half as high as the masts had once stood. The whole midships section of the *Bounty* had been caught and the wind was blowing some of the flames low over the water and the smoke onto the beach.

Christian steered the cutter through the half-concealed rocks and made towards the beach, riding in high on a roller, and sweeping in the last fifty yards when it curled over and broke. The women waded out to meet it, clutching the gunwale as if it were their last and inadequately small bastion of security now that their ship was gone. They were all wailing in a chorus of grief and some were tearing their hair and beating their fists against their temples.

Jack Williams leaped over the side with the grapnel and line, and pushed them aside in order to reach the beach before the boat was swamped. The rest of the men followed him.

Few of the party ate any of the dinner the women had prepared. Quintal and McKoy had some of the baked breadfruit taken from the embers of the fire and drank some coconut milk before lying down to sleep off their grog. Most of the rest just sat on the rocks watching the *Bounty* drift towards the shore, the flames increasing in height and extent until they reached from stem to stern, and the whole ship was consumed by the inferno.

It was remarkable how long the fire took to burn itself out. At dusk the flames began to diminish slowly, though their brightness gave the opposite impression, and an hour later the sparks in their thousands were still shooting up, racing higher than the clifftops before extingushing themselves in the illuminated clouds of smoke.

The women scarcely let up their wailing for a minute, and with the coming of darkness the spectacular but melancholy spectacle caused many of the men, the white mutineers as well as the natives, to cry in chorus with them. Voluntary exiles the white men may have been, but the end of the *Bounty* was like the slamming of the cell door in their new prison; while for the conscripted natives and most of the women, it was the end of any hope of returning to their Tahitian homes and families.

By midnight the *Bounty* was burnt to the water. She had not drifted far from her anchorage. Her bottom had soon struck a submerged rock, and now she lay some three hundred yards out from the shore with the waves washing over her, extinguishing piecemeal the outline of her hull etched red against the black water. Poop and forecastle had long since been consumed and only one or two of her ribs still rose, scarlet and curving, above her corpse. These remained flaming a while longer like torchlights above a ceremonial funeral carriage, before they collapsed with a hiss into the sea.

By the early hours of the morning only a faint glow out in the bay lit up the last of the smoke drifting above them and over the island.

All the settlers, brown and white, at length fell asleep, and the last of the *Bounty* sank in the shallow waters of the bay that was to bear her name for ever.

No one seems to have thought of punishing, or even remonstrating with, Mat Quintal for burning the *Bounty*. The natives regarded it as an act of fate, like a hurricane or the spread of a fatal disease. Some god had deemed that they deserved to suffer this catastrophe, and Quintal's hand had only been used to carry it out. He was not to blame. McKoy believed that his friend had done the right thing. The opinions of the others, led by Christian, was that this was no time to fall out among themselves. Quintal and McKoy had always needed careful watching. They were violent men at any time, knowing nothing of self-discipline; and on this little island they would need to be watched more carefully than ever.

Besides, there was too much to do. It would be easy enough to survive here like animals. But if they were going to create a civilised community there must be order and routine in their lives, and to achieve them required a lot of hard work.

The morning after the *Bounty*'s fire, the sea brought in on the tide a mass of charred splinters, and black ash, which covered the rocks along the shore as if that ancient Pitcairn volcano had erupted again in the night. Here and there blackened, half-burnt timbers could be seen cast up among the rocks. Their first task was to retrieve these before the next high tide took them out to sea again. Not all could be saved. It was heavy work shifting them above the high-tide limit and many escaped before they could be reached. For weeks after these valuable lengths of timber, the fruit of an oak forest 10,000 miles distant, were seen in the ocean about Pitcairn, or cast up on some inaccessible part of the shore.

Gravity, the settlers soon learned, was the first enemy on Pitcairn. Except for the small plateau of flat land above and to the west of Bounty Bay, it was uphill or downhill work wherever you walked, and as they were always carrying heavy loads, a full day's work left them exhausted.

The first and most difficult task was to drag their stores and supplies to this plateau—over three hundred feet up the rocks and dusty red soil of the cliff-face. The burden was relieved in two ways. Ropes and pulleys salvaged from the ship, secured to the trunks of palms, were used to provide a lift for the heavy stores piled up on the beach. Then Isabella discovered a footpath. It was scarcely discernible through the undergrowth and was broken by erosion and falls of rocks over the years. Only a Polynesian would have recognised it for what it was. But it was evidently cut out of the cliff by the early settlers who had chosen this same bay for their landing place, and, perhaps centuries earlier, had faced the same problems of raising from the beach the stores they had brought—perhaps from Tahiti, too—to the island's uplands.

The natives were overjoyed and encouraged in their work by this evidence that their forebears had lived here. Later, when Christian showed his wife the remains of the settlement, the familiar carvings still recognisable on old lengths of wood, the foundation stones of their houses, and the carvings and paintings in a cave in an inlet on the south side of the island, she and the other women were so reassured that they scattered about the islands in groups in the hope of finding fellow natives who perhaps had hidden in fear on the arrival of the *Bounty*. It was, of course, a fruitless search. But the knowledge that others of their own race had been here, had cultivated the land—the breadfruit plantation in the centre of the island proved that—and worshipped in *morais* like their own at Tahiti, greatly comforted them and made them more contented in their subservient role.

By the end of February 1790 the stores and all but the heaviest lengths of timber had been hauled up the cliff-face from Bounty Bay and piled on the level land where they intended to build their dwellings. Christian had surveyed the island more accurately now and had decided to put it to the other white men that the flat land and the rolling land in the centre of the island, with its shallower valleys and good natural drainage, should be divided into nine equal parts, each a private estate for one of them. Here they would grow their own crops, sharing between them the services of the six native men for the heavier work as they required them.

The arrangement was agreed to by the others, and the division of the island went ahead without any fuss, the lines of demarcation following the twisting valleys through the woodland. Some were better off than others in the lie of their land or its readiness for clearance or its distance from the proposed site of the village. But the merits and the demerits worked out fairly evenly, and on an island as richly endowed as Pitcairn, it seemed unnecessary to quarrel about small advantages. The discovery later on one of the estates of a number of cloth plants aroused jealousy for a while, but Christian asked the owner to divide his crop equally among the others and this, too, was settled agreeably.

'The natives,' one reporter noted later, 'became contented slaves.' For the present, and no doubt because of the natural promiscuity of the Polynesians, the sharing arrangement, with only three women between the six of them, caused no resentment.

During these first months they were all too busy to give much thought to the confined nature of their environment, to the potentially dangerous imbalances and injustices of their community, and to the problems that must lie ahead when they realised that they could live as well idly as industriously. Homemaking is an absorbing occupation and there was no time for brooding.

In clearings chopped out from the miro, banyan and palm trees on the plateau, the families built their houses, using as material both the *Bounty*'s timbers—these formed the foundations and corner uprights—and the wood they had felled on the sites. The standard pattern was of two rooms, one above the other, the lower raised a foot or two off the ground, the upper sleeping area reached by a ladder. A wide area was left open on the sides on both floors, and the pitched roof was covered with thickly matted palm leaves. To save the carrying of water, a wooden gutter ran along the sides to catch the rain which was fed into one of the *Bounty*'s casks. These houses combined the best in European and Polynesian design and materials for the mixed-race community that was to live in them. Advice was proffered from family to family, but no rules were laid down. All that Christian insisted on was that they must be invisible from the sea. The banyan tree provided the perfect screen and a long line of them was left on the seaward side of the community like a permanently drawn curtain.

Jack Williams from the Channel Islands, the slim dark sailor who had often acted as armourer's mate to Coleman in the *Bounty*, set up the forge in one part of the village; and nearby the sawing pit was dug for the cutting of planks. By the middle of the year—it was winter but the fall in temperature was scarcely discernible—the village was beginning to assume a more orderly aspect, and the white men began to go out in the mornings with their tools to clear their land and plant their crops. Since they had arrived, the taro plant had been discovered, another useful staple food—there seemed no limit to the natural riches of this island. And now these new farmer-sailors began planting the yam and sweet-potato seeds, the sugar cane, banana and plantain plants they had brought from Tahiti and Tubai.

The natural ecology of the little island suffered another fearful shock when they decided to let loose the livestock. It seemed much less trouble to allow them to run free to breed and fend for themselves than to contain them in enclosures where they would have to be fed daily, although most households often kept one fattening pig in a sty and a tethered goat for its milk. Some would probably escape anyway, and with their good supply of powder for their seventeen muskets, they could at any time be shot for food. The chickens lived communally and scratched about the village wherever their fancy took them, the unusual but evocative sound of the cock crowing providing the white men with a morning reminder of home.

But the hens were not willing layers in this climate, and never met the islanders' need for eggs. It was this failure that led to the community's first tragedy.

The sea birds nested thickly on the cliff-faces, unafraid of man, and the women went out daily to collect their eggs. In October, even before Jack Williams had completed work on his house, his wife Pashotu slipped and fell to her death down the cliffs. It was their first loss—but by no means the last on these dangerous cliffs—and Williams took it hard.

A few days later, Isabella gave birth to a son, the first native-born Pitcairner. She and Christian prosaically named him after the day of the week and the month, Thursday October Christian, and he was baptised by Will Brown, now Christian's closest friend. And so their numbers were brought up again to twenty-eight, one of mixed race. But only briefly. Tinafanaea, the woman shared by the Tubaians Oho and Tetaheite, fell ill with a growth on her neck. She died mysteriously within a few weeks. So now the six natives had only two women between them.

By the end of 1790 the community had settled down into a routine of work and recreation. The cutter was used for fishing when the weather allowed, and the natives began building two canoes for their own fishing when they were not needed in the fields. The women helped one another about the village, kept the fires going, washed the clothes and made new ones from the *Bounty*'s sails, and did the cooking and housework much as they would have done on Tahiti. The white men went out with muskets when they wanted meat and shot the hogs, which were breeding fast and could only be kept out of the plantations by close fencing.

The native men lived at peace with one another and relations were good with most of the white men. Only Quintal and McKoy remained a trouble, and everyone on the island except Christian more or less feared this tough inseparable pair, whose violence was uncontrollable when they were drunk, and bad enough when they were sober. There was speculation on how they would get on when they had exhausted their own supplies of wine and liquor.

Quintal and McKoy had little to do with the other white men, who formed themselves into two groups, Jack Adams and Ned Young who had adjoining gardens and houses and lived more closely with the natives, and were judged by the others to exchange wives freely with each other and the native men; and Christian, Martin, Mills and Brown.

Fletcher Christian's friendship with Ned Young had died a slow death since the mutiny. These two were the only men who at first shared the secret of the mutiny, and the growth of Christian's regret and remorse was matched by his feeling of resentment towards the man who had incited him on, until he began to believe—with some reason—that the tragedy would never have occurred but for the malevolent intervention of this dark intriguer who had taken none of the risk and in a court martial would hardly be implicated.

For his part, Ned Young, a highly educated and articulate young man, felt he was being treated shabbily and detested Christian's pious moodiness. It was not he who had acted violently. His motive in suggesting that they should rid themselves of their tyrannical commander was to relieve his friend of the burden hanging from his neck—to show him the way out of his private hell. In Young's eyes it was Christian's decision alone which had started the mutiny.

As to Jack Williams, he remained a lonely figure, Pitcairn's only widower, unhappy and increasingly resentful. He had little to do with the others and kept himself occupied at his forge, where there was always plenty of work mending and making tools, converting the cutlasses into billhooks, and keeping an edge on the axes.

Williams, Quintal and McKoy were the sources of potential danger in the community. But nobody discussed them for the present. It was as if there was a pact of silence among the islanders. In this tight community the delicate balance of relations could so easily be upset.

There were other, and inevitable, strains and stresses which revealed themselves. Although the white men knew that they could never safely leave the place, they all pined for their homes—Isaac

Martin for Nantucket, Ned Young for St Kitts, Christian for Cumberland and his brothers, especially for Edward, and Jack Adams for the hurly-burly of Wapping on the Thames where he had lived all his life.

The women, too, were showing signs of restlessness. Even those who had come of their own free will now felt an acute longing for the wider spaces of Tahiti and the gossip and familiar faces of Matavai.

Added to the danger that no one wanted to be here was the fact that Pitcairn was just not big enough. Its remoteness and inaccessibility, ruggedness and smallness, all the things that made it an ideal refuge also made it domestically unsatisfactory, especially for a disgruntled mixed-race community. Rousseauism was all very well, but it first needed space, and the claustrophobia of a small island is a desperate disease. No doubt this is why the early Polynesian community had fled; it is certainly the reason why the smaller Pacific islands used rarely to be inhabited for long by the same tribe, and those huge double-hulled canoes sailed from island to island on their eternal odysseys.

If the Pitcairners had but known it, the awful lesson was there, 1,200 miles to the east, where the nearest inhabited island of Easter had known nothing but ferocious civil war and every other evil for centuries past.

Strong leadership, and a tenacious grip on the Christian faith, could have saved them. Christian, who lived up to his name until the time of the mutiny, made no attempt to preserve the formalities and services of the Church of England which Bligh was always so punctilious about, although he had preserved the *Bounty*'s Bible and prayer book among the other books from Bligh's old cabin. Only on one Sunday, soon after their arrival, did he read Divine Service.

As the most intelligent, best educated and most introspective of all these first Pitcairners, none suffered the agonies of loneliness and claustrophobia more acutely than Christian himself. One of the strongest traditional tales of the early days of Pitcairn that has been handed down through the generations, is that he would disappear for long periods after the community had been established and his authority as a leader had diminished. He would, it is said, make the long and dangerous climb up to a cave—inevitably known today as Christian's Cave—high above the cliffs west of the village. There he would sit for hours on end, staring out to sea, thinking dark thoughts of his past, aching for the old smells and sights and weather of Moorland Close and the company of his family, half hoping for and half dreading the sight of a sail. He always went armed with a musket and ample shot and powder, perhaps to defend his eyrie to the end—its tactical position was almost unassailable—perhaps to blow out his own brains? Or was it in fear of what was about to happen?

During the eighteen months from the beginning of 1791 to the middle of the following year, the decline in the spirit and morals of the Pitcairn community continued unabated, and every week brought new and ominous evidence of its break-up. On the one hand Ned Young and Jack Adams became increasingly familiar with the natives and increasingly promiscuous; while Quintal and McKoy abused and made life a misery for their wives and the native men. Animosity led to violent scenes. Christian declined into longer and longer moods of black depression and was sometimes not seen for days on end; and Jack Williams became a dour, lonely figure in his enforced bachelorhood.

Mills, Brown and Martin led more sober and industrious lives and tended their estates assiduously. In all the plantations the crops did well, and Brown gave advice when it was asked for. Food was always abundant and varied. When flesh or fowl were needed the white men went out with their muskets and shot birds along the cliff-tops or hogs or goats, according to their inclination. Quintal's wife Sarah produced a baby boy, who was named Matthew after his father, and McKoy had a boy, too, who was christened Daniel. Jack Mills's wife Vahineatua bore a girl, named Elizabeth, and Isabella had a second son, which Christian named, more orthodoxly this time, Charles.

Then, some time in the middle months of 1792, Jack Williams, deciding that he had had enough of celibacy, confronted Christian and told him that he intended to take by force one of the natives' wives. Christian was outraged and said that he must be mad. 'They have but two women for six. This can only lead to violence,' he said. 'Put the idea out of your mind, Jack.'

Williams, surly and defiant, approached in turn the other white men. From all of them, even McKoy and Quintal, he received the same response. There would be trouble. They might outnumber the natives but in this small community the tearing of a woman from the minority race would be fatal. 'Don't do it, Jack.' Everyone was sympathetic; no one would give him support.

After this there was silence from Williams for some weeks. But it was not the end of the matter. He returned to the attack several times, threatening and pleading in turn, until after a while they ceased to take him seriously. Then one day he asked Christian to call together all the white men. He had something important to tell them.

There was no formal centre to the village—no place of worship, no meeting place. But the women had formed the habit of gathering in one spot under the shelter of a great banyan tree which was within sight of most of the houses. Here the ground had been worn and there were logs for sitting on. And here the white men collected on this day to listen to Williams. Christian, still the formal leader but now seldom exercising any power or influence, called for silence.

'There is no place for me here,' Williams began. 'I am leaving the island. You have your *tyo*s and your children. That is something for you. I have nothing. It is my right to leave. You have refused me a woman so I must seek one elsewhere. I would rather be captured and taken back to England in irons and hanged at Spithead than remain on this island any longer.'

Christian and the others suddenly realised that Williams was serious; that he really was prepared to face almost certain death either by drowning or exposure, or at the end of a rope. It was a serious situation for them, too. For Williams was the only one among them who could handle the forge, make new tools as they wore out, or repair the muskets, or create from the *Bounty*'s iron the hundred-and-one things they would need in the future. They could live without him, without nails, or tools, or firearms, or cooking utensils, but they would be condemned eventually to a primitive existence.

'What boat will you have, Jack?' someone asked.

'The cutter. It is the only one for the open sea. And it is my entitlement if I am to have no woman.'

The natives had their own canoes now, but the cutter was the only craft the white men knew how to handle safely for fishing about the island.

'The cutter? But the cutter belongs by right to all of us. What boat do we have if you take it?'

Christian now realised that Williams was in a strong bargaining position. If they shut him away, besides being always a risk, he would refuse any longer to act as armourer. Nor could they hope to guard the boat day and night. They could prevent him by force from taking one of the natives' wives, but not the cutter.

Christian spoke quietly to Brown and Mills. 'We shall have to yield to Jack,' he said. 'He has too much the advantage of us. The Indians must give up one of their women.'

He turned to Williams. 'Who is it you will have, then?'

Williams, truculent in his moment of triumph, spoke sharply. 'Nancy or Mareva. Either will do.'

None of the others dared make further objection, though all were seized by fear of the consequences.

'We shall draw, then,' said Christian decisively. 'Will, take two sticks, one short and one long,' he instructed Brown. 'The short one is for Nancy, the long for Mareva.'

Brown presented his two fists to Williams, the ends of the sticks projecting above his thumbs. Williams drew one out. It was the shorter of the two.

That evening while Talaloo and Nancy were eating their evening meal in their house they saw the nine white men approaching, all armed with muskets, Christian leading them. Talaloo knew why they were coming and what they were after, for word travelled faster than sound itself on Pitcairn. Nancy had long wanted to leave him for the lonely white man, and would have done had she been allowed to. Like Mareva she felt of a lower caste than the other women with their white-skinned men.

'Nancy, you are to live with Jack Williams,' said Christian. 'He has been without a woman for too long.'

Nancy nodded and looked fondly at her new mate, then came to him.

The other white men were looking anxiously for Talaloo, whom they had seen from a distance. He was nowhere to be found inside the house nor near it. He seemed to have vanished. Then one of them spotted a distant dark figure. He was running fast uphill and soon disappeared among the trees.

Nancy went away willingly with Williams to live in his house, and the next day all the community went about their business in the normal way, except Talaloo. He was hiding somewhere, at the west end of the island some of the natives reported. The white men carried their pistols in their belts and tended to keep together more than they usually did. Brown and Christian whose gardens adjoined at the west end of the village talked apprehensively of what might now happen. If it came to civil war on the island, only Menalee, who regarded himself as Christian's *tyo*, might remain loyal to them. The muscular Tetaheite and his friend Oho, both from Tubai and once volunteer slaves to Christian, had long since turned surly and distant. The others, Timoa and Nehow, from Tahiti, went about their daily duties silently and inscrutably.

Nothing more happened for several days, although a heavy feeling of imminent doom seemed to hang over the island. There was still no sign of the deprived native Talaloo.

One evening at the very end of September when the women were gathered together in their favourite place in the centre of the village preparing the food for their men, singing and talking, Isabella and Brown's wife Teatuahitea overheard Nancy singing a song quietly, as if for them alone, in Tahitian. It was a simple, extemporised song such as they often sang, but in the theme they picked out this warning 'Why do the men sharpen their axes? To cut off the white men's heads.'

The two women slipped away and hastened to their husbands with the message. Christian acted instantly and alone. Loading his musket with ball, he hurried to the house where the native men always gathered in the evenings after the work of the day and burst in on them. They were all there, except Menalee. Talaloo had come back, no doubt to organise the massacre. As further confirmation of Nancy's warning there were axes lying about.

Talaloo was moving silently and slowly towards the handle of the nearest axe. As he bent down Christian raised the musket and aimed it at him.

There was pandemonium in the little room, and in the shouting and confusion Talaloo, followed by Timoa, fled towards the entrance. Christian pulled the trigger at point-blank range but the musket misfired. Then he, too, fled and reached his house without injury.

Later Menalee told him that the plot was indeed real, that the natives had conspired to attack the white men as they lay asleep, that their hate and hostility were boundless, and that Talaloo and

Timoa had fled into the hills and would not return until the others had retrieved Nancy. Oho had left separately later, armed with an axe and swearing vengeance.

Three days of armed truce passed during which there was no communication between the white men and the native men except Menalee, who seemed to have thrown in his lot wholeheartedly with the white cause. On the fourth day Nancy disappeared. Isabella later told Christian what had happened.

In the afternoons the women often made their way down the old track and fished by line from the rocks bordering Bounty Bay. Timoa and Talaloo had surprised them there, appearing as if from nowhere, had seized Nancy and disappeared. They were both armed with axes and the women were helpless. Oho had taken no part. No one had seen him since he had run up into the hills, though he was believed to be hiding somewhere at the extreme west of the island where no one ever went.

When Christian heard of this kidnapping, he again called the white men together. They decided that only with the death of Talaloo could there be peace again on Pitcairn, and Menalee was given the role of *agent provocateur*. Christian briefed him carefully. He was to pretend that he had changed sides and was now loyal to the native cause and disgusted with the tyrannical conduct of his master. Isabella would cook three puddings. One would be poisoned. Menalee must go up into the hills with these puddings, and armed with a concealed pistol, seek out Nancy and the two Tahitians.

'You must say to them, "I have brought you food to sustain you",' Christian instructed his *tyo* carefully. 'Then you must say, "Soon we will rise and kill all the white men". Then you must give Timoa and Nancy each a pudding, and the third pudding to Talaloo. If he does not die you must shoot him.'

The next morning Menalee carried out his orders, soon disappearing among the valleys and trees. He did not return until evening. He was alone with Timoa and Nancy. Together the three Tahitians told of the events of the day.

'I was a long time finding them,' said Menalee. 'They were high Up-in-Ti concealed among the bushes.'

'I was glad to see him come,' said Nancy, 'for I knew that you had sent him and that I should soon return to the village and the white men.'

Timoa took up the tale. 'He had three puddings, and he said they were for us as we must be hungry. He told us that all the natives, the men and the women, would rise up against the white men. But I knew that this was not true and that Menalee had been sent by Christian. Menalee made Talaloo take one of the puddings and we all sat down to eat.'

Nancy said, 'But Talaloo would not eat his pudding. He threw it into the' bushes and took mine and ate it instead. Menalee asked, "Why do you throw away your good pudding?" But Talaloo did not answer. He only ate.'

'So Talaloo still lives?' said Christian. 'We shall have to hunt him down. We are not safe while he is alive.'

'*Mămōō, mămōō*, master,' said Menalee impatiently. 'This is not the end of the story. Next I said to Talaloo, "I have brought Mareva with me. She wishes to speak to us. She is over there." And I pointed across the valley where a path winds up the side to Mr McKoy's plantation.'

'I led the way,' continued Nancy, 'Timoa behind me, Talaloo behind Timoa and Menalee at the end. We walked some way along the path like this . . .'

Menalee interrupted excitedly, eager to show himself a hero in Christian's eyes. 'I pulled out my pistol and held it to the back of Talaloo's head and pulled the trigger. But there was only a little sound, not a big sound. It did not fire. Talaloo turned and saw the pistol in my hand. He looked at me with fear in his eyes and ran into the forest. I ran after him.'

'He ran fast,' broke in Nancy.

'I ran like the wind,' Menalee cried proudly. 'Talaloo could not run so fast. I held him and together we rolled on the ground striking at each other. Talaloo was calling his wife to help—"Come, Nancy!" When she came,' he said with relish, 'he must have thought, "Now we will kill Menalee".'

'Talaloo did not know how much I hated him,' said Nancy as a calm statement of fact. 'I took up a stone and landed on the two fighting men. And I beat at his head with the stone—my husband's head, not Menalee's,' she added, looking at him.

Timoa was saying nothing. He stood some way apart, looking the other way but remembering the scene. He remembered how Menalee had freed himself from Talaloo's grip and grabbed a big stone and fell on the struggling man and his wife.

'I beat his head until he was dead,' said Menalee triumphantly. 'Blood and brains on the earth.'

'And I beat him, too, many times.'

Christian turned to Timoa. 'And you did nothing?'

'There was nothing for me to do. He is dead, is he not?' Timoa added truculently.

Brown had come up to listen to the end of this tale of murder. 'This is only the first killing,' Christian said to him. 'The blood will flow fast on Pitcairn now.'

'If we can do away with the most violent of them quickly we may yet survive,' said Brown.

But were they not all violent? Was not Menalee violent, perhaps the most violent of all? And could any of them be trusted—even Menalee, who had committed this murder for them?

'None of us will be safe now,' said Brown. 'We must sleep with our muskets loaded, and we must not trust our wives.'

'You mean Isabella? My own wife?'

'No one. Not even one another. Do not trust me. And certainly not Ned Young. He is too much with the natives,' said Brown.

It was a quiet evening and for once there was no wind. The sea birds were silent, the tall palms along the cliffs which in a gale could bend like bowing courtiers, stood upright and still. One of the babies was crying somewhere, but otherwise the village was quiet too. As if exhausted by the terror of the murder, no one seemed inclined to talk any more. Nancy had slipped back quietly to Williams's house. The steam and smoke from the cooking rose straight up into the darkening sky.

Later, when it was quite dark and they had eaten, Christian and Brown, Mills, Martin, Williams, Quintal and McKoy talked together softly in Christian's house. They spoke of their present fear and their fear for the future.

'We told you there would be killings if you had your way,' said Christian at one point to Jack Williams.

'That is past now. She wanted to be my wife. She has told how she helped kill Talaloo. She hated him. He misused her. She told me so.'

'Yes, it is past,' Brown agreed. 'Now we must protect ourselves.'

'We should kill them all,' muttered Quintal. 'We should have killed them all long ago.'

'And have their other woman,' added McKoy. 'We have been

soft with them. Look at you, Mr Christian. You treat your Menalee as if he was your brother. Will is right. Trust none of them. And kill Oho now. He is out there somewhere still. That one is a plotter.'

Not even his friend Quintal would agree that all five native men should be killed. They were useful with the hard work. But there was a strong feeling that Oho must go. He was their greatest danger. Perhaps Tetaheite, too. But certainly Oho.

'Send Menalee again,' Martin suggested. 'He is a good killer.' To which someone else added tartly, 'He needs a woman with him to help.'

At length it was agreed between these white men that Christian should send his *tyo* out on the hunt again the following day; that he should use guile to attract Oho back to the village and then kill him from behind as he had tried to kill Talaloo. If he succeeded they would trust him in future. If he failed he would be regarded as a traitor and shot.

On the next morning Christian carried out the plan as agreed except that, at the last minute, he sent Timoa, too, as support, offering them rich rewards if they succeeded in finding and killing Oho and saying nothing of the fate that would befall them if they failed.

Menalee and Timoa found Oho alone, hungry and frightened. They pretended to commiserate with him, pledging revenge on the white men. Then at a moment when Oho's back was turned Menalee drew out his pistol and killed him with one shot in the head.

For a long time after this second murder it seemed that the natives had been cowed into submission. The only result of their own plot had been the loss of two of their number. Brown had been proved right. But trust was not re-established, even after six months without further bloodshed, either between the natives and the white men, or between the men of the same race. Young and Adams took no part in their old shipmates' affairs, living together in isolation in the houses they had built on their adjoining gardens. While Christian, Brown, Mills and Martin were increasingly watchful of the natives—even of Menalee.

McKoy and Quintal treated them more harshly than ever, frequently beating them. These two were more or less drunk all the time now. They had reached the end of their share of the *Bounty*'s wine and spirits, but McKoy, who had once worked in a whisky distillery in Scotland and knew the secrets, devised a still from an old kettle and succeeded in making a brew from the root of the tee plant, which grew freely everywhere on the island. It was more potent alcohol even than navy rum. On one day Menalee stole a pig which McKoy had been fattening for a feast. McKoy found him cooking it and attacked and beat him unconscious. Timoa, too, was found guilty of the theft and was strung up and publicly beaten. Every fall of the lash marked an addition to the uneven score which one day would have to be balanced.

The women's lives were more miserable than those of any of the men. They despised their fellow countrymen for their inferior status and, except for Isabella who remained a loyal wife to the end and was expecting a third child, had lost respect for the white men whose behaviour was as bad as that of the lowest castes on Tahiti. These were no longer the mysterious white-skinned masters who had once so strongly attracted them with their fine clothes, their covetable possessions, their ardent passions. The white men were no longer even white men. They rarely washed. Their clothes had long since worn out and they dressed like the natives with no more than a belted skirt about the waist and a hat to keep off the sun. They, too, went barefoot, and their manners were increasingly brutish. Above all, the women were suffocatingly restless. They were not just homesick. They wanted desperately to be away from this tiny precipitous island where there was no room and no happiness. This was no place to bring up their children.

The native men, too, wanted to get away. But under the severe discipline now imposed on them, the four survivors saw no hope. First they would have to destroy the white men.

The plotting began again in September 1793. Only Menalee again remained loyal, first discouraging his fellow countrymen, then standing aloof so that he was not included, except as a possible victim, in the final plans. This time, they knew, they would have to have firearms. Young and Adams had instructed them in their use, taking them out to shoot birds and hogs. Musket work did not come easily to them. They were alarmed by the noise and discouraged by the difficulty of hitting the target except at the shortest range. Tetaheite was the best shot.

This time they succeeded in keeping the plot a secret. None of the women were told. They did not want another exposure like Nancy's last time. On the morning of 20 September the natives' plot began quietly to unfold. It was planting weather, and the best planting season. All the white men except Young and Adams were out in the fields, with Menalee helping Mills, who was behind with his planting. The other native men, too, began the day by working for their masters on the plantations. Then, one by one, the three of them—Tetaheite, Nehow and Timoa—stole away and made for the village, and unnoticed by the women, each succeeded in stealing a musket and ammunition.

The natives crept up first on Jack Williams, the man who had started all the trouble. He was repairing his fence where some hogs had got through and caused havoc among his newly planted yams. They shot him in the back of the head as he was leaning over securing a post, and he died instantly.

Among those who heard the shot was Isaac Martin. Assuming that Brown or Mills was out hunting, he called across the valley to Christian, who was invisible but within earshot, 'Well done! We'll have a feast today.'

The three natives were working towards Christian's garden when they heard Mills's voice, and they changed their plans cunningly and speedily. Tetaheite, who could see Mills and Menalee working close together and recognised the danger, decided to split this potentially dangerous combination. 'Yes,' he called as if in reply to Mills. 'Yes, we have shot a great hog. We need Menalee to help us carry it.'

Mills released Menalee from his work, presuming that Young or Adams was out hunting with the natives. There was no sound from Christian, who must have heard this exchange but was still out of sight behind some trees.

Menalee did as he was ordered and strode off towards Williams's plot. He was almost on top of the body before he saw it, lying beside the fence with half the head shot away. Then he saw the three natives. So it was a white man and not a hog he was expected to help carry.

Menalee turned as if to run away. But Tetaheite, who was as strong as two men, held him and whispered threateningly, '*Mămōō!* Be with us or you will die. All the white men are to die!'

By unhappy chance, Menalee's own *tyo* was to be the next victim. Knowing that to sound a warning would lead to instant death,

Menalee remained in agonised silence as they crept up behind Christian, who was bent over his spade digging in yams, a pile of roots on the gound nearby.

Tetaheite again carried out the execution, with speed and skill. He leapt forward the last few steps with the musket raised and fired into the back of Christian's head.

Christian died almost instantly. But as he lay on the newly tilled soil, he called out—not very loudly, not in a tone of agony or anger—simply, 'Oh, dear!'* Then Tetaheite called for an axe which Nehow passed to him, and Tetaheite struck again and again at the face until it was unrecognisable.

Two white men heard Christian's death cry, for McKoy had come into Mills's plantation to ask him something. Now alarmed by this second shot and the sound of the voice that had followed it, McKoy said to Mills, 'That was surely some person dying?'

'I think it was only Isabella calling her children to dinner,' Mills replied.

A moment later Menalee appeared in the clearing. He was panting as if he had run far, and he spoke in a tense voice. 'Your house is being robbed by Tetaheite and Nehow. Go there quickly!'

McKoy ran down the valley, now acutely alarmed. Had those earlier shots been aimed at hogs—or his fellow white men? He knew the answer before he reached his house. He was about to go in when a third shot rang out. It came from inside, the ball whistling past his head. So Menalee had tricked him. 'Do not trust anyone!' Brown had said. Now all four natives had risen in revolt.

McKoy ran back up the hill. He was a fast runner still in spite of the drink and easily outpaced the heavier pursuing Tahitians. As he ran he called out a warning to Mills. 'They are murdering us all— hide yourself.'

McKoy made first for the spot where he believed Christian to be working. Instead he found his corpse, the blood from his head wound soaking into the soil, staining it a darker red, one side of the head as terrible a sight as the other.

Another musket-shot sounded, scarcely a hundred yards away. McKoy did not learn until later that his warning to Mills had come too late. Menalee had acquired a pistol from Tetaheite, had run up to Mills as if to warn him of the danger. Mills, unsuspecting, had

* There is a large rock, shaped like a gravestone, just off the south coast of the island which was later named after the last two words Fletcher Christian spoke.

gone to meet him and was shot in the face at point-blank range. He had been, at forty-one years, the oldest man on Pitcairn by a wide margin.

Now McKoy ran to give the news of Christian's death to Isabella. Shortly after Christian had left for his work, she had gone into labour. When McKoy burst into her house to tell her of her husband's death she was already giving birth to her third child, with Nancy acting as midwife.

Menalee had run amok in his new-found freedom and wanted more blood. He saw McKoy leave Christian's house and guessed that he would make for the house of his friend Quintal. He ran through the trees to get there first, picking up a large stone on the way—he did not know how to reload the pistol, nor did he have ball or powder for it.

McKoy and Menalee reached Quintal's house together, with McKoy panting out, 'Mat, get to the woods with your musket!' When Quintal left his house he saw the two men struggling on the ground beside his pig sty, with Menalee beating at McKoy with the stone. McKoy had been wounded but was proving the stronger of the two. Like all Polynesians, Menalee had put on a lot of weight since maturity from overeating. McKoy was lither and more muscular.

As Quintal raced to his rescue, he saw McKoy lift Menalee up bodily and hurl him over the fence into the sty among the pigs, where he lay still. He might have been stunned or dead, but they did not wait to find out. Quintal grabbed another musket for McKoy and told his wife Sarah to run to warn the other white men. They had had enough and both made off up into the hills to await the outcome of this day of murder.

Isaac Martin did not understand what was going on. He had heard shots and shouts but went on working on a piece of land close to his house, where his wife Paurai was doing the chores. He had heard no word of warning, though he must have been mystified by the number of musket shots. Perhaps there was a big shoot for hogs going on. It would not be the first time for they had recently become a pest.

Next he saw three armed natives coming across his land. Still unsuspecting—he had heard that Young and Adams were in the habit of lending the natives muskets—he awaited their arrival. He recognised Tetaheite, Timoa and Nehow. Tetaheite came straight up to him, with Timoa at his side. They were laughing and they put the barrels of the muskets to Martin's belly as if this were a practical joke—they loved practical jokes.

'Do you know what we have been doing this morning?' Tetaheite asked.

Martin shook his head. 'No.'

'We have been doing the same as shooting hogs'—and the two natives pulled the triggers together.

There were two clicks, and Martin joined them in their laughter. It was like old times, when they had often laughed together at simple jokes.

Tetaheite and Nehow recocked their muskets and, still laughing, again pulled the triggers. This time both muskets fired. By some miracle of chance, the shots did not kill Martin. He fell to the ground, but like a savagely wounded animal rose again at once, and clutching his stomach ran off, not to his own house which was nearer, but to Brown's. He got there before his pursuers, uttering shouts of warning at the same time.

He was shouting and bleeding, doubled up in pain when he got inside and collapsed on the floor. Brown was already there, driven indoors by fear at the renewed shooting, reaching for his own musket.

Menalee was the first of the natives to arrive, wild with blood lust. As he burst in he glimpsed one of the *Bounty*'s sledgehammers hanging from a hook on the wall, seized it and beat out Martin's brains as he lay on the floor.

Thus died the first American on Pitcairn Island.

Menalee turned next on to Brown who was frantically trying to load his musket in the farthest corner of the room. Two more natives arrived then and a shot rang out. It missed him, but Menalee got in a savage blow with the sledgehammer before Brown burst past him, racing for the entrance, dodging past Nehow and Tetaheite.

Then an odd thing happened. Timoa was outside, musket reloaded and raised. For some reason Timoa had taken a fancy to Brown—or perhaps it was only sudden pity. No one would ever know. But as Brown dashed past, Timoa said in English, 'Fall when I fire.'

Brown ran and when he was a dozen yards from his house, he heard a shot and at once fell to the ground, feigning death. When the other three natives emerged, they saw Timoa with the smoking musket in his hands, and Brown lying on the ground. This did not satisfy Menalee. He had left the sledgehammer inside beside the corpse. Now he took up a stone and ran to Brown, striking him a terrible blow on the head.

Brown rose to a sitting position, holding his bleeding head and calling out for mercy. 'If you are going to kill me, let me see Teatua-hitea first,' he begged.

Timoa held Menalee's arms. 'Let him go, he is no danger,' he said in Tahitian. Reluctantly, Menalee allowed Brown to get to his feet and walk slowly, unsteadily, towards the centre of the village in search of his wife.

Brown did not get far. Suddenly Menalee snatched a musket from Nehow, and before Timoa could stop him, shot him in the back from one yard.

Thus died the gardener from Kew.

Sarah Quintal raised the alarm first at Adams's house. He was work-ing in a field nearby, and when she called out to warn him of the danger he only looked up momentarily and then bent to his work again. Sarah did not wait but ran back to the village calling out for her husband.

Five white men were already dead. But the natives could no longer hope to finish their business as stealthily as they had begun it. Women everywhere were raising the alarm. Down in the village pandemonium had broken out. Calls of warning and shouts for help reached as far as the hills and echoed back from the forests. The dogs were barking hysterically and the children were crying out. The whole island had awoken to the catastrophe in their midst, suddenly, fearfully, aware that no intended victim could hope to escape for there was nowhere to escape to. Whether it was one man who had gone berserk or a dozen bent on murder, there was no telling now who was killing who, where the next shot might be fired, or who might die.

Even Jack Adams had recognised that something wicked was

going on. He put down his tools and made for Brown's house where he heard the sound of the last shots. He saw no bodies. But, leaning on the butts of their muskets as they had often seen the white men do, the four natives were standing about the entrance, recovering their strength and discussing their next move. Adams regarded them all as his friends and was not at first put out by the sight of the four muskets.

'What is the matter?' he called out.

They all turned together, threateningly, raising their muskets at the same time. '*Mămōō*!' they replied in warning. They did not look as if they were going to shoot. They just wanted him out of the way. Adams did not linger.

From the cries of lamentation and alarm from the village Adams at last judged the truth, that the natives had risen, that no white man was safe, even he who considered himself their friend. For the present at least, he must seek refuge in some remote part of the island, just as Timoa and Tallaloo had done earlier. But first he needed supplies and some warm clothing, for the nights could still be cold out in the open.

So Adams emerged briefly from the forest and made his way stealthily to Williams's house. Williams was the only one with a warm coat, the envy of all the others even though there was seldom need to wear it. When he arrived he found Nancy there, alone in her grief.

'My *tyo* is dead,' she lamented, beating her fists against her temples. Her voice rose in a shriek. 'All the white men are dead!'

Adams did not wait to commiserate, nor to dispute her statement. He grabbed Williams's coat from its hook and ran off again into the forest, making for his own house, which was close to the cliff-edge on the northern shore of the island. He was hastily filling a bag with some yams when all four natives, who must have been lying in wait for him, burst in. Menalee had a loaded musket again and he fired across the room as Adams struggled to escape through the window. The ball struck him in the back of his shoulder and passed out through his neck, sending him tumbling on to the ground outside.

Menalee was the first to reach him, racing round the house, holding the musket by its barrel. He hurled himself on to the wounded man, beating him again and again with the butt. Adams attempted feebly to ward off the blows, breaking his thumb against the musket. Tetaheite was the next to arrive. His musket was still loaded and he held it to Adams's body as he lay on the ground and pulled the trigger. But again it misfired, no doubt because it was reloaded unskilfully and hurriedly.

Adams was a strong man and there was plenty of life in him yet. He struggled to his feet and ran fast inland, leaving a trail of blood but easily outstripping his pursuers.

Timoa got nearest to Adams in the race and he called out to him to stop. 'It's all right,' he was shouting.

At a safe distance and from a safe height above the natives, Adams paused. He needed the rest anyway, and he needed to staunch the flow of blood. He turned back and looked down at them. They would not hit him from this distance with a musket.

'Why is it all right?' he called to them. 'You want to kill me.'

'No,' replied Timoa. 'We do not want to kill you. We forgot what Mr Young told us about leaving you alive for his companion.'

Adams considered his situation carefully. He badly needed attention to his wound. If they were determined to kill him, they must get him in the end. There was little to lose by putting his trust in them for what it was worth, and that was nothing.

Holding some palm leaves to his neck, Adams walked slowly back to the four natives, and together they made their way, as if by a prearranged plan, towards Christian's house.

Ned Young had taken occupation of Christian's house as a matter of course just as Christian had moved into Bligh's cabin in the *Bounty*. Many of the women were there, too, partly to seek protection from the natives, partly to help his wife Susan to protect the last of their white men, for they believed that all the others were now dead. Quintal's wife Sarah was missing, but Nancy was there, still stunned, as they all were, by this day of terror. A mass orgy of grief was taking place, but it was subdued out of respect for Isabella who lay on her bed, nursing her new child, a baby girl, soon to be named Mary.

No one present realised that the one white man, around whom they were gathered, had brought about this massacre, briefing and inciting the four native men, just as he had earlier spurred on Christian to take the *Bounty*. And as before, he had had no need to take part, absenting himself discreetly while the cruel deeds were done.

Into this crowded little house came Jack Adams, pale and drawn from the effects of his wound, bewildered by the size of the gathering, shocked and in pain. His appearance created yet another sensation. Seeing his injuries and his escort of armed natives, all looking wild after their bloodbath, they leaped to his side, his wife Paurai holding his arms and leading the chorus of pleas for mercy addressed to the natives. It seemed as if their appeal succeeded, for after words with Young they went off again.

While Paurai and the two other native women attended to his wounds, uttering expressions of pity and concern, Adams spoke to his friend. Young was sitting in a chair Christian had made. It might have been the throne to which he had succeeded, and Ned Young looked the part—the new and undisputed king of Pitcairn. Like Adams, Young had often spoken of the unjustness in the division of the women and the uprising it must one day cause. But Adams had had no knowledge of this plot, nor of Young's instigation of it.

'Why did you do it?' Adams asked now, talking quickly in English so that the women would not understand.

'They would do it one day themselves. This island is like Tofua, always erupting. Soon it would have gone up in a great explosion. It is better to control an explosion as I have done.'

Young was quite calm about it, like a general who never leaves his tent during a victorious battle. Now there would be no shortage of women. He had already planned to have Isabella as a second wife. He had always admired her looks, and the house Christian had built for her. It was very comfortable here. He would have Nancy, too, making three in all. A small harem.

Although Young waited a few days before putting these plans into effect, he spoke now of Adams's likely choice, thinking it might cheer him to discuss his future wives. Quintal and McKoy were not yet dead, but what of their wives, Sarah and Mary? They were handsome women, too.

In fact at that moment Sarah had succeeded in rejoining Quintal up in the hills where he had fled earlier with McKoy. Here they built themselves a shelter in a good tactical position and awaited the inevitable attack by the four natives. It was not long coming. But the natives were cautious in their approach for they had suffered many months of fear from these two men and had little confidence in their own skill with their muskets.

Their attack was a brief and abortive business. They fired a few shots without effect, and when they approached closer and the fire was returned, they fled back to the village, where they were severely rebuked by Young for their lack of courage.

The wave of violence had run its course but the massacre of the whites solved no problems and brought new jealousies and passions in its backwash before the next wave broke. The women's grief was followed by a vengeful hatred of their fellow countrymen who had murdered their husbands and made fatherless their children. Down in the village tempers flared quickly and the native men watched one another with caution and guarded their claims on the unwilling women. Young did nothing. He just watched expectantly, like a cockfight spectator between rounds.

Only one week after the massacre, in the evening when many of the natives were gathered about in the centre of the village, Menalee became jealous of the attention Timoa was showing Susan. Susan was playing on a fife—a survivor of the *Bounty*—and Timoa was singing to it, a harmlessly romantic enough scene, one would have thought, if the killing madness had not seized all the men on Pitcairn.

Suddenly Menalee could bear it no longer, took up a musket and shot at Timoa, wounding him.

'Fetch me a musket,' Timoa begged of Susan as he lay bleeding on the ground.

While Susan ran into Timoa's house, Menalee re-loaded his musket, took aim again at Timoa and shot him dead.

Others had now gathered round, shouting and wailing and threatening to kill Menalee. Tetaheite arrived, and Nehow after him. When they saw Timoa dead on the ground they attacked Menalee, who fled from the village with his musket, outpaced his pursuers, and was never seen alive by them again.

Quintal and McKoy caught sight of Menalee soon after this killing. From their hide-out at the western end of the island where the land rises to above one thousand feet, they saw him approaching, and that he was armed with a musket. They seized their own weapons, and were about to fire at him when he called out, 'I have come to be your *tyo*. Do not kill me.'

'Put your musket down on the ground,' Quintal ordered. 'Then you may come to us.'

Keeping the native covered with his own musket, Quintal told McKoy to fetch Menalee's weapon. He turned to Sarah. 'Go to Mr Young in the village. He will not harm you. Ask him why Menalee has come to us.'

Sarah returned later with a letter from Ned Young. It told how Menalee had killed Timoa, how he was mad, and recommended that they should kill him if they valued their lives. All the native men were now mad, Young continued. For his part, he intended to arrange for the death of Nehow and Tetaheite. Then when Menalee was also dead, it would be safe for them to return to their homes.

Quintal and McKoy had already made up their minds to kill the native. It was an easy execution, carried through without any compunction. McKoy shot him in the back with his own musket. They left him where he fell.

But fear and mistrust had now both grown to such a pitch that Quintal and McKoy believed that Young might have laid a trap for them in the village and that the two surviving natives would kill them as soon as they returned. For the present, then, they would remain clear, and on their guard.

Three days passed. It was 4 October 1793. Young's wife Susan appeared from the village with another message, confirming that the two natives were now dead and that they could safely return.

'We do not believe your master,' McKoy told her. 'Tell Mr Young that we need proof.'

They did not have long to wait for it. When Susan returned the next time she carried a bag, and inside it were the severed hands of Tetaheite and Nehow.

'You see they are dead,' she told them triumphantly.

So McKoy and Quintal with Sarah and Susan returned from the hills to the village, believing that their troubles were at last over.

McKoy and Quintal learned that one of the last murders had been committed in bed. That seemed appropriate. Two people were in

Young's plot, Brown's widow Teatuahitea and his own wife Susan. Jack Adams, still recovering from his serious wound, was unable to participate. Teatuahitea was to lure Tetaheite into her bed, but was to avoid putting her arm under his head while they slept. At a word from Young, Susan was to steal into the house with an axe, while Young himself went to Nehow's house with a musket, wake him up and suggest that they should go hunting for Quintal and McKoy. Susan was to call out when she had completed her task.

Everything went according to plan except that Susan was not strong enough to cut off the heavy Tubaian's head with one blow. Tetaheite rose up bloodily in bed beside Teatuahitea when the first blow was struck. Susan delivered another blow with all her strength, and though she did not succeed in severing his head she managed to kill him.

Young was talking to Nehow and loading his musket when he heard Susan's voice. Nehow saw that he had loaded only one barrel. 'Load both barrels, Mr Young,' he reminded him. 'There are two men to kill.' Young followed the Tahitian's suggestion, cocked both triggers and fired both barrels at Nehow's head, almost blowing it off. It was Ned Young's first direct act of violence. But not his last.

Peace of a sort did come to Pitcairn on that bloody October night, but little happiness came with it. The rest of this parable of bloodshed and terror and racial hatred can be quickly recounted. Now that the number of men had been reduced from fifteen to four, the women found themselves searching for a man to share a bed with. Young, as has been told, took two besides his wife Susan. McKoy took Teatuahitea as well as his Mary, and Quintal took on Nancy as an addition to his household and his bed. Jack Adams claimed Vahineatua and Jenny. But this was a purely nominal arrangement. Only the original wives remained all the time in the same house. The other women moved from bed to bed as their fancy, and the men's fancies, took them.

With peace and security and the end of the racial struggle, the women became restless again. For them, as for all their race, contentment could be found only on a large island in a crowded community, or in a nomadic existence. Some months after the murders, Ned Young wrote in his journal that 'since the massacre, it has been the desire of the greater part of them to get some conveyance to enable them to leave the island'. New urgency was added to this need by the treatment they received at the hands of McKoy and Quintal. These two, after their days of fear and hiding, were back to their old drinking habits, and having no native men to beat they beat the women instead.

One day a sail was sighted to the north-east. It threw the community into a ferment. In the evening the men fled up into the hills with their muskets, while the women took advantage of their absence to light fires to attract attention. By the morning it had disappeared. But if the sight of that ship had terrified the men, it had inflamed still further the women's longing to quit Pitcairn. In April 1794 Jenny told Young that they were going to build their own boat, and no one was going to stop them. And to ram home her point, she began dismantling the timbers of one of the houses.

Young and Adams discussed this new challenge to their authority with some anxiety and decided to humour the women. They could build their own boat if they wished, they told Jenny. Moreover, the men would help them. The women's boat was a lost cause, and at the same time a tragi-comedy, from the start. It was designed and largely built by the four white men, with female assistance, only to prove the impossibility of the project. They had neither the tools, the equipment nor the expertise. However, a boat of sorts was in the end completed by August. On the 13th of that month the women examined the result of their weeks of labour with excited expectation.

Two days later, when the weather was suitable, the boat that was to take them home to Tahiti was launched in Bounty Bay. 'According to expectation she upset,' noted Ned Young dryly in his journal.

In one last desperate attempt to get away from Pitcairn, the women conspired to murder the white men and leave in the *Bounty*'s cutter. The plot was disclosed in time by one of their number, but the men went through another period of fear and suspicion before they were satisfied that they were out of danger. Time was the best cure for the women's restlessness and dissatisfaction—time and the community's fecundity. By the early months of 1795 the population had so increased that even Jenny could see that they could never all pack into the cutter with their children, even if they did succeed in killing the four white men.

The pace of events on this unhappy island at last slowed down. McKoy continued to drink himself to death. He nearly succeeded in 1796 when he fell from a coconut tree and seriously injured himself. Soon after he had recovered he disappeared. His body was later discovered at the foot of the cliffs below Christian's Cave. He had evidently bound his own hands and feet and tied a weight about his neck before leaping to his death.

The death of McKoy had a fearful effect on Mat Quintal. He, too, drank as heavily as ever and led a life separated from the rest with his wife Sarah, whom he beat mercilessly. One day, in 1799, Sarah, too, was found dead at the bottom of the cliffs. Quintal said that she had gone searching for birds' eggs. Now he demanded Jenny in her place, threatening Jack Adams and Ned Young with instant death if she was not handed over.

The two men realised that Quintal had lost his reason, just as McKoy had done, from the alcohol of the tee root, and that he was as likely to take their lives as McKoy had taken his own. So, with an axe, they battered in the head of the man who burnt the *Bounty* while he was lying in his house in a drunken stupor.

This final murder on Pitcairn had a profound and reforming effect on Young and Adams. First they gave up all alcohol themselves, and forbade their women from drinking it too. Then, as if they and the island on which they lived had now been exorcised of all evil with the death of every man who had landed there with them almost a decade earlier, they suddenly gave themselves up to the Christian faith, and its propagation, with the zeal of early evangelical missionaries. Shame for their past misdeeds must have been one reason for this rapid conversion. But there was a second. Young had been unwell for some time. He was losing weight, and towards the end of the year his dark face had assumed a gaunt appearance. He found difficulty in breathing. He was, as he knew, dying of asthma, a disease from which he had long suffered.

Now Jack Adams was scarcely literate. Brought up among the wharves of London's docks, he had had little religious training and knew the Bible only from the formal services on board H.M. ships. Knowing that Ned Young would soon be dead, leaving him as the father of this flock of women and children, he took reading lessons from his companion every day so that he would be able to officiate at Divine Service and lead them in hymn singing after he was gone.

When Ned Young—dark progenitor of violence, mayhem and murder—finally died on Christmas Day 1800, Jack Adams, the rough sailor from Wapping, suddenly found himself having to officiate at the Christmas services, at his friend's funeral and burial. But it seems that he rose to the responsibilities splendidly, warmly supported by the womenfolk and the older children, to whom, at the age of thirty-three, he was already like an aged prophet, at once their undisputed temporal and clerical leader, their shepherd and counsellor.

It was a curious experience for these stout Polynesian women to find themselves so rapidly converted to the Christian faith. On one day, it seemed, they were bedding with and suffering at the hands of

for the Lord's Day Morning

Suffer me not o Lord to Waste this Day in Sin or folly But Let me Worship thee with Much Delight teach me to know more of thee and to Serve thee Better than ever I have Done Before that I may Be fitter to Dwell in heaven, where thy worship and Service are everlasting Amen

John Adams

'Reckless Jack' Adams's handwriting. Ned Young taught him to write and to read a bunch of murderous villains, both dark- and light-skinned. The next they were having to attend morning service and evensong, Divine Service and prayer and Bible readings. In his enthusiasm, Adams was perhaps excessive in his teaching. He did, for example, misunderstand the prayer book's reference to Ash Wednesday and Good Friday being fast days, and insisted for many years that the islanders should fast every Wednesday and Friday—which was a very considerable sacrifice for these voracious eaters, and they would sometimes faint at their work in the fields. But at least the community remained united and at peace, and the women's restlessness was soothed by prayer and the new spirit of love which the Good Book, and Jack Adams, had brought to Pitcairn.

McKoy's still was, of course, soon destroyed, and all the remaining alcohol on the island followed the blood of black men and white men into the dusty soil.

For eight more years the outside world remained ignorant of this tiny reformed community and its patriarchal ruler. The women grew fatter and middle-aged and their children began to cast about for wives. Thursday October Christian, the second oldest man, surprised everybody by asking McKoy's elderly widow to marry him. Mary gave birth to a child, Charles, in 1808, her fifth, nearly twenty years after her first on Tahiti.

In the same year a sail was again sighted. This time it did not disappear in the night. In the morning it was seen out in the bay. It came in closer and then there was the rattle of chains as the bower anchor splashed into the water.

The sailing ship *Topaz* of Boston, Massachusetts, had left her home port in the late months of 1807, had worked her way down the South American coast to Patagonia, and doubled Cape Horn in February. Captain Mayhew Folger was one of the first of the enterprising sealers to pursue his prey in the Drake Strait and the southern Pacific, and by chance had followed the track of Carteret over forty years earlier. It had not been a particularly successful voyage, and by the end of August 1808 Folger and his crew were in acute need of water and fresh provisions. The sight of the abrupt silhouette of an island on the evening of 28 September came as a surprise and a relief, just as it had to Christian, for no navigator had yet corrected the only record of this remote island.

Folger closed the island in the last light of the day, noting with disappointment an iron-bound coast and the white line of breakers on the inhospitable shore. By the time darkness fell he had ruled out any chance of a landing the next day. Later in the night, however, Folger identified lights on the shore which indicated that the island was inhabited and therefore might after all be able to meet their most urgent needs. Folger stood off and on through the night, and at dawn closed a bay on the north-east coast which seemed to offer some sort of shelter.

The sun had already risen when the *Topaz* dropped her anchor in Bounty Bay, and now Folger studied the coastline more carefully through his glass. He saw figures gathered on a narrow strip of shelving beach, a building that looked like a thatched boathouse, and a track zigzagging up the cliff behind. Smoke was rising from behind trees on a level piece of land above.

Folger had decided that it would not be safe to attempt a landing in one of his ship's boats when he saw an outrigger canoe put out from the beach, lift over the breaking rollers, and head towards the *Topaz*. Within half an hour the canoe, rising high and falling deep into the troughs of the waves, had come alongside the sealer, and Folger could look down from the bows of his vessel to see the three young men who had braved these heavy seas. They were waving their paddles above their heads and calling out.

To the astonishment of Folger and his crew, the canoeists spoke in English. 'Where do you come from?' the tallest of the three called from the stern of the canoe. 'Will you not come ashore?'

'Come on board, we will not harm you,' Folger replied. He ordered two lines over the side, the boys paddled alongside and climbed up on to deck, staring about them in wonder. They were all tall and muscular, dusky rather than brown-skinned, with full lips and wide-set black eyes. Polynesians all right, Folger judged, but not pure blood.

'What is the name of this island?' Folger now asked.

'Peetcairn, sir.'

'Were you born here, are you English?'

'Yes, we are English.' He pronounced it 'Eengleesh', and 'v' as 'w'. The eldest lad was answering the questions, and asking them:

'Are you English?'

'No, we are American.' This appeared to mean nothing to the boys, though they seemed to be relieved.

Like his companions, the tallest boy wore a cloth round his waist with a knife stuck into the belt. This one also wore a straw hat decorated with cocks' feathers. Now he introduced himself, with the odd name of Thursday October, the others as his brother Charles, and James Young. 'We were born here. But not our mothers and fathers. They came here a long time ago in a ship as big as this.'

'Where are your mothers and fathers?'

'Our fathers are dead. They died long ago. I am the oldest man,' said Thursday proudly. 'Except for Mr Adams of course.'

'Who is Mr Adams?'

'He is a wery old man. He teaches us about God. He would like to see you if you are not English.'

Captain Folger explained about his need for water. Did they have plenty of water? Could they tow some casks ashore and fill them, ready for the ship's longboat to collect them when the sea became calmer? They would be well rewarded. And did they have plenty of fruit? They needed fresh fruit and vegetables, and meat too if they had it?

Thursday answered quickly and enthusiastically: 'Yes!' 'Yes!' 'Yes!', the cocks' feathers in his hat bobbing in the sun.

One of the *Topaz*'s crew accompanied the boys in their canoe and supervised the towing of the five empty casks on a long length of line. The canoe put off, and disappearing intermittently into the troughs of the waves, made its way back towards the beach. Here there were many willing hands to catch it as it came sweeping in, and to help drag up the casks.

Later, Folger succeeded in getting ashore, too, and was led up the steep cliff-track. Everything about this little island community was strange. Their houses and fences, their tools and implements and cooking utensils, were unlike anything this seasoned sailor had seen before, being half primitive, half Western. At first it seemed like a fairy-tale village of children. There were children everywhere, all half-breeds, all dark and beautiful and well proportioned, speaking an odd dialect in which he could recognise English words as they ran along beside him. Then he saw one or two older women standing outside their houses, fat and dark and handsome, pure Polynesian, smiling and waving shyly as they watched him walk by.

Folger was brought at last to a middle-aged man sitting outside his house with two women beside him. You could see at once that he was pure European, a stout and stooping figure, with long grey hair falling over his shoulders but balding at the front. His features were fine, with a long nose and steady brown eyes, but his face was deeply pitted with smallpox scars, and there was a pale, wrinkled scar on one side of his neck. His broad shoulders, his deep chest, and his legs, too, were covered with tattoo patterns.

The man rose when Folger approached and extended his hand in greeting. 'I hear you are from our old English colonies in America. My name is John Adams. We are glad to welcome you to our island.'

On that day Adams related to the American captain in detail the story of the *Bounty* and her men since she had last been seen sailing out of Matavai Bay nineteen years before, from the early days of hope and earnest endeavour, through the collapse of morals and the decadence of the mid-1790s, and the death by murder or suicide of all but one of the male community. Then he spoke proudly of their reformation, of his conversion of his flock of women and children to the word of God, of his own timely spiritual retrieval before all was lost, and of his hopes for their future. 'We are happy today. May God preserve us as we are.'

Later, Adams learned with amazement and relief that Bligh and many of his men had survived to return to England, and that those who had chosen to remain on Tahiti had been brought back to a court martial. Some had been hanged, Folger remembered, but he could not remember their names or how many.

Then Adams asked what else had been happening in the world outside for the past twenty years. Folger told what he knew, which was mostly of his own country, about Adams's namesake as Federalist and President, of Thomas Jefferson and troubles with the French. None of this made much impression on Adams, but his interest was aroused when Folger told him of England's war with France, and of the great naval victories of the Nile and Trafalgar. When he heard of Nelson's last great victory Adams's old patriotism was so strongly aroused that he stood up, and according to Folger, raised his hat and exclaimed, 'Hurrah! Old England forever!'

Folger re-embarked when his longboat could get in close enough to the shore to take on the filled casks of water and as much fresh food of all kinds as it could carry. In addition, Folger brought with him, as presents from Adams, the *Bounty*'s old chronometer made by Kendall of London and the ship's azimuth compass.

'We will return to you in eight months,' were his last words to Adams.

The *Topaz* continued her voyage and never returned. The consequences of this sealer's chance call at Pitcairn were surprisingly slight, both for the island and the world outside. Life continued its serene and uneventful course. Folger had corrected the calendar, which had been a constant preoccupation and comfort in the early days on Pitcairn. First Christian and then Young and Adams had kept it faithfully. But earlier in his long search about the southern Pacific, Christian had failed to allow for the *Bounty*'s crossing of the date line; so, ever since, they had lived one day behind, holding the Sabbath on a Saturday. This was now corrected, as was the name of Christian's first-born son. After the *Topaz*'s visit, Thursday October changed his name to Friday.

The story of the fate of the *Bounty* mutineers and the rediscovery of Pitcairn Island was not heard in England for another five years. Folger's sealing voyage took him to Juan Fernandez—back round the Horn and at last to Boston. The War of 1812 with Britain cut off most communications between the two countries, but a letter from Folger from Nantucket arrived at last at the Admiralty in London in 1813. It was noted by some clerk, filed away and forgotten. The Lords Commissioners were too busy with more important things to be bothered with some doubtful tale about a long forgotten mutiny. As far as the Royal Navy, and Bligh, were concerned, the mystery of the *Bounty* and of the fate of Fletcher Christian remained unsolved.

Among the Admiralty's problems at this time—a minor one, perhaps, more an irritation—was that of the American frigate *Essex* which had for some time been seizing British whalers off the coast of South America. Two frigates were sent out from England to intercept and destroy this raider. They were the *Briton*, Captain Sir F. Staines, and the *Tagus*, Captain Pipon. These two men-o'-war, proceeding in company, were *en route* from the Marquesas Islands to Valparaiso to begin their search when they sighted Pitcairn. No correction had yet been made to the position of Pitcairn since Carteret's inaccurate charting of the island, and at first Staines believed that he had made a new discovery.

The arrival of these two warships caused consternation on Pitcairn as soon as news that they were flying the British flag was brought to Adams. His wife, the other women and the older children, had long known that their leader was a hunted man—wrongly, of course, for he had told them that he was innocent of any participation in the mutiny. They also knew that it was only the authority and inspiration of this man that held together their community, that without his example the colony must soon break up and return to its old evil ways.

Like the *Topaz* six years earlier, the two vessels stood off and on through the night and came to anchor in Bounty Bay at dawn. And again Friday October and one of Ned Young's boys came out in a canoe to greet the ships' commanders: the sons of two mutinous midshipmen facing the Royal Navy's authority for the first time, and each determined to protect the last of their fathers' shipmates.

They need not have worried. These officers were kindly men, compassionate and curious, harbouring no vengeful feelings about the remote event in the Royal Navy's history when they gleaned the extraordinary truth from these two young men. Captain Pipon himself wrote of Friday October:

'He was then, when we saw him, about twenty-five years of age, a tall fine young man, about six feet high, dark black hair, a countenance extremely open and interesting. . . . He is of course of a brown cast, not however with that mixture of red, so disgusting in the wild Indians. With a great show of good humour, and a disposition and willingness to oblige, we were very glad to trace in his benevolent countenance, all the features of an honest English face.' He spoke English, Pipon continued, in a 'manner vastly pleasing. I could not survey this interesting personage without feelings of tenderness and compassion.' Young, too, he found 'a very fine youth'.

After being assured that the Royal Navy intended no harm to any of them, Christian and Young took the two commanders ashore by canoe, almost upsetting and drowning them in the surf. They talked at length to this man who long ago had held Captain Bligh at bayonet point in his cabin. Now his piety and seriousness, the Christian simplicity of the life he had created on this beautiful little island, convinced Staines and Pipon that it would be 'an act of great cruelty and inhumanity' to arrest him and take him home to inevitable court martial and execution. So they left him there, with the Royal Navy's blessings.

One last picture of this remarkable man has come down to us. It is eleven years later, and Adams is almost sixty years of age, to the young people of Pitcairn a living legend of their stormy past. Another British naval vessel has anchored in Bounty Bay. The young men of the island bring Adams out to the ship, and after asking permission in accordance with service custom, he climbs on board in his special visiting day uniform. There he stands, half revered island patriarch, half common seaman, treading, still with a trace of anxiety, the decks of a British man-o'-war again for the first time for thirty-five years.

'He was unusually strong and active for his age,' writes one eyewitness, 'notwithstanding the inconvenience of considerable corpulency. He was dressed in a sailor's shirt and trousers and a low-crowned hat, which he instinctively held in his hand until desired to put it on. He still retained his sailor's gait, doffing his hat and smoothing down his bald forehead whenever he was addressed by the officers. His mind naturally reverted to scenes that could not fail to produce a temporary embarrassment, heightened, perhaps, by the familiarity with which he found himself addressed by persons of a class with those whom he had been accustomed to obey.'

'Reckless Jack' Adams, as he had once been known, died four years later, deeply mourned by his wife and his old mistresses, his children and grandchildren. He remains today the most honoured figure in Pitcairn's history, his grave—set alone among orange and lemon and banana trees, close to the centre of the village and to his original home—is tended with special care all through the year and is always decorated with flowers. The example of his piety saved Pitcairn when it was so nearly too late, and has endured for another one and a half centuries.

11

'The worst of serpents'

William Bligh of his officers

✣

THE court martial that assembled on board H.M.S. *Duke* in Portsmouth harbour to try the ten officers and men of the *Bounty* was a great British *cause célèbre* of the autumn of 1792. Those who stood trial were Midshipman Peter Heywood, the armourer Jo Coleman, James Morrison, bo'sun's mate, the carpenter's mate Charles Norman and one of his crew, Tom McIntosh, and the five able seamen Tom Ellison, Tom Burkett, John Millward, Will Muspratt and blind Michael Byrn. Under the presidency of the Right Honourable Lord Hood, Vice-Admiral and C.-in-C. Portsmouth, eleven Royal Navy captains sat in judgement on the prisoners.

In the three months since the arrival of the prisoners at Portsmouth many influences had been at work in favour of the accused and against Bligh. His absence on the other side of the world gravely compromised his position and reduced the power of the prosecution. It was held to be a travesty of justice that the court martial should sit at all without the chief prosecuting witness, the man who had been the first victim of the mutineers. Even before his departure in the *Providence* he had done a number of things which compromised his popular reputation.

Public opinion in England in the late eighteenth century was a very small and very sensitive barometer, just as those who wielded power were few in number. A large and powerful family, with connections in the law, in the civil service, in politics and the armed forces and the seats of learning, could speedily destroy the good name of a man who lacked these supports. Both the Heywood and Christian families were of this calibre, and Bligh showed a grave lack of wisdom in his failure to recognise the dangers lying ahead after enjoying his rapturous reception in London.

The Heywoods were in an especially strong position to attack Bligh. Peter Heywood was the apple of the family's eye, an endearing, lively, pretty boy, adored by his sisters and his mother, and only fifteen years old when he had left home to join the *Bounty*. His father had died just two months before Bligh returned to England, and when his grief-stricken mother wrote anxiously to Bligh asking for news of her son, he replied:

Madam:
I received your letter this day, and feel for you very much, being perfectly sensible of the extreme distress you must suffer from the conduct of your son Peter. *His baseness is beyond all description*, but I hope you will endeavour to prevent the loss of him, heavy as the misfortune is, from afflicting you too severely. I imagine he is, with the rest of the mutineers, returned to Otaheite.
I am, Madam,
Wm. Bligh

Heywood's uncle, a colonel in the army, also wrote anxiously for news of his nephew. Bligh wrote back promptly: '*His ingratitude is of the blackest dye*, for I was father to him in every respect, and he never once had an angry word with me through the whole course of the voyage, as his conduct always gave me much pleasure and satisfaction. I very much regret *that so much baseness formed the character of a young man* I had a real regard for, and it will give me much pleasure to hear that his friends *can bear the loss of him without much concern.*'

After this the Heywoods were left in an agony of suspense about the fate of their boy for almost two years, certain only that he could never have committed the crime of which Bligh had accused him, the suspicions about Bligh feeding on themselves and growing abundantly. Then at last there arrived a letter from Peter, dated 20

November 1791 at Batavia, describing the mutiny and entirely exonerating himself from any guilt.

'My ever-honoured and Dearest Mother,' it began, 'At length the time has arrived when you are once more to hear from your ill-fated son, whose conduct at the capture of that ship in which it was my fortune to embark, has, I fear, from what has since happened to me, been grossly misrepresented to you by Lieutenant Bligh.'

Even before young Heywood's arrival in England the battle for his life was being waged, and the letter from his mother, which awaited him at Portsmouth, told how they were 'at present making all possible interest with every friend and connexion we have, to ensure sufficient support and protection at your approaching trial'.

Mrs Heywood wrote to all her friends and relatives with naval connections—to the Bertie family, one of whom, Captain Albermarle Bertie, was later selected among ten others as members of the court; his uncle Commodore Thomas Pasley, whose ship the *Vengeance* was at Portsmouth when Heywood arrived there with the other prisoners. Pasley replied to the family's appeal: 'Every exertion, you may rest assured, I shall use to save his life.' The commodore took the trouble to seek out future witnesses at the court martial like Fryer, Cole, Purcell and Peckover, all of whom confirmed Heywood's innocence.

Later, Pasley had a word with his friend Captain Montague of the *Hector*, in which the prisoners were confined to ensure that 'every attention and indulgence possible' was granted to Heywood. He also closely interrogated the young man himself and was able to reassure his family that he was confident that Peter had played no active part in the mutiny; and arranged for him to get the best possible legal advice from a Mr Aaron Graham, a highly experienced judge-advocate at courts martial.

Captain Edward Edwards's treatment of the prisoners, his loss of his ship, the story of the four prisoners going down in the *Pandora* because he had refused to allow their irons to be removed, became widely known and tended to bring public sentiment round in favour of Heywood and the other prisoners, and, by implication, more strongly than ever against Bligh. Why had he chosen to sail away before the men he had accused had been brought home, leaving behind him doubtful and even slanderous evidence? Why had so many officers, several from respectable families, risen up against him?

This was not a time of soft justice in England, least of all softness to mutineers and pirates, but as stories of Bligh's behaviour before the mutiny, of his unsubstantiated accusations, spread through society and the corridors of the Admiralty itself, people began to think that there was more to this notorious mutiny than met the eye.

The trial began on the morning of 12 September, and the evidence for the prosecution occupied the first three days. From the outset it was evident that Coleman, Norman and McIntosh would be acquitted as Bligh had left behind a deposition which exculpated them. It was also pretty clear that four of the seamen who had been seen bearing arms during the mutiny—Ellison, Burkett, Millward and Muspratt—had little hope of escaping the gallows, though the first had some narrow chance because of his youth. The interest in the trial, apart from the usual morbid fascination, lay in the fate of Heywood and Morrison, especially Heywood.

During the first two days evidence for the prosecution was given by Fryer, Cole, Purcell and Peckover, each in turn describing the events of that fatal morning as they remembered them, offering little that was contentious or unpredictable, and much that helped to build up a detailed and altogether fascinating minute-by-minute picture of every stage of the mutiny. Between them, Fryer and Cole had seen Burkett, Muspratt and Millward under arms. Cole spoke in favour of Heywood—'All along he was intending to come away but was kept below against his wishes.' He also spoke up strenuously for Morrison. Purcell said he thought that Millward had been forced to take part; and that Heywood had been no more than a victim of his youthfulness and the excitement of the moment. Yes, he said, he had seen Heywood with a cutlass in his hand, but as soon as he had asked him, 'In the name of God, Peter, what do you do with that?' he had at once dropped it. 'I looked upon him,' continued Purcell, 'as a person confused . . . In my mind he had no hand in the conspiracy'.

Fryer and Purcell, who considered themselves to have been so ill-used by Bligh, were clearly doing all that they could to give a favourable impression of those among their old shipmates who were not, by any judgement, deep-dyed mutineers. All four officers were cross-questioned by the prisoners and spoke well of their previous behaviour.

Not until the third day did the tone of the court change. The reason for this was the calling as witnesses of Hayward and Hallett, who had of course been, after Bligh, the next targets of Christian and the mutineers, and who had suffered not one but two gruelling open-boat voyages on account of 'the piracy of those who stood in the dock'. They had no reason to love any of these ten men, and they proceeded to show in their statements and during the cross-questioning that they were anxious to see them all swing from the yard arm, except only the three who had been already exonerated.

Under cross-examination, Hayward said he thought Morrison had assisted the mutineers, his 'countenance was rejoiced'; that he supposed Heywood was 'on the side of the mutineers'. Hallett claimed to have seen Morrison bearing arms and to have called out in a jeering manner; and Heywood had laughed, turned round and walked away after Bligh had said something to him.

The fourth day was Heywood's. The others, too, offered their defence. But in the length and professionalism, and also the emotionalism of his presentation, Peter Heywood dominated the proceedings. He had been briefed to attract the sympathy of the court on several grounds, and when this tall, good-looking, fair young man stood up, at nine o'clock on the morning of 17 September in the great cabin of H.M.S. *Duke*, he caught the eager attention of the court, the officials and guards and every member of the public.

His first step was a bold one. After the 'long and severe confinement I have suffered I am afraid I am not capable of delivering [my defence] with that force of expression which it requires', and desired the court's permission that it might be read by his legal adviser, Mr Const, instead. 'Appearances probably are against me but they are appearances only, for I declare before this court and the tribunal of Almighty God I am innocent of the charge. . . .'

Heywood's defence rested first on his youth and innocence, second on his confusion and ignorance of exactly what was going on, and thirdly on his fear—a fear, he hastened to add, which was shared by Tom Hayward and a number of others. 'To be starved to death, or drowned, appeared to be inevitable if I went in the boat and surely it is not to be wondered at if at the age of sixteen years with no one to advise with and so ignorant of the discipline of the service (having never been to sea before) as not to know or even suppose that it was possible that what I should determine upon might afterwards be alleged against me as a crime—I say under such circumstances, in so trying a situation, can it be wondered at if I suffered the preservation of my life to be the first, and to supersede every other, consideration?'

Heywood then proceeded to demolish Hallett's case. Hallett had unfortunately earlier confessed that he could remember neither the day nor the month on which he had arrived at Tahiti in the *Pandora*. How then, asked Heywood, could the court believe that he had accurately remembered the time and sequence of events, amidst the hurly-burly of a mutiny, three and a half years earlier? How also —in connection with the dangerous evidence that he had laughed at Bligh—had Hallett managed 'to particularise the muscles of a man's countenance' at the distance Heywood was able to show he was standing from Bligh at the time? When he had finished with him, Hallett was certainly a discredited witness, and even appeared to have been guilty of perjury.

Heywood brought his evidence to a shattering emotional climax: 'My parents (but I have only one left, a solitary and mournful mother who is at home weeping and trembling for the event of this day) thanks to their fostering care taught me betimes to reverence God, to honour the King and be obedient to his laws and at no time have I resolutely or designedly been an apostate to either.'

Morrison's case, though shorter and less emotional, also showed a touch of professionalism; and Byrn told a short and true heart-rending tale of anxiety and confusion. Coleman, Norman and McIntosh were also brief. The four seamen put up as good a case as they could against hopeless odds. They were certain they were doomed.

At nine o'clock on the morning of 18 September the court assembled and was then cleared while Lord Hood passed sentence on the ten men standing manacled in the dock.

'It is agreed,' he began, 'that the charges have been proved against the said Peter Heywood, James Morrison, Thomas Ellison, Thomas Burkett, John Millward and William Muspratt, and I do adjudge you and each of you to suffer death by being hanged by the neck on board such of His Majesty's ship or ships of war . . .'

The President went on to 'humbly and most earnestly recommend the said Peter Heywood and James Morrison to His Majesty's Royal Mercy'. The rest went free.

The Heywood family were condemned to another period of agonising doubt after the findings of the court martial were made known. Peter's sister Nessy wrote to the Earl of Chatham, the First

Lord of the Admiralty—'I assure you, my lord, that he is dearer and more precious to me than any object on earth—nay, infinitely more valuable than life itself—that, deprived of him, the word misery would but ill express my complicated wretchedness. . . .'

But all was well, both for Heywood and Morrison, and a free pardon was sent down from London to Portsmouth two weeks later. On Commodore Pasley's recommendation, Lord Hood himself offered to take Heywood in his flagship *Victory* as a midshipman, and Lord Spencer agreed to his promotion.

To acquit, and at once to promote, an officer who had been one of Bligh's chief targets, was a public rebuke to the absent captain, and everyone recognised it as such. Heywood rose to the rank of post-captain ten years later, and died, an admiral, in 1831, after forty-two years of honourable service. The dictionary he compiled on Tahiti while awaiting a ship was eventually published and, it is said, proved of great value to the first missionaries when they began work on the island before he died.

Morrison, too, had no difficulty in finding a ship. He bequeathed his remarkable journal* to Heywood, and extracts from it, somewhat mutilated, appeared for the first time in a book called *The Mutineers of the Bounty* (1870) by Heywood's stepdaughter, Lady Belcher. He died at sea when serving as a gunner in H.M.S. *Blenheim* in 1807.

Of the four mutineers condemned to death, Will Muspratt cleverly won a stay of execution, and eventually his freedom on a legal technicality; and so, of the twenty-five who remained behind in the *Bounty*, only three met the common fate of every mutineer—Tom Ellison, the boy who had once been recommended to Bligh by Campbell and was only sixteen when he had thrown in his lot so joyfully, more as a prank really, with Christian; John Millward, a 'man of great education and capacity', according to one witness who met him shortly before his execution; and Tom Burkett, another eager supporter of Christian.

The executions, due to be carried out on board H.M.S. *Brunswick* on 29 October, aroused even greater excitement than the court martial. Among the better classes there was satisfaction that the well-born and likable Peter Heywood, and the less-educated but highly articulate James Morrison, were both pardoned. Locally in

* See below, page 312.

Portsmouth there was some disappointment that the spectacle would only feature three ordinary seamen. 'According to great murmurs and the vulgar notion,' wrote one gentleman visitor from London, 'money bought their lives, and the others fell sacrifice to their poverty.'

This same witness—an unidentified fellow but obviously of some importance—managed to get on board the *Brunswick* the evening before the ceremony. He discovered, to his astonishment, that the prisoners 'tripped up and down the ladders with the most wonderful alacrity; and their countenances, instead of being (as I expected) the index of a woeful depression of mind, were perfectly calm, serene and cheerful'. On that last evening Millward read Dodd's Sermons to his two companions.

'At nine o'clock the next morning the fatal gun was fired, and the yellow flag displayed the dreadful summons to claim the attention of all the fleet. Boats from every ship assembled, and, in a short time, the ship was crowded with officers and men. Along the shore, and even afloat in wherries, were men, women and children, to the amount of thousands, as if, instead of a solemn scene of sorrow, it had been a spectacle of joy.'

The prisoners were brought up from below and were escorted, one to the starboard yardarm, the other two to the port yardarm. 'The officers and men were arranged along the deck in column; the yard ropes stretched along in each man's hand. On the cathead Millward addressed the ship's company, confessed the errors they had been guilty of, acknowledged the justice of their sentences and warned them by his fate to shun similar paths of impropriety: his speech was nervous, strong, and eloquent, and delivered in an open and deliberative manner.'

James Morrison himself, who had so narrowly escaped their fate, had requested the privilege of performing the last offices to his three friends. The gun was fired—'and their souls took their flight in a cloud'.

With the violent deaths of three more of the *Bounty*'s crew, it is worth glancing back to the fates of the men on Christian's watch at the time of the mutiny three and a half years earlier. Within a year from the date of the hanging, which disposed of Burkett and Ellison, Christian, Mills and Martin had all been murdered.

Quintal was, in effect, executed on Pitcairn a few years later. The two midshipmen, Hayward and Hallett, who had done their best to see that Heywood and Morrison were both hanged too, met violent ends soon after, Hallett in H.M.S. *Penelope*, Hayward out in China when the sloop in which he was serving foundered in a typhoon.

Of these nine men, then, three died at the hands of white men, three at the hands of natives, two by storms, leaving only one survivor, the shark-watcher, the man we remember as a dreamy eccentric, Charles Norman of the carpenter's crew, who survived the hell of the *Pandora* and was acquitted at the court martial. He returned safely at last to his wife and children.

The eighteen-month-long period between William Bligh's return home in the *Providence* and his next employment in the Royal Navy was one of anxiety and unhappiness for him. The proceedings and findings of the court martial were known throughout the land. Everyone knew that this had been no ordinary mutiny, conspired only for evil purposes by ignorant seamen. The evidence for the prosecution had revealed the uneven behaviour of Bligh and the incident of the stolen coconuts. From answers to questions put by the members of the court martial it became evident that Fletcher Christian, a man of gentle birth and good education, had been abused by Bligh, that 'he had been in hell for a fortnight'.

The fact that the court, and the Lords Commissioners, had between them hung only three of the ten accused and bent over backwards to be as lenient as the law allowed, was not lost on those who wielded power and influence in the country. As soon as the court martial was over fierce contention broke out between the five chief families involved, the Bethams, Blighs and Hallets on one side, facing the Christians, determined to retrieve the good name of the family, and the Heywoods, who with their name triumphantly vindicated, now turned relentlessly to exact revenge on the Blighs.

Fletcher's brother Edward appointed himself the leader of the faction which set about the destruction of Bligh's reputation. He possessed the power, the learning and the distinguished reputation —all the weapons—to succeed. Soon after Bligh's return home, Edward Christian published at his own expense an abbreviated edition of the *Minutes of the Proceedings of the Court Martial,* contributing his own long Appendix. According to your prejudices, this might be read as a piece of special pleading on behalf of his brother and his allies, or as a revelation of the real truth behind the mutiny. Either way, as might be expected, it was a very clever piece of writing.

It was not his intention, insisted the elder Christian, to pervert truth or justice. Quite the reverse. Mutineers should be 'punished with inexorable rigour'. But 'every friend of truth and strict justice must feel his attention awakened to the true causes and circumstances, which have hitherto been concealed or misrepresented of one of the most remarkable events in the annals of the Navy'.

In his assiduous search for truth, Edward Christian had contacted survivors of the open-boat voyage with Bligh and survivors of the *Pandora* shipwreck, including, of course, Fryer, Peckover, Purcell and Heywood, and McIntosh, Byrn, Coleman, Muspratt, Morrison and others. Then, in the presence of men like the Canon of Windsor, the Chaplain to the Bishop of London, eminent barristers, and one of the Wordsworth family, he had questioned them at length about the events that led up to the fatal day, and the mutiny itself.

Skilfully sewn together, this volunteered evidence revealed far more than the court martial about the true causes of the mutiny. It made public for the first time, for example, that Christian had first tried to escape from the 'hell' of the ship, that this was no premeditated mutiny, that the 'young gentlemen' and others among the officers had been harshly ill-used (so they said) for many weeks past, and that Bligh had threatened to throw the officers overboard before they reached the dread Endeavour Straits.

This Appendix attacked not only Bligh by implication but also the veracity of his own published narrative. It spoke of the 'poignancy of Christian's distress' at Bligh's abuse in front of the ship's company, and the Tahitian chiefs—'if he would only find fault with him in private'. It attacked Bligh for stating in his narrative that his boat-load 'were turned out to certain destruction' when, as Edward Christian wrote, 'it is proved before the court martial, that most of the persons went into the launch voluntarily'.

Edward Christian was much too wise a man even to hint that he condoned his brother's crime. His intention was to bring new light to bear on it, on the man who was the victim of the mutiny, and his own brother who had initiated it. The idea of the mutiny was put into Fletcher's head by others, Edward Christian suggested, at a time when he was at the limit of his endurance. Everyone had loved him for 'his amiable qualities'. 'All those who came in the boat, whose sufferings and losses on his account have been so severe, not only speak of him without resentment and with forgiveness, but with a degree of rapture and enthusiasm'; and he went on to quote some of these comments, like, 'He was a gentleman and a brave man; and every officer and seaman on board the ship would have gone through fire and water to have served him.'

Edward Christian concluded his long Appendix:

The crime itself in this instance may afford an awful lesson to the Navy, and to mankind, that there is a degree of pressure, beyond which the best formed and principled mind must either break or recoil. And though public justice and the public safety can allow no vindication of any species of Mutiny, yet reason and humanity will distinguish the sudden unpremeditated act of desperation and frenzy, from the foul deliberate contempt of every religious duty and honourable sentiment; and will deplore the uncertainty of human prospects, when they reflect that a young man is condemned to perpetual infamy, who, if he had served on board any other ship, or had perhaps been absent from the *Bounty* a single day, or one ill-fated hour, might still have been an honour to his country, and a glory and comfort to his friends.

Bligh was obliged to reply to this damaging publication, which had a wide readership, and he in turn sought out some of the witnesses who had lent their names in support of Edward Christian. Some denied what they had previously sworn. All except Peter Heywood must have become weary with this quarrel raging about them, and afraid that they might, even now, become legally implicated. One of them, McIntosh, confessed 'that he had been threatened for what he had mentioned'. John Hallett declared that no officer or seaman had been accused of theft after the *Bounty* left Nomuka, no matter what anyone else had said. Edward Christian came back once more with a Short Reply to Captain Bligh's Answer, and had the last and most telling word with a declaration from the steady and reliable Bligh-man, Will Peckover, that the facts in Edward Christian's Appendix were substantially accurate.

Although Britain was now at war with France, the Lords Commissioners did not feel able to employ Bligh while all this was going on, and he was kept on half-pay, an embittered and penurious officer with few people prepared to support him. His wife, as always, stuck loyally behind him, firing off outraged letters to anyone who might support her husband. To add to their troubles, she now gave birth again, this time to twins, both boys. To the couple's lasting grief they died a day later.

While his contemporaries were gaining distinction in battles culminating in the great victory of the Glorious First of June, and adding to their fortunes with prize money, Bligh remained unemployed by the Navy. The Admiralty would not even support the publication of his narrative of the second and successful breadfruit expedition and he certainly could not afford to subsidise it privately. His chance came at last, when the controversy with Edward Christian and his other opponents was dying down, in April 1795. He was appointed to the command of the *Calcutta*, which was ordered to join the fleet of Admiral Adam Duncan in the North Sea, blockading the Dutch Fleet. In the following January he was given the command of the much larger *Director*, of sixty-four guns.

Dull, uneventful and frustrating blockade duties occupied the *Director*'s company for many months. Never had the Royal Navy been harder pressed at sea than at this time. Conditions and pay were appalling, and it had been necessary to press into service a great number of lawbreakers and tavern drunks. These men became ripe material for mutiny on a giant scale, organised by opportunists as well as idealists, and by men who had caught the infection of revolution that was spreading all over Europe.

After a period in port the *Director* rejoined Duncan's fleet in March 1797. Bligh was soon aware of a new and dangerous spirit running through the ship. Six men refused or neglected their duties. Bligh served out lashes to them all, and to five more a few days later. The normal running of the ship became more and more difficult and Bligh soon realised that this was no passing restlessness. He took the *Director* into Sheerness, and there, at nine in the morning of 19 May 1797, he was ordered ashore and to yield up his command.

It was the second time he had been ordered off his ship by mutineers. But this time he was in good company. For the whole Nore command of the Royal Navy, with its immense responsibilities in the North Sea and the Channel, had risen up against their officers, demanding improved pay and conditions. This was the infamous Mutiny of the Nore, which put Britain at the mercy of her foes for a month. Bligh took an active and responsible part in the closing stages of the mutiny, in which the Admiralty yielded to many of the most important demands of the ringleaders, a number of whom were then hanged.

Bligh experienced a new taste of battle at Camperdown, a few months after this mutiny; and again at Copenhagen against the Danish fleet in April 1801. He was proud for the rest of his life of the part he played in both these battles, and was always eager to reminisce about them.

But even when fighting for his country Bligh seemed unable to avoid controversy. There is no reason to doubt that he behaved as gallantly under the pressure of battle as he did in the midst of hostile natives on Hawaii as a young man, or during that awful open-boat voyage in his maturity. Yet doubts were cast by his enemies on Bligh's fighting spirit at both battles, and unfortunately the record shows that he claimed undue credit for the part he played in the capture of the Dutch flagship at Camperdown, and that in Duncan's despatch no mention was made of the part taken by his ship.

Bligh was nearing the end of his active service in the Royal Navy. His reputation as a navigator and hydrographer, as naturalist and scientist, was quite untarnished. He had been presented with the Gold Medal by the Royal Society, of which he was now a Fellow. The Admiralty despatched him on surveying voyages. His family life remained blissfully happy, and there was no more loving and anxious father. Yet his professional life was rarely free from discord, and Betsy seemed to be forever involved in support and defence of his reputation.

In June 1799 there was another court martial. The master of the *Director*, Joseph Ramsey, was in trouble with Bligh, accused of improper behaviour and impertinence. 'If I am not able to work the ship,' he is stated to have said to Bligh, 'it is better to have some person else here.' 'The charge against him is proved,' declared the court, and Ramsey got his way, and nothing worse, when he was 'dismissed from his situation as master of the *Director*'.

Bligh's next court martial occurred in 1804. At this time he was commander of the *Warrior*, in which his second lieutenant was an officer called John Frazier. There had obviously been a lot of trouble between these two before Frazier had an accident, injuring his leg by falling between casks loaded in a launch. Frazier claimed that he was unable to walk. Bligh, considering him a malingerer, refused to excuse him his duties, and gave him until nine o'clock to appear on deck.

'What can I do? My good God, I wish I was able to keep my watch,' Frazier said in his appeal to the ship's surgeon.

Without much ado, Bligh placed his lieutenant under arrest and had him charged with 'contumacy and disobedience'. On the surgeon's evidence, Frazier was acquitted.

The lieutenant wasted no time in pushing home his advantage and reported that Bligh 'publicly on the quarter deck . . . did grossly insult and ill treat me . . . by calling me rascal, scoundrel and shaking his fist in my face and that at various times . . . he behaved himself towards me and other commissioned, warrant and petty officers of the said ship in a tyrannical and oppressive and unofficerlike manner.'

When the news of this accusation reached the Admiralty from Bligh's C.in-C., it was decided to court martial him in turn. The *Warrior* court martial, as it came to be called, was the last, inglorious event in Bligh's naval career. Unlike the court martial of the *Bounty* mutineers, this was no public *cause célèbre*, and the minutes and findings were not publicised. Bligh's Victorian detractors missed this significant event in his career altogether, and it was left to Mackaness, Bligh's sympathetic twentieth-century biographer, to reveal in detail this wounding and humiliating episode in his life.

In fact the evidence at this court martial adds little to what we already know about William Bligh. What it does is to colour more strongly the man's weaknesses as a leader and at the same time underlines his good intentions. The phrase has been coined, for a man of impatience and high standards, that 'he does not suffer fools gladly'. Bligh could not suffer fools, or weak, or temperamental characters. He could not afford to, any more than Cook, in solitary responsibility for many lives, under many hazards, in remote corners of the world for years at a time.

The *Bounty* episode had scarred Bligh's whole personality. After 1789 he became more insecure, more defensive, more conscious of the presence of real or supposed enemies than ever. He swore, we can be certain, more roundly and fluently and readily than before. He was watching out for his subordinates' weaknesses more keenly than before. He was more than ever determined, because it was more than ever necessary, to give a good account of himself to his superiors, and to his ever-loyal patron, Banks.

But Bligh could never hope to acquire that serene self-confidence so vital to a successful commander, especially after his public combat with Edward Christian in 1794–5. His enemies were too many, his reputation, justly or unjustly, was too flawed. He was irrecoverably wounded.

We can see, with sinking heart and with awful clarity, Bligh as commander of H.M.S. *Warrior*, threatening and cursing like the caricatured version of the earlier Bligh in Charles Laughton's film, overplaying the same part he had played years before out in Polynesia. We can see it all again, more sharply than ever, in this ship —the uneasiness and unpredictability of the man, the loyal officers who would see him through everything, those other officers who recognised weakness in this posturing and cursing and the over-reacting to minor episodes which most commanders would shrug off or deal with summarily and then forget.

At first one feels, 'Will this man never learn from his mistakes?' And one has to answer that he was too proud and too unsure of himself. The next moment one is in sympathy with him, asking, 'What diabolical turn of fate burdened this great navigator, wherever he sailed, with so many weak, unrealiable officers?'

Lieutenant Frazier was abused as roundly and was as publicly humiliated as Christian. Of that there can be no doubt. Another lieutenant swore that he heard Bligh claim that 'I will rule the officers of the *Warrior* with a iron rod,' and that if an officer fell within his power—then 'woe be to them! mercy, no by God, I will show them none'. A third witness at the court martial declared that Bligh was 'sometimes passionate and sometimes very cool'.

It was this unevenness that destroyed men's confidence—the establishing of favourites and the sudden irrational outbursts against those who supposed themselves favoured. Where leadership should have come naturally, he was seen to be trying too hard. We see it again and again in the *Warrior* court martial. The outcome was inevitable. His officers might, as Bligh complained, 'turn out to be the worst of serpents', but the court martial's considered opinion was that 'the charges are in part proved, and we do therefore adjudge Captain William Bligh to be reprimanded and to be admonished to be in future more correct in his language'.

Bligh was restored to his command and wrote without delay to Banks, complaining about everything—the court martial, the findings, and his officers; and begged Banks to use his influence to get some of these officers removed. 'Instances of my doing good,' remarks Bligh to his patron, 'and rendering service are numerous since my youth to this moment. I defy the world to produce one act of malevolence or injustice.'

While Bligh is suffering this further crisis in his naval career, steps are being taken that will end for the time being his long period of misfortune. A new and seemingly golden opportunity comes his way, and again it is the powerful hand of Sir Joseph Banks that offers it to him. On 15 March 1805 Banks writes to Bligh on board the *Warrior*: 'As I hope I never omit any chance of being useful to a friend whom I esteem, as I do you, I lose not a minute in apprising you of [this offer].' Banks continues:

I have always, since the first institution of the new colony at New South Wales, taken a deep interest in its success, and have been constantly consulted by His Majesty's Ministers, through all the changes there have been in the department which directs it, relative to the more important concerns of the colonists. At present, King, the Governor, is tired of his station; and well may he be so. He has carried into effect a reform of great extent, which militated much with the interests of the soldiers and settlers there. He is, consequently, disliked and much opposed, and has asked leave to return.

Banks's offer was the governorship of New South Wales, no less, with a salary of £2,000 a year, a pension of £1,000 a year, and no loss in his naval seniority. It was an opportunity that Bligh could not pass by, especially in view of its timing. The one serious drawback was that he would have to leave behind his 'beloved Betsy' and his children. As he explained sadly to Banks in his reply, Elizabeth could not possibly undertake such a long sea voyage. Her nerves had suffered on account of her husband's troubles and the valiant fight she had put up on his behalf. 'The sound of a gun or thunder' was unbearable to her, and even when Bligh's ship was in port she could remain on board for only a few hours.

Acceptance of this magnificent offer therefore meant separation from his family for more than four years. However, 'to procure a little affluence' as he put it, they both agreed that it was the right thing to do, and in February 1806 he bade his wife and five of his daughters farewell at the house in Durham Place, Lambeth, in south London, where they had lived for so many years. His daughter Mary accompanied him. She had married a naval officer, John Putland, who had agreed to act as Bligh's lieutenant during his governorship of the colony.

This party of three embarked in the transport *Lady Madeleine Sinclair*, one of a number of ships carrying men and women convicts and colonists out to Botany Bay, and the convoy was commanded by Captain Joseph Short in H.M.S. *Porpoise*.

The wisdom of Mrs Bligh's decision to remain behind was soon proved. Short and Bligh were soon at loggerheads and quarrelled all the way out—over where they should stop, the course they should steer, and even about who was in command. At one point Short ordered shots to be fired across the bows and astern of Bligh's ship, in order to force him to alter course. The third shot was aimed to strike the ship, and Putland was to have fired it—at Short's orders.

Clearly, Bligh had met more than his match at sea; but on land, in New South Wales, where Short had decided to settle and had sold up all he had in England and had brought with him his wife and seven children on the promise of a grant of 600 acres, Bligh got his own back. When Short refused to obey Bligh's order to give up the command of his ship, Bligh had him arrested and sent back to England with his family for court martial. His wife and one of his children died from the rigours of the voyage in an old leaky vessel. At the court martial Short was honourably acquitted, and the evidence and findings were highly unfavourable to Bligh.

Bligh found conditions in New South Wales far worse than Banks had described them, far worse than he could have dreamed possible. The corrupt, violent, drunken and immoral community consisted of rum pedlars and rum drinkers, all controlled by a ruthless military junta. The New South Wales Corps had originally been created, from the dregs of the British army, to guard the convicts and administer martial law. As numbers increased and free settlers arrived, the Corps held on to all its early special privileges, perverted justice to its own ends, and above all seized monopolistic control of what was collectively the colony's food and currency—its rum.

The settlers, the farmers, the convicts, men and women, with few exceptions, had all succumbed to alcoholism. Women sold their bodies, men their land and their stock, for rum. The officers of the Corps saw that they got it, at a price, and made vast fortunes from it.

The Governor, Bligh discovered to his chagrin, was regarded as no more than a cypher. Previous governors had either accepted the situation, dabbling a little themselves, or had fought for reform, as his predecessor had done, and failed. Bligh, needless to say, decided that he was going to fight, and win. That was why Banks had entrusted him with the post.

Bligh made many enemies during his first months. His main antagonist, the man who was to break him, was John McArthur, one of Australia's early folk hero-villains, a man of gigantic ambitions and negligible scruples, boss of the rum corps. McArthur had resigned his commission in the New South Wales Corps and got a corner in everything that led to profit and power.

Bligh fought valiantly but unskilfully against the gangster regime of McArthur and his cronies. He was quite out of his depth in this world of chicanery and corruption. He swore and resorted to sledge-hammer tactics. His motives were admirable—such as the banning of stills and the manufacture of spirits, and his endeavours to bring some sort of just civil government to the colony. But his methods could never hope to prevail against the solidly entrenched power of men like McArthur—who were as quick as any naval officer to spot weakness in a leader.

Here, in this remote outpost, without the support of law, military strength, or influential friends, Bligh was more helpless than he had ever been in the past. There was no Betsy, no Banks, to support him. His daughter could do nothing, his son-in-law was dying of consumption. The small company of friends he had made when he had first arrived, dissolved away.

We have seen several pathetic pictures of William Bligh since that savage April dawn in his cabin in the *Bounty*, but none more heart-rending than that of 26 January 1808, the day McArthur got Major George Johnston, the commanding officer of the New South Wales Corps, to arrest him in Government House.

Several hundred men of the Corps, with fixed bayonets and muskets loaded with ball, marched from the parade ground of their barracks, led by Johnston and his officers, towards Government House. They were accompanied by the band playing 'The British

Grenadiers', and by a large number of the citizens enthusiastically encouraging them on. At the house, Johnston drew up his men, stood them at ease, and sent in a party to arrest Bligh and his staff. They were opposed, according to one witness, only by Bligh's daughter Mary, who 'hastened to the gates and gallantly opposed their entrance, setting the bayonets at defiance and exclaimed, "You traitors, you rebels, you have just walked over my husband's grave and now you come to murder my father!"' She had to be dragged away—a true Bligh.

The manner of Bligh's arrest is the most memorable and controversial event in the notorious Rum Rebellion. All that is known for sure is that he took a lot of finding and that he was eventually discovered in a back room underneath a feather bed, wearing his naval uniform and the gold medal he had earned at the Battle of Camperdown. Was it cowardice that sent him there, or did he hope that the soldiery and the mob might eventually look for him elsewhere, thus enabling him to escape? Bligh, as so often before, is his own stoutest and most convincing defender:

> For twenty-one years I have been a Post-Captain, and have been engaged in services of danger, not falling within the ordinary duties of my profession—for four years with Captain Cook in the *Resolution* and four years more as a Commander myself, I traversed unknown seas, braving difficulties more terrible because less frequently encountered . . . In the Battle of Camperdown the *Director*, under my command, first silenced and then boarded the ship of Admiral de Winter; and after the battle of Copenhagen, where I commanded the *Glatton*, I was sent for by Lord Nelson to receive his thanks publicly on the quarterdeck. Was it for me then to sully my reputation and to disgrace the medal I wear by shrinking from death, which I had braved in every shape?

After suffering numerous humiliations and vicissitudes, quarrelling with and straining the hospitality of his replacement as Governor, Colonel Lachlan Macquarie, who was sent out from England with proper military support and dictatorial powers, Bligh sailed from New South Wales on 27 April 1810, arriving in London six months later.

Once again he found himself involved in strife and litigation. Some of the leading figures in the Rum Rebellion, Johnston and

McArthur among them, were already in London, or arrived shortly after him. Factions were again hard at work discrediting Bligh. A second officer who was sent home by Bligh for court martial was acquitted; McArthur threatened civil action against Bligh for £20,000 damages.

The legal arguments dragged on, the Crown seemed curiously reluctant to institute proceedings. At last, in May 1811, a court martial was assembled to try Johnston for mutiny. It was a long-drawn-out and unsatisfactory trial for all parties. No one showed up well, even Bligh, the one man who had at least attempted to bring order and justice to the unhappy colony. Johnston was found guilty and sentenced to be cashiered.

After this ordeal, the last of so many, Bligh applied for promotion to flag rank; and it is with relief that one learns that his request was granted. He never hoisted his flag, never went to sea again, but at least he could retire from his full-blooded, turbulent public career as an admiral—no longer that derisory, corpulent character 'old Breadfruit', but William Bligh, Rear-Admiral of the Blue, who had fought alongside Nelson, Hyde-Parker and Duncan, and one of the greatest navigators and explorers of his day.

This last court martial, at which her husband had given two full days' evidence and all the unpleasantness and anxiety that accompanied it, were too much for Eliazbeth. Bligh's devoted, highly strung, dedicated and intelligent wife, fell ill and died, worn out by life, on 15 April 1812 at Durham Place. Bligh buried her in Lambeth Churchyard, where her body lies alongside her husband's today.

Bligh was deeply distressed at this loss of his 'beloved Betsy', the last and bitterest consequence of the last and bitterest court martial in which he was involved. Taking solace from the love of his four unmarried daughters, he moved from London to a house at Farningham. Here he built up a quiet social life in the tranquillity of the Kent countryside, travelled sometimes to London to see his friends, corresponded affectionately with his old patron Banks, and sat on one or two Admiralty committees, which comforted him with the knowledge that the world still needed him.

On 7 December 1817, on one of his increasingly frequent visits to his doctor in London, he was taken ill and died of cancer aged sixty-three.

I2

'A crime
of so black a nature'

✢

LIQUOR, in the end, did for both Bligh and Christian—McKoy's illicit still on Pitcairn, and McArthur's in New South Wales. Bligh's career, and Christian's life, ended in divided, corrupt, alcoholic and isolated communities far from home and the forces of law and order.

The solution to the mystery of the *Bounty* mutiny lies somewhere in the passage between Tahiti and Tofua, and in those words spoken in secrecy and anguish by Christian to Peter Heywood on the black volcanic beach of Matavai Bay before the *Bounty* left Tahiti for the last time.

To understand what may have passed between these two young North Countrymen it is necessary to step far back and look at a little considered side of life in the Royal Navy.

At the end of the eighteenth century the moral standards in the Royal Navy had never been lower. Winston Churchill's definition of the Navy's record in war as resting on 'rum, sodomy and the lash' is superbly apt. Sex at sea had been a problem since men first left coastal waters on passages to distant ports. Long sexual abstinence led to restlessness, disaffection and 'unnatural practices' from the earliest years of Egyptian exploration. It was a recurrent problem with the Portuguese, Spanish, Venetian, English, French and Dutch explorers and traders of the fifteenth, sixteenth and seventeenth centuries. Tucked away among the early narratives are references to the awful punishments meted out to men found guilty of sodomy. Magellan had two cases of it before he had even crossed the Atlantic on the first-ever circumnavigation. Every nation, every navy, every commander at one time or another had to face up to the problem. It was worst in time of war; and at no time was it a greater problem than in the Royal Navy during the second half of the eighteenth century when numbers in the lower deck were swollen by pressed men in thousands, many of them of a low or criminal character.

To reduce the dangers of sodomy the navy encouraged women as well as wives to come on board—prostitutes at home, natives abroad—whenever the ship was in port. This was all very well, and even romantic in our eyes, in Matavai Bay during the *Bounty*'s stay there. The scene was less edifying in home ports, especially through the eyes of the officers' and men's wives and children. 'These all inhabit the same deck,' a contemporary eyewitness reports, 'where, whatever be their age or sex or character, they are huddled promiscuously together, eating, drinking and sleeping, without any adequate means of separation or privacy, for the most part even without the slightest screen between their berths; and where, in the sight and hearing of all around them, they live in the unrestrained indulgence of every licentious propensity which may be supposed to actuate inmates of this description.'

After many months of blockading duties during the Napoleonic Wars a man-o'-war sails into Spithead. 'Immediately upon arrival,' an officer recounts, 'crowds of boats flock off with cargoes of prostitutes. Having no money to pay for their conveyance, the waterman takes as many as his boat will hold, upon speculation, and hovers round the ship until she is secured at her anchors and the necessary work done; when he, with others, is permitted to come alongside. The men then go into the boats, and pick out each a woman (as one would choose cattle), paying a shilling or two to the boatman for her passage off.'

No one can say whether this sort of conduct in port was successful in reducing sodomy at sea. The subject is never mentioned in contemporary memoirs. The reports of courts martial that have survived reveal numerous cases of sodomy, not always punished with death although technically a capital offence. Usually the charge was milder—'Disgraceful conduct', 'Indecency', 'Gross indecency', 'Indecent conduct and attempted sodomy'—these are the charges against two lieutenants, a mate, an acting master, two marines, three seamen and a boy over one period.

Section 29 of the Articles of War at this time was explicit on the subject. 'If any person in the fleet shall commit the unnatural and detestable sin of buggery or sodomy, with man or beast, he shall be punished with death, by the sentence of a court martial.'

But for every case that was brought to court, there were certainly many hundreds which went unpunished.

Those who attempted to bring about a moral reform in the navy had no doubt at all that the encouragement of prostitution and licentiousness on shipboard actually encouraged sodomy at sea. One contemporary pamphleteer angrily demanded to know, 'What can be more *unnatural*, more contrary to all the feelings of our common nature, than the open, undisguised, unblushing, promiscuous concubinage, which now takes place on board His Majesty's ships of war? Is it not the person who has been tutored in this school of impurity and licentiousness, and who must there have bid adieu to those feelings which operate the most powerfully as a restraint on new modes of criminal indulgence, less likely than others to shrink from any abomination which may be suggested to his mind? ... Who are the men most likely to be guilty of unnatural practices; —those who had for weeks inhabited the lower deck of a man of war, and been witnesses and actors in the brutalising scenes we have described; who had had their imaginations contaminated by all sorts of obscenity, and their consciences scarred by the sight and participation of all sorts of polluting exhibitions;—or the men who, whatever may be supposed the force of their unnatural passions, had never passed through so debasing and demoralising an ordeal?'

From this sort of protest—one of many—we can judge how widespread 'unnatural practices' were in the Navy at that time—and for many years before and many years after, and among all ranks. The length of time at sea—many months, perhaps several years— was one reason. Another was the confined conditions on board—in the *Bounty* nearly fifty young men and boys restricted to a vessel with an *overall* length of ninety feet, the greater part of the accommodation being given up to stores and the breadfruit garden. She took little short of a year to reach her destination, and for much of that time her company had little with which to occupy themselves. There were few of the distractions and entertainments of shipboard life that occupy the long uneventful hours today. Most of the men were illiterate.

Intimate friendships were made on these lonely voyages. It would be surprising if these did not sometimes develop homosexual tendencies. So long as they were not damaging to discipline, the commander turned a blind eye to them, and they were accepted as a normal part of shipboard life. Many of the men who participated enjoyed a normal and happy married life at home.

The ship's commander, with his own cabin and the privilege of privacy, and with his special responsibilities as Bligh had—for his 'young gentlemen' like Peter Heywood on his first voyage, was also in a special position to enjoy intimate relationships. Even in the overcrowded *Bounty*, Bligh's command was a lonely one, especially after he ceased to share meals with his surgeon and master. We can imagine that he was glad to have company for midday dinner, and especially for supper and the long evenings. There was nothing unusual about this. Every commander invited his officers to share his table.

Of all the midshipmen in the *Bounty*, Bligh's friendship with Christian, as we have seen, was the most intimate and long lasting. This was their third voyage together. It is clear that Christian was singled out for special favours in the *Britannia* and later in the *Bounty*. With the key to Bligh's liquor store, when on watch he would often send down one of the men to fetch him a tot. He is reported as having supper with Bligh every other night.

There were disputes between the commander and his protégé before they reached Tahiti, but they were few and not of a very violent nature. At Tahiti the close relationship was broken, with Christian ashore all the time, living a full-blooded heterosexual life with the native women, while Bligh, with Cook as an example, lived a sexually abstemious life half on shipboard and half on shore with the royal family. If he had wanted a female *tyo*, it would not have conformed to his dignified status to take one.

Let us look back to early April 1789. Bligh is angry at the state of the ship and the slackness of officers and men. For more than five months he has seen them all enjoying themselves with the women. These women are superbly beautiful, and Bligh is the first to appreciate this. He is thirty-four, corpulent, pale, not too fit, and now angry. The young man, Fletcher Christian, whom he has indulged and instructed and lived closely with for so long, has been sharing his bed with a particularly beautiful young woman, the daughter of a chief, in a state of delightful self-indulgence, for a long time. He is slack, careless, handsome, his muscular brown body patterned with tattoo marks. He is suffering from venereal disease as the result of his earlier philanderings. If Bligh has been experiencing sexual jealousy, which is extremely likely, then his first target for vengeance will obviously be Christian.

It is at this time—according to all accounts—that Fletcher Christian's ordeal begins.

With the knowledge that Bligh was appalled at the condition of his ship and her company, and on the supposition that he was jealous of the lax and easy life and the sexual indulgences which all his officers and men had enjoyed, now is the moment when he will vent his fury as he smartens up his ship for the long and arduous voyage ahead. He does more than this. However one looks at them, the days between Matavai Bay and Tofua reveal a commander who is at the end of his tether, behaves violently and irrationally, shows extreme possessiveness and a truly fearsome venom towards his officers, and towards Christian in particular.

Now this could be difficult to account for. But it could be explained if we knew—but we never shall for sure—that Bligh and Christian had enjoyed for a long period a homosexual relationship, a relationship going back to their first voyage together in 1785, when Edward Lamb saw Bligh's 'partiality for the young man'. Christian, perhaps experiencing a feeling of disgust, is now unwilling to renew this relationship with the older man who has insulted him in front of his lover and her relatives on Tahiti and has singled him out for special abuse the moment the *Bounty* is again at sea.

We know only that Christian confided something in secret to Peter Heywood before the two separated for the last time at Tahiti; that Heywood was asked to pass on a message to Christian's family —probably to Edward, the brother to whom Christian was closest— which might mitigate the crime in his eyes; that Heywood, after careful consideration, decided against saying anything, the secret of the message dying with him.

For Peter Heywood, family friend and closer than ever to the Christians after the court martial, to refrain from divulging this message—the last word they could ever hear from him—suggests that it was either deeply shaming to the family, deeply wounding, or too dangerous. It could hardly have been that Christian had caught a dose of venereal disease, an accepted and easily curable mariner's risk which had affected nearly a half of the *Bounty*'s crew.

The most likely supposition is that Christian wished at least his brother to know that he had been under unbearable pressure to renew an intimate relationship with his commander which had benefited him greatly in the past but which, after five months in the paradise of Tahiti, was no longer congenial. After refusing to spend the evening with Bligh for the last time, Christian, in a deeply disturbed state of mind, determines on a step so dangerous that it amounts to suicide, is foiled, is offered an alternative course of action which at any other time he would not have contemplated, and which he almost instantly regrets—'It is too late,' is his *cri de cœur* to Bligh. 'I have been in hell.'

Peter Heywood was the most suitable confidant and messenger, for family reasons and because Christian could rely on him to say nothing to anyone else. And for another reason. For, to extend further this hypothesis, Heywood was Bligh's second favourite on board, and—judged on Bligh's claim that he 'was father to him in every respect' and that Heywood's 'conduct always gave me much pleasure and satisfaction'—had also enjoyed an intimate relationship with his commander, whether or not of an improper nature. This would certainly account for Bligh's later uncharacteristically cruel and vindictive behaviour towards the boy and his family. Heywood's acquittal at the court martial and his family's alliance with the Christian family to blacken Bligh's name were seriously damaging to his career.

If the *Bounty* was entirely free from 'the unnatural and detestable sin', she was a most unusual vessel. If it seems odd that in the heat of the court martial and its aftermath no one spoke out with this accusation against Bligh, there are three possible explanations. The first is that no one knew for sure. The second that it might implicate others. The third that it was a dangerous accusation to make at any time (there had to be a witness and proof of *res in re*), and against a commanding officer especially dangerous.

For, as John McArthur (a different one) wrote in his *Treatise of the Principles and Practice of Naval Courts Martial*, published in the year of the *Bounty* court martial, 'It is an offence so easily charged, and the negative so difficult to be proved, that the accusation should be clearly made out; for, if false, it deserves a punishment inferior only to that of the crime itself. In the few instances of accusation of this nature, brought before naval courts martial, that have not been clearly and positively proved, the prosecutors have been stigmatised in the sentences passed, by the courts declaring the charges malicious, vexatious, oppressive and ill-founded—a trivial compensation for the accusation of a crime of so black a nature.'

I believe that the solution of the *Bounty* mystery lies somewhere in this forbidden darkness. But circumstances, timing, conditions and the nature of the other men among whom these two lived played their full part, too. Somewhere between Tahiti and Tofua, between the 4th and the 27th April 1789, the same ship's company which had survived the physical hell of the Horn cracked under the emotional strain of life on a tranquil, tropical ocean, heading for home, the most difficult part of their mission accomplished, and possessing all the provisions and good health anyone could ask for.

First, let us accept that the *Bounty*'s company were a pretty idiosyncratic lot. There were too many clever young men, too many men with chips on their shoulders, in the ship. Anxious to respond to the appeals of persuasive and influential relatives and friends, Bligh accepted with too cursory examination the Halletts and Haywards, the Stewarts and Youngs. None of them contributed usefully to the *Bounty*'s role as an armed floating nursery garden.

Bligh had chosen for his crew a weak master, a drunken surgeon, an awkward carpenter, mainly second-rate petty and warrant officers, and a bunch of well-born 'young gentlemen' of negligible experience, together with the usual collection of roughs—Churchill, Quintal, Mills, Smith and the rest.

Above all, Bligh had Christian. These two made what we call today a highly strung pair. Passion it was called then, and it was a characteristic these two very different men shared. As we have seen, their relationship may well have been intimate as well as passionate, certainly until the *Bounty*'s arrival at Tahiti.

Bligh's qualities and weaknesses as a leader are now clear to us: an unsurpassed foul-weather commander who reveals his lack of self-confidence only when the going is good; courageous, dutiful, a superb seaman and navigator, but fretful, impatient and seriously lacking in imagination. Shrewd people who met him for the first time would see the short, stout figure with wide-set mariner's legs, small, bright, angry blue eyes set against a wax-pale complexion, and they would think—'There is a difficult man! I would go through hell and high water with him, but not for one day in the same ship on a calm sea.'

The aggressiveness is so poorly concealed that it is almost as if Bligh wants you to know there is going to be trouble. Yet he can also be a delightful companion—not witty, but well-informed, eager to pass on his skills and knowledge. A rum customer indeed!

The Victorians loathed him; recent judgements have been more generous, partly in reaction to Sir John Barrow and others, partly to refute Charles Laughton's picture of him in the 1936 film, all bombast and lashes. A short little-known comment on him, written by David Hannay in *Blackwoods* in April 1910, comes closer to the truth than many more laboured, more psychological studies:

> Bligh was a man who had a quite wonderful capacity for breeding rebellion. He was not only mutinied against at sea, but was deposed for his government in New South Wales by seditious soldiers. We know of no single act of gross tyranny he committed. His valour and his strength of body and character are not to be disputed. But he was notorious, even in the rough navy of the eighteenth century, for a foul mouth . . . and he did not know how to stop. He was a nagger.

Christian, on the other hand, exposed shamelessly his insatiable appetite for affection; and like so many of his kind, because of his fetching ways and handsome appearance, usually received it. Bligh, who pretended to himself that he was above such things, fell under the spell of Christian's charm and liveliness.

Long after his death was known in England, Christian's friends and family still thought of him with love. When Byron was harsh on him in one of his poems, Christian's old schoolfriend Isaac Wilkinson from Cockermouth addressed a verse in reply to the great poet, as if his friend had been some Ariel:

> In milder strains thy tuneful harp had sung,
> And softer accents would have graced thy tongue,
> Hadst thou but known the chief of Pitcairn's Isle,

Young Christian—victim to a tyrant's guile.
His heart was open, generous and humane,
His was a heart that felt for others' pain.
Yet quick of spirit as the electric beam,
When from the clouds its darting lightnings gleam.

Yes, Christian's charm was difficult to resist. So were his transparent kindness and his anxiety to please. Several times during the mutiny we can see him standing back in dismay at what he was doing. It is not only that he is putting the lives of all his shipmates in danger. He is making enemies. And to add to his anguish, he knows that it is too late.

Even after he had in effect condemned Purcell the carpenter and Bligh to certain death, Christian attempted to ingratiate himself in front of Bligh by pressing for the return to Purcell of his precious tool chest. Yet, as the realistic Mat Quintall hastened to point out, Purcell with his tools could build a boat, and thus increase the chances of the castaways' survival, and, in turn, the likelihood of Christian's and his mutineers' eventual capture and death.

Recall, too, how Christian—after the mutineers' demand to blow the bugger Bligh's brains out—presented Bligh with his own sextant and nautical tables. We can almost hear the anxious, even apologetic note, in Christian's voice as he reassures Bligh: 'There, this is sufficient for every purpose.' The sextant, he tells him eagerly, is a good one.

Bligh promoted above his ability this weak, moody, temperamental and sentimental young man. Christian was no leader. Where Bligh had moments of magnificence as a leader, Christian had none. Just as he destroyed the community of the *Bounty* with an explosion ignited by pent-up despair and shame, so he later brought about the destruction of the community he had founded on Pitcairn by a failure to rise to the responsibilities of leadership. There was just not enough fibre in him to endure the harsh treatment and the humiliations he suffered under Bligh, or the guilt and remorse, the self-pity and loneliness, that led him to abdicate power on Pitcairn.

Over-promotion of naval officers, under the patriarchal system of patronage, was as great a threat to the order of things in the late eighteenth century as it is in commerce and industry today. The patronage system usually worked well and gave all round satisfaction. When it did not, the results were disastrous.

Just as Bligh had his own patron ashore in Banks, so he in turn had his own protégés, notably Christian, Heywood, Stewart, Hallett and Hayward—all family friends or relations. Bligh was expected to spend as much time instructing them as he and others had enjoyed from Cook years earlier. You expected much from your protégés—your students—because if they turned out well they were regarded as a credit to yourself. The reverse also applied.

Bligh took endless pains in the *Britannia* and the *Bounty* to instruct Christian in all branches of seamanship and was proud of his progress. In return he expected loyalty and respect. When Christian was offered higher responsibilities—as when he was promoted acting lieutenant and second-in-command—Bligh expected him to rise to them. Bligh was affronted and angered by the failure of the young man in whom he had placed such high trust. His pride and self-esteem, both so sensitive and so well-developed, were hurt.

Bligh did not demote or punish Christian. Instead he raged at him and publicly humiliated him, and then with the storm over, offered him the hand of friendship, expecting everything to be forgotten and the hand to be taken. Christian found this a bewildering and exhausting experience, part of the 'hell' of which he so vehemently complained, and of which the world was to hear so much.

Was all this enough to drive Fletcher Christian to mutiny? Not at first perhaps. Knowing him as we do we are not surprised that he preferred to slide out of his crisis. It needed a Ned Young—the *Bounty*'s Iago—to put steel into Christian's resolve, and to bring about the most celebrated mutiny of all time.

Chronology

1787	*23 December*	*Bounty* sails from Spithead
1788	*26 October*	Anchors in Matavai Bay, Tahiti
1789	*4 April*	Sails from Tahiti
	22 April	Anchors at Nomuka, Friendly Islands
	28 April	The day of the mutiny
	28 May	*Bounty* anchors at Tubai
	6 June	*Bounty* anchors at Tahiti
	14 June	*Bounty*'s launch arrives at Coupang
	16 June	*Bounty* leaves Tahiti
	12 September	*Bounty* leaves Tubai
	23 September	*Bounty* leaves Tahiti with Christian and eight mutineers
1790	*15 January*	*Bounty* arrives Pitcairn Island
	23 January	*Bounty* burns and sinks
	14 March	Bligh arrives at Portsmouth
	22 October	Bligh tried by court martial for loss of his ship
1791	*23 March*	*Pandora* arrives at Tahiti
	8 May	*Pandora* leaves Tahiti with fourteen prisoners
	28 August	*Pandora* shipwrecked
1792	*12 September*	Court martial of ten surviving prisoners
	29 October	Three mutineers executed at Spithead
1793	*20 September*	Christian and four other white men on Pitcairn murdered
	4 October	Murder of the surviving native men on Pitcairn
1808	*28 September*	Discovery of the Pitcairn community by Captain Mayhew Folger

Note on Sources

William Bligh, Fletcher Christian and the mutiny on board the *Bounty* have all been written about many times since, just 180 years ago, that small handful of mutineers was tried, found guilty and executed at Spithead. The new documentary material in this book stems mainly from my researches in Cumberland, in the Naval Library and Public Record Office in London, and the Mitchell Library in Sydney, that vast and priceless store of *Bountiana*.

Papers in the Public Library at Whitehaven and the Brooker Papers at Carlisle revealed new light on Fletcher Christian and the Christian family, and the other Manx-Cumberland families directly and indirectly involved in the mutiny. The Mutiny Collection, and Papers and Pamphlets on health, food and morals in the Naval Library were of special value. Ships' logs of the *Providence*, the *Resolution* and the *Discovery* in the Public Record Office in London also offered me previously unpublished material on Bligh's voyages to the Pacific before and after the *Bounty*'s. In the Mitchell Library the Brabourne Collection in the Bligh Papers, Miscellaneous Papers, and Bligh's letters to his wife, all provided pricelessly valuable information that was new to me, especially on the events at Batavia and Cape Town on Bligh's arrival after the mutiny, on his passage out to New South Wales, and the voyage of the *Providence*.

Many of the contemporary illustrations and maps taken from original journals and narratives are reproduced for the first time.

The value of historical sightseeing is more difficult to calculate. All I can say is that I should have felt very much less adequately equipped to write this book if I had not, by great good fortune, sailed the Cape Horn waters where the *Bounty* took such a beating, watched the skyline of Rarotonga loom out of the morning haze as Christian—now the lonely mutineer—had seen it, made my choppy way into Bounty Bay, Pitcairn Island, evading the exposed rocks, to land on that tiny beach, eaten breadfruit on Point Venus, Matavai Bay, and visited in a launch little bigger than Bligh's a number of the islands inside the Great Barrier Reef in Queensland.

I have occasionally modified the punctuation, the spelling and sometimes the sentence construction in ships' logs, narratives, journals and reports in order to clarify the meaning without altering the sense. Reported dialogue is always a difficult problem. Most of it I have reproduced verbatim. Here and there I have translated evidence given at the court martial, for example, into dialogue. Thus, the exchange between Burkett and Peckover when the launch is alongside the *Bounty* (page 161) appears in the proceedings of the court martial: 'Whilst we were lying under the stern, Thomas Burkett came and asked me if I wanted anything. I told him I had only what I stood up in, a shirt and a pair of trousers; he told me if I would send my keys up, he would go and get me some clothes.' That is Peckover's evidence. Burkett's evidence was: 'Mr Peckover told me to get him some clothes and a pocket book.'

The events on Pitcairn Island present a special case. Up to the time when the *Bounty* left Tahiti for the last time there can be little questioning of the facts or the sequence of events. It may not be possible to authenticate the exact words spoken at any time, remembered months or even years later. Nor the exact timing, nor even the exact shape of things that happened. But allowing for prejudices, fallible memories, and chance, the story is probably as historically accurate as most 200-year-old history—and more accurately recorded than many events for there is nothing to embellish, nothing to romanticise: all the ingredients of a great romantic saga are already present.

At Pitcairn the events enter a parable phase—the Pitcairn Parable. Here we have to rely on less trustworthy sources—Jenny's reminiscences nearly thirty years later, the stories handed down to the children and grandchildren of the original settlers, notably Quintal's son Arthur, John Adams's accounts given to several visitors before he died, and traditional legends—sometimes unexpectedly fresh—to be heard still on Pitcairn today.

There is a good deal of disparity between the recorded times of events but a surprising unanimity on what happened and in what order. There is no reason to doubt that the main outline of the story of the founding and dissolution of the Pitcairn colony is true.

It is a parable, and a non-parable, if we stick strictly to dictionary definitions. We can list the main events with their supposed dates; or we can create a compound of all the many stories originating from the islanders and their ancestors, shaving off a little doubtful edge here, highlighting what most evidence points to be the truth, fitting the characters we now know well and allowing them to react, and to speak, as we believe they would have done. I have chosen the second course.

Select Bibliography

A complete *Bounty* Bibliography would be a formidable affair indeed and no useful purpose would be served by including it here. These are the books and periodicals which have been most useful:

Askew, J., *Guide to Cockermouth*, Cockermouth, 2nd edn, 1872.

Barney, S. and Christian, E., *Minutes of the proceedings of the court martial held at Portsmouth . . . with an appendix containing a full account of the real causes and circumstances . . .* London, 1794.

Barrow, J., *The eventful history of the mutiny and piratical seizure of H.M.S. Bounty . . .* London, 1831.

Beaglehole, J. C., *Captain Cook and Captain Bligh . . .* Wellington, 1967.

Beechey, F. W., *Narrative of a voyage to the Pacific . . .* 2 vols. London, 1831.

Belcher, D., *The mutineers of the Bounty . . .* London, 1870.

Bligh, W., *A narrative of the mutiny on board His Majesty's Ship Bounty . . .* London, 1790.

Bligh, W., *A voyage to the South Sea . . .* London, 1792.

Bligh, W., *An answer to certain assertions . . .* London, 1794.

Brodie, W., *Pitcairn Island and the islanders in 1850 . . .* London, 1851.

Cameron, H. C., *Sir Joseph Banks*, London, 1952.

Christian, E., *A short reply to Captain William Bligh's answer*, London, 1795.

Cook, J. and King, J., *Voyage to the Pacific Ocean . . .* 3 vols. London, 1785.

Danielsson, B., *What happened on the Bounty*, London, 1962.

Darby, M., *Who caused the mutiny on the Bounty?* Sydney, 1965.

Darby, M., *The causes of the Bounty mutiny*, Uppsala, 1966.

Dawson, W. R. (ed.), *The Banks letters . . .* London, 1958.

Du Rietz, R., *The causes of the Bounty mutiny*, Uppsala, 1965.

Lee, I., *Captain Bligh's second voyage to the South Seas*, London, 1920.

Lloyd, C. and Coulter, J. L. S., *Medicine and the Navy*, 4 vols, vols 3 and 4, London 1957–63.

Lonsdale, H., *Worthies of Cumberland*, London, 1876.

Mackaness, G., *The life of Vice-Admiral William Bligh*, Sydney, 2 vols., 1932.

Moorman, M., *William Wordsworth*, London, 1957.

Murray, T. B., *Pitcairn: the island, the people and the pastor*, London, 1853.

Nicolson, R. B., *The Pitcairners*, Sydney, 1965.

Rutter, O., *The true story of the mutiny of the Bounty*, London, 1936.

Rutter, O., *Turbulent Journey: a life of William Bligh*, London, 1936.

Rutter, O. (ed.), *The court-martial of the Bounty mutineers*, London 1931.

Rutter, O. (ed.), *The voyage of the Bounty's launch*, London 1934.

Rutter, O. (ed.), *The Journal of James Morrison*, London 1935.

Rutter, O. (ed.), *The log of the Bounty* . . . London 2 vols., 1936–7.

Rutter, O. (ed.), *Bligh's voyage in the Resource* . . . London, 1937.

Rutter, O. (ed.), *John Fryer of the Bounty* . . . London, 1939.

Samwell, D., *Captain Cook and Hawaii*, London, 1786.

Shapiro, H. L., *The heritage of the Bounty*, London, 1936.

Shillibeer, J., *A narative of the Briton's voyage to Pitcairn's Island*, London, 1817.

Sparks, J., *Memoirs of the life and travels of John Ledyard*, London, 1828.

Thomson, B., (ed.), *Voyage of H.M.S. Pandora* . . . London, 1915.

Woof, R. (ed.), *Wordsworth's Hawkshead by T. W. Thompson*, London, 1970.

Gentleman's Magazine, 1790, 1792.

Journal of the Manx Museum, 1936.

Journal of the Polynesian Society.

Mariner's Mirror, 1928, 1932, 1936, 1941.

United Services Journal, 1829, 1831, 1834.

James Morrison's *Journal* presents something of an enigma. It has all the marks of authenticity. Where the detail can be corroborated it is confirmed as truthful. He is a splendid observer and raconteur— a born diarist, full of colourful prejudices, sometimes a seaborne Boswell to Christian's Dr Johnson. His strongest prejudice is against Bligh. From the outset of the voyage he detests the man. He plays a canny role during the mutiny, watching the sway of power, deciding finally that it is safer to remain on board than commit himself to that overloaded boat yet succeeding in appearing as a neutral. An odd fellow, in fact, like so many of that ship's company, devious, shrewd, articulate.

But how could he have retained what purports to be a day-to-day journal through all that followed? Those five months in Pandora's Box, the shipwreck, the island ordeal, the open boat voyage to Batavia? He claimed to have been in the water for one and a half hours and to have been ordered tied down in the boat, by a commander who was hardly likely to have kept such a damaging document for him. The likeliest explanation is that it was impounded or destroyed by Edwards, and that under less rigorous circumstances he re-wrote it from memory while awaiting the court martial. This would account for the hints that appear here and there that the author is writing with the advantage of hindsight. It remains a document respected by all present day *Bounty* scholars.

Jenny is another curious figure in the fascinating cast of the *Bounty* saga. When she was John Adams's *tyo* on Tahiti he tattooed his initials (as they then were) on her arm—AS/1789. She was a pretty woman when young, but like the rest soon became overweight. On Pitcairn she became Isaac Martin's wife but had no children by him. After he was murdered she vigorously espoused the cause of female emancipation. She, above all the women, longed again for Tahiti and her family. She got her way in the end, too. But not until 1817. In that year the American ship *Sultan* called at Pitcairn, and she persuaded her commander, Captain Rogers, to take her on board. It was a long and circuitous journey home for her, via Chile and the Marquesas. By this time the first Christian missionaries were at work on Tahiti, and to one of these Teahuteatoaonoa (she had reverted to her native name) gave her first account of the events since she had left the island in 1789. It was published in the *Sydney Gazette* on 17 July 1819. The text of another account appeared in the *Bengal Hurkaru* many years later.

Much reliance has been placed on Jenny's accounts by subsequent Pitcairn historians, and the confidence does not seem to be misplaced. Although her story is much shorter than Morrison's she has the same eye for detail, which, where it can be checked (for instance, in the early days, by Morrison's journal) appears to be accurate. She slips up here and there; she says that one of the mutineers was mortally wounded on Tubai whereas only two were lightly wounded. But in Jenny we see a tough, vigorous, determined and intelligent middle-aged woman who is also a crisp reporter.

Index

Compiled by F. D. Buck

References in italic indicate an illustration

315